INEFFABILITY AND RELIGIOUS EXPERIENCE

Pickering Studies in Philosophy of Religion

Series Editor: Russell Re Manning

Forthcoming Titles

Natural Theology in the Scientific Revolution: God's Scientists
Katherine Calloway

Hegel, Love and Forgiveness: Positive Recognition in German Idealism
Liz Disley

Eighteenth-Century Dissent and Cambridge Platonism
Louise Hickman

INEFFABILITY AND RELIGIOUS EXPERIENCE

BY

Guy Bennett-Hunter

LONDON AND NEW YORK

First published 2014 by Pickering & Chatto (Publishers) Limited

Published 2016 by Routledge
2 Park Square, Milton Park, Abingdon, Oxon OX14 4RN
711 Third Avenue, New York, NY 10017, USA

Routledge is an imprint of the Taylor & Francis Group, an informa business

© Taylor & Francis 2014
© Guy Bennett-Hunter 2014

To the best of the Publisher's knowledge every effort has been made to contact relevant copyright holders and to clear any relevant copyright issues. Any omissions that come to their attention will be remedied in future editions.

All rights reserved, including those of translation into foreign languages. No part of this book may be reprinted or reproduced or utilised in any form or by any electronic, mechanical, or other means, now known or hereafter invented, including photocopying and recording, or in any information storage or retrieval system, without permission in writing from the publishers.

Notice:
Product or corporate names may be trademarks or registered trademarks, and are used only for identification and explanation without intent to infringe.

BRITISH LIBRARY CATALOGUING IN PUBLICATION DATA

Bennett-Hunter, Guy, author.
Ineffability and religious experience. – (Pickering studies in philosophy of religion)
1. Religion – Philosophy. 2. Ineffable, The.
I. Title II. Series
210-dc23

ISBN-13: 978-1-84893-471-9 (hbk)
Typeset by Pickering & Chatto (Publishers) Limited

CONTENTS

Acknowledgements	vii
Introduction: Philosophy of Religion in the New Style	1
Part I: The Problem of Ineffability	
1 Ineffability and Religion	7
2 Philosophical Defence of the Concept of Ineffability	23
Part II: Attempted Solutions to the Problem of Ineffability	
3 Two Attempts at Theological Appropriation	39
4 Karl Jaspers's Philosophical Position	77
Part III: Ineffability Revisited	
5 The Nature of Philosophical Evocation of the Ineffable	105
6 The Aesthetic and Ritual Embodiment of the Ineffable	133
Notes	155
Works Cited	187
Index	197

ACKNOWLEDGEMENTS

This book is a revised and expanded version of my PhD dissertation. Accordingly, I should first of all like to thank my supervisor at the University of Cambridge, Dr Russell Re Manning, for agreeing to supervise the writing of that thesis, and for his incisive questions and supportive encouragement as it came into being. Without him, the argument of this book as a whole would be much the poorer. It has been a great pleasure to work with Russell, whose enthusiasm for philosophical and theological ideas is subtly infectious.

I would like to thank Professor David E. Cooper, Emeritus Professor of Philosophy at Durham University, whose philosophical work and supervision of my undergraduate dissertation initially inspired me to pursue the path of thinking of which I have written here. Although that path is recognizably the same one on which I embarked as an undergraduate, I hope that my further advancement along it is marked by some improvement and refinement of my thinking and writing.

I am grateful to the institutions that provided the funding for the research of which this book is the result. I would like to thank the Master and Fellows of Selwyn College, Cambridge for electing me to the Gosden Scholarship for three years. I am also grateful to the Research Degrees Panel of the Archbishops' Council of the Church of England; I would especially like to thank Dr David R. Law for arguing my case and the Chair of the Panel, Professor David Brown, for being convinced by that argument. Without the funding that Selwyn College and the Archbishops' Council provided, the research for this book would have taken a great deal longer to complete. I am grateful, too, to the Institute for Advanced Studies in the Humanities at the University of Edinburgh for awarding me a Postdoctoral Research Fellowship, towards the end of which I was able to revise and add to this research and to begin to prepare the manuscript of this book for publication.

My thanks go, too, to my erstwhile editor at Pickering & Chatto, Dr Philip Good, for his enthusiasm and support for the publication of this book, and to project editor Frances Lubbe for copy-editing the manuscript.

I would like to thank my parents for their love and support throughout my life and continuing education. I am grateful to my father, Mr Ken Bennett-Hunter, for provoking in me a passion for philosophy at a very early age (if I recall, by arguing the case for a form of idealism), for my early introduction to the theatre and for our continuing discussions on philosophical and other topics. I would like to thank my mother, Mrs Janice Bennett-Hunter, for inspiring and encouraging my continuing love of literature. Although she humbly claims not to understand what I now write, that writing would be less humane without her profound literary influence. It may be a little late to change the subject of my studies and research from Philosophy of Religion to English Literature but I have my parents to thank for my continuing and fruitful interest in the arts, especially literature and drama.

Finally, but by no means least, I should like to thank my wife, Dr Julia Candy, for her unstinting love, support and willingness to engage in recondite discussions throughout the research for and writing of this book. Were it not for her, I should probably have lost hope long ago and never discovered what the subtitle of one (still unread) handbook calls the 'peaks', as opposed to the 'troughs', of research. I am most grateful to her for believing in the work I have been doing and for believing in me. Although her humility prevents her from accepting the fact, I am sure that, without her, this book would not exist.

G. B.-H.
Scotland, December 2013.

INTRODUCTION: PHILOSOPHY OF RELIGION IN THE NEW STYLE

Is it time that we lost our faith in philosophy of religion? That discipline, which is sometimes referred to as 'natural theology', is still often associated, if not identified, with the traditional philosophical arguments concerning the existence and nature of God. As the existentialist theologian John Macquarrie succinctly expresses this narrow interpretation of its purpose, it is 'to supply rational proof of the reality of those matters with which theology deals'.[1] Many philosophers have attempted to answer the old question 'What has Athens to do with Jerusalem?'[2] (theologians having mostly tended to treat it as a less urgent matter), and their answers have often taken the form of elaborate systems of philosophy of religion, thus narrowly interpreted.[3] As a work of philosophy of religion, this book implicitly engages with Tertullian's question in a rather different way, in a way that demands a broader interpretation of the terms 'philosophy of religion' and 'natural theology'. The implied answer to my opening question, therefore, is a qualified negative.

I shall spare the reader from yet another detailed criticism of the traditional arguments; as Macquarrie remarks on such overfamiliar analysis, 'it has been done again and again'.[4] Here, I simply record my agreement with his two main reasons for being dissatisfied by that general programme. The first reason is that the traditional attempts to prove or justify God's existence by appeal to evidence and rational argument are doomed to philosophical failure. Just as there are continued attempts to restate the old arguments in newer philosophical terms, so the counterarguments made famous by Hume and Kant continue to be revised in the light of those restatements.[5] The two Enlightenment thinkers seem to have dealt blows to the traditional arguments from which they have never fully recovered, at least not yet. As a result, it has become difficult to believe that anything short of a genuinely new kind of argument (as opposed to an old one, revised and adapted) could succeed in proving the existence of God or in demonstrating that it is more rational to accept that God is real than it is to deny God's reality. It will suffice here to quote Macquarrie's succinct disposal of the main arguments which justifies his suggestion, and my own, that we should transcend this confined vision of what philosophy of religion is.[6]

As far as the ontological proof is concerned, the point that existence is not a predicate seems to me to count decisively against it; as regards the *a posteriori* arguments, it has to be admitted both that the evidence itself is ambiguous and that the attempt to move from empirical evidences to transempirical conclusions involves a logical jump that has never been satisfactorily explained.[7]

The second reason for being dissatisfied with philosophy of religion, narrowly construed, is associated with the sense that the religious or theological claim to faith in God is not really, solely or primarily, as advocates of the narrow interpretation have been assuming, a belief that a hypothesis is true. This reason is expressed in Macquarrie's claim that '[t]he God who is the conclusion of an argument ... is not the God who is worshipped in religion'.[8] This point echoes, *inter alia*, Hume's famous and probably ironic statement at the end of his treatment 'Of Miracles', in Section 10 of the *Enquiry Concerning Human Understanding*, that '[o]ur most holy religion is founded on *faith*, not on reason', a statement that has itself also been echoed in John Cottingham's recent attempt to downplay what he calls 'doxastic freight' as characteristic of the main, substantial difference between theism and atheism.[9] Even if we imagine, for the sake of argument, a scenario in which the traditional arguments for God's existence were found to be persuasive, the imagined consequences are difficult to identify as having anything to do with religious faith on any conventional understanding. The main consequence would presumably be that all rational beings would accept the existence of God either as proven or as the most reasonable explanation of the existence and nature of the observable world. It would in that case be irrational to reject the proposition that God exists or less rational to deny than to affirm it. But what would have been established, in this imagined scenario, is nothing like the solid rational foundation for religious commitment for which philosophy of religion has traditionally aimed. All that would have been established is the truth of a scientific or logical hypothesis: that an omniscient, omnipotent, benevolent being is very likely to exist or, logically, must exist. Any *religious* commitment beyond this (for example, the kind of commitment reflected by engaging in religious practices) would remain an act of faith. And if the truth of Classical Theism were established in this way, it is doubtful that the members of any religious group would or could worship this Classical god as their own. Surely, when it comes to the question of what God is, most members of such groups are already committed to rather more than the bland theism, which, on the narrow interpretation in question, a successful philosophy of religion could, at best, establish.

For both these reasons, Macquarrie (whose major systematic work, *Principles of Christian Theology*, was published back in the 1960s) pessimistically describes as 'ruinous' the condition of what he prefers to call 'natural theology in the old style'.[10] He believes that natural theology, so construed, should be abandoned –

and, on this, I share his opinion. But, as he recognizes, sole reliance on 'revealed' theology, natural theology's supposed alternative, would be equally undesirable, if not more so; rational supports are necessary if theology is to be protected, and indeed distinguished, from illusion and superstition.[11] As is well known, Freud found the rational arguments in favour of religions, their holy books and teachings wanting but he also deftly demonstrated the circularity of the appeal to revelation for which one might be tempted to reach as an apparently self-sufficient alternative. If we cannot convincingly argue for the existence of God as the supposed author of religious texts and source of religious teachings, we might be inclined to appeal to revelation instead. But, as Freud pointed out, 'that assertion itself forms part of the teachings that are to be examined as to their credibility – and no proposition, as we know, can prove itself'.[12] Taken together, the lack of convincing rational arguments and the circularity of the appeal to revelation imply, for Freud, the inescapably superstitious and illusory character of religion. Whatever we make of his conclusion, we can be sure that the non-rational (if not irrational) nature of the appeal to revelation, together with its circularity, guarantees that it will be no replacement for natural theology in the old style.

Fortunately, then, Macquarrie advocates and develops a 'natural theology in the new style' that provides rational support for religion, bridging the gap between ordinary experience and faith. It takes over, to that extent, old-style natural theology's basic function but without the attendant weaknesses: it owes to the phenomenological method, is descriptive rather than purely deductive and attends not just to the rational arguments but also to the conviction that underlies and motivates them. It takes seriously the measure of participation involved in religious faith, a feature that might enable it to be a far more effective apologetic tool than abstract argument alone. Finally, it is existential rather than purely rational, taking the concrete, lived condition of human existence, which undoubtedly includes a rational dimension, as its starting point.[13] Taken together, these features of natural theology in the new style actually entail, for Macquarrie, the blurring, if not the abandonment of the old, traditional distinction between 'natural' and 'revealed' kinds of theology.[14] If God is the source of everything, this must include knowledge or experience of God's self. Not only, therefore, could there be no 'unaided' experience of God, so that all theology must claim to be 'revealed' in that sense, but even all 'revealed' theology must come to us via our human faculties of apprehension and is, to that extent, 'natural'. The resultant conception of natural theology is not of a second route to religious experience alongside God's self-revelation, nor does it reflect the desire to undermine the role of rational reflection in critically testing religious experience. Rather, it is of an appeal to the general possibility of revelation, or religious experience, which is accessible to any being with our human faculties, including, but not limited to, our rational ones.[15] Towards the beginning of his Gifford

Lectures, Macquarrie describes this definition of natural theology as broader than the one pejoratively held by Hume and Kant but as no less consonant with the terms of Lord Gifford's foundation:

> When he says that the subject is to be treated as a 'natural science', he cannot mean that God is to be treated as a phenomenon of nature, but that the enquiry is to be carried out by the natural human faculties that are common to all, without appeal to some special source of knowledge. This is how the word 'natural' was traditionally understood in the expression 'natural theology'.[16]

Tertullian's question, it seems, will not go away – nor, in my view, should it – but the answers that continue to be provided by practitioners of revised and updated forms of traditional philosophy of religion remain as philosophically and religiously unsatisfying as Macquarrie found them nearly half a century ago – and for the very same reasons. Few philosophers have taken up the gauntlet and considered the possibility of a broader, and perhaps more satisfying, kind of philosophy of religion in response both to Tertullian's question and to criticisms like the ones Macquarrie skilfully summarizes. This is perhaps forgivable on the grounds that, if familiarity does indeed breed contempt, it presumably does so as much in philosophy as in other spheres of human life; the philosophical arguments in defence of old-style natural theology are well-worn, after all. And we may find it reasonable to forgive philosophers who continue valiantly in the attempt to rebuff the criticisms of old-style natural theology when there is a clear need for something that fulfils its basic function yet, for all the criticisms, no obvious positive proposal for a more satisfactory kind of programme with which it might be replaced. Although Macquarrie, who was one of the first scholars to make Heidegger's philosophy available in English, helped to pioneer the application to religion of the existential phenomenological style of philosophizing, his own positive proposal concerning philosophy of religion has been neglected and has remained undeveloped.

This book is intended to serve as one, belated (or overdue) instance of a new kind of philosophy of religion, what Macquarrie calls a 'natural theology in the new style'. It attempts to show, in the process, what a revised, broadened form of philosophy of religion, appropriately informed by significant developments in twentieth-century and contemporary philosophy, might look like. It is written from a philosophical perspective, in agreement with Freud that 'there is no authority higher than reason' (at least until reason demonstrates its own limitations).[17] But, at the same time, it tries to heed Macquarrie's desiderata and to deploy that authority as part of a coherent philosophical method that is phenomenological and existential as well as rational: the (presently rather unfashionable) method of existential phenomenology. As an instance of the broader form of philosophy of religion advocated by Macquarrie, it attempts to establish, by means of this philosophical methodology, the extent to which religious experience or revelation is generally possible. In this way, it challenges the old distinction between 'natural' and 'revealed' kinds of theology by establishing the possibility of religious experience, insofar as it can be established, on a philosophical basis. It thereby acknowledges the continuity of the 'natural' form of theology with its supposedly 'revealed' counterpart. The book's specific focus is on the unjustly neglected concept of ineffability (of that which is, in principle, resistant to conceptual formulation and therefore literal linguistic articulation), a concept which, in its theological application, appears to be in greatest philosophical tension with the thought that religious experience is possible: if the divine is entirely mysterious, how can it possibly be experienced?

Part of the proposed answer lies in the thought, articulated by William James, that the experiential dimension to religion is deeply interconnected with the pragmatic dimension, perhaps more so than with the doxastic dimension. In this respect, the book is part of the recent turn in philosophy of religion away from a restricted focus on belief and on purely linguistic forms of expression towards experience and practice. (The names of John Cottingham and Mark Wynn, among others, are associated with what might be called the 'humane turn' in philosophy of religion.)[18] This book therefore attempts to overcome a major philosophical obstacle to acceptance of the general possibility of religious experience and thereby to serve as an instance of a broader, more humane kind of philosophy of religion: a philosophy of religion in the new style.

This book is divided into three parts. The first part outlines and engages philosophically with the problem of ineffability in religion, the second part critically engages with philosophical and theological attempts to solve the problem, while the third part develops my own constructive proposal for a solution in the light of the foregoing analysis.

The book opens with the observation that the notion of ineffability has been largely ignored by philosophers, even though it is clearly a central one in the Christian mystical tradition and in more recent apophatic theological developments. Mid-twentieth-century philosophical discussions of mysticism invoked the idea and a number of phenomenologists share a sense that the meaningful human world is answerable to some 'background' that is inarticulable and mysterious. But, despite this, the logical implications of the notion of ineffability for religious experience, language and practice have not been explicitly and systematically thought through. This book, restricted to a dual focus on twentieth-century and contemporary philosophy and on the Christian religion, attempts to address this neglect.

After reviewing the philosophical, and some theological, literature on the notion of ineffability in religion, this book's first two chapters identify and respond to the problem of ineffability: a philosophical tension between the notions of 'ineffability' and 'answerability', between the idea that the ineffable is beyond conceptualization and the thought that some kind of experience, language or practice connected with it is required if the notion is to be meaningfully invoked, let alone (as in a religious context) serve as the measure for the meaning of the human world and of human life. In this connection, the meaning of the word 'God' is interpreted as a reference to the concept of ineffability. A recent philosophical defence of the concept is endorsed which, rooted in existential phenomenology and (as is shown in detail) Heidegger's later philosophy, resolves this tension.

In the third and fourth chapters, the detail of theological attempts, by Paul Tillich and John Macquarrie, to accommodate this line of thought as directly inherited from the phenomenologists (especially Heidegger) is examined and criticized, as, eventually, is a more promising possibility represented by the unjustly neglected philosophy of Karl Jaspers.

In the fifth chapter, the rational status of existential phenomenology (its relation to discourse conditioned by the subject–object dichotomy) is revisited and examined more closely in the light of the engagement with Jaspers's thought. It is concluded that phenomenology's specifically philosophical way of evoking the ineffable is necessarily that of a rationally based dialectic.

The final chapter points to spheres outside philosophy, aesthetic and ritual, which may be understood to cultivate the experience of the ineffable without such dialectic. Concluding with a focus on religion's pragmatic dimension, it offers an 'aesthetic account of ritual meaning' and concludes by showing how the Christian Eucharistic rite can be understood, in philosophical terms, as a vehicle for religious experience and expression – the evocation and invocation of the ineffable.

1 INEFFABILITY AND RELIGION

The central concept to be addressed in this book is that of 'ineffability'. The specific way in which I understand the term will, I hope, become clear in the next chapter but, by way of initial orientation, it seems appropriate to make some initial remarks. By the term 'ineffable', I mean to refer not just to the concept of that which is inexpressible or in practice unknown but to the notion of what is *in principle* resistant to conceptual grasp *and* (therefore) literal linguistic articulation. 'Ineffability', in my sense, should therefore be taken also to include a non-disparaging sense of 'mystery'. It may seem obvious that this concept has long been at work in Christianity, indeed this fact is part of what motivates me to write a book about it. But I first want to distinguish between two lines of religious thought, both of which look, at first glance, like promising sources for the notion of ineffability in Christianity. I label these the 'theological conception' of 'mystery' and the 'apophatic premise'. The initial interest in the theological conception is provoked by its attempt to explore the connection between mystery and religious practice (especially ritual), which is one of my eventual aims. Although the mystical writing produced by those committed to the apophatic premise has inspired most of the (very little) existing philosophical treatment of the notion of ineffability in the period of interest, both lines of thought have received twentieth-century and contemporary philosophical defence. The main aim of this first chapter is therefore to review, and critically to engage with, representative examples of that philosophical treatment.

The Theological Conception of Mystery

There is a line of thought, originating in early twentieth-century theology, whose focus is on 'mystery'. Albert Plé, for instance, starts from the conception of mystery as it is found in New Testament, especially Pauline, texts. He defines it, curiously, as something *revealed* in Christ and in the teaching of the Apostles, as something manifest and spoken of, though perhaps previously hidden.[1] He locates one major piece of biblical evidence for this definition at Colossians 1:25–7 but thoroughly supports each part of it with further biblical evidence.[2] In this conception of mystery there is a Christological focus, since Christ is thought of as the medium for the hidden, invisible, inaccessible God and is believed to manifest God in his own physical and sensible being.[3] But Christ, as much now as he was for Paul, is inaccessible to the senses because he is believed to be 'at the right hand of God'.[4] Thus, until the *parousia*, the Church (as Christ's mystical body) and its Eucharistic liturgy constitute '*for us*' the necessary media of faith.[5] In this same volume, under Plé's editorship, Louis Bouyer contrasts the notion of '*mysterion*' as it is understood in Greek paganism (where mysteries were secret rites, rather than doctrines, and which were revealed only to initiates)[6] with the Pauline usage, which he thinks the first in Christian literature, where it refers to God's plan of salvation to be fully revealed at the end of time, already revealed in Christ, especially in his parables and in the events of his life.[7] It is on the basis of this contrast, Bouyer thinks, that the difference between pagan secrecy in connection with '*mysterion*' and, to take one example, St Ignatius of Alexandria's description of 'mysteries to be cried aloud' can best be understood.[8] Following on where Plé's essay left off, Bouyer takes up the line of thought reflected in the translation from the Greek '*mysterion*' to the Latin '*sacramentum*',[9] where the notion of mystery takes on a liturgical significance as many writers, especially in the Constantinian era, apply terms that were applied to the pagan rites to the Christian liturgy and to the actions, objects and rites associated with it.[10] These new allusions, Bouyer claims, were added to the Pauline sense of 'mystery' without suppressing it and it was in this context that the word 'mystery' and its cognates came to be applied to the Christian sacraments in general and to the Eucharist in particular.[11]

Whatever we may make of the historical arguments made by Plé and Bouyer, arguments of this kind certainly lie behind and inform the not uncontroversially influential[12] work of Odo Casel.[13] Casel states his point of departure in his initial answer to his own central question, 'What is the essence of the mystery?', namely, *revelation* whose primary source he believes is holy scripture.[14] With Plé and Bouyer, Casel suggests that, although the Church rejected the ancient mystery religions, it has always used their language in relation to its own liturgy and to clarify the meaning of its rituals.[15] He accepts St Paul's identification of the religious mystery with the reality of Christ and his life and defines 'the mystery of worship' as the presentation and renewal of that first mystery ('the mystery of Christ') by means of which access to it and participation in it are possible.[16] Casel's view that 'mystery' and 'liturgy' mean the same thing considered from two viewpoints is summarized as follows:

> *Mystery* means the heart of the action, that is to say, the redeeming work of the risen Lord, through the sacred actions he has appointed: liturgy, corresponding to its original sense of 'people's work' ... means rather the action of the Church in conjunction with this saving action of Christ's.[17]

George Guiver provides an interesting gloss on Casel's interpretation of the New Testament's sense of 'mystery' operative in the work of Plé and Bouyer:

> (a) it is the divine presence, (b) it is Christ, (c) Christ is God's hidden plan for his creation, (d) now no longer hidden but made manifest in the saving events, (e) this manifesting of the Mystery at the time of those events now lives on in the sacramental life of Christ's body the Church.[18]

Aside from his annoyance at Casel's error of translation,[19] Gordon-Taylor's reason for paying relatively little attention to his work is its neglect of the apophatic dimension which, Gordon-Taylor feels, cannot but be acknowledged in any decent discussion of divine activity.[20] He observes that Casel does not anywhere in his work deal with the apophatic implications of the concept of mystery and their bearing on a theology of divine presence in the liturgy. On the contrary, Casel seems to assume Christ's objective presence in the Eucharist.[21] The fact that, in the secondary literature, Casel's 'mystery' (which appears to be, if not the apotheosis of the theological conception, then at least its most influential statement) is taken to refer to no fewer than two distinct realities cursorily indicates a substantial distance between this theological conception of mystery and my notion of ineffability.

This is not the only reason that I do not take my cue, in this book, from the theological conception. To my mind, even given their not unproblematic dependence on scriptural authority, there is something odd about the arguments provided by Plé, Bouyer and Casel in support of the theological conception. That is that similar biblical texts and in some cases the very same texts, here used to support the idea, were used a little less than three centuries earlier to support arguments *against* the idea of a Christian mystery. In his famous *Christianity Not Mysterious*,[22] John Toland covers some of the same Pauline ground as Plé, notably the basis of Plé's definition at Colossians 1:25–7, and many similar New Testament texts.[23] Toland's interpretation of the relevant kind of biblical passage displays a deep affinity with that of Plé: 'the Mysteries of the Gospel were certain things in their own Nature intelligible enough, but call'd Mysteries by reason of the Vail under which they were formerly hid'.[24]

However, there follows for Toland a very different 'promis'd Conclusion'; rhetorically, and with biting sarcasm, he asks:

> Now in what Sense could this Mystery be said to be reveal'd, this Secret to be made manifest, to be made known to all Nations by the Preaching of the Apostles, if it remain'd still incomprehensible? A mighty Favour indeed! to bless the world with a parcel of unintelligible Notions or Expressions, when it was already overstock'd.[25]

Thus it appears that the difference between Toland and Casel is over the meaning of words, or rather the key word 'mystery'. Whereas, for Plé, the religious mystery is defined as something revealed, Toland does not appear to see how it could possibly be both revealed and a mystery. That such a major disagreement is possible suggests that, in each case, different concepts lie behind the same word. The way in which I understand the term (in sympathy with Toland) leads me to the conclusion that what Casel calls 'mystery' is not the same concept as that which I denote with the term 'ineffability' and which is of interest to me here. It is not necessarily that the arguments for the theological conception fail but rather that they defend a different concept to that of ineffability. My preference, in this book, for using of the word 'ineffability' and its cognates, rather than, say, 'mystery' owes partly to my wish to distinguish my own arguments from those in support of, and otherwise connected with, the theological conception. The word is also adopted partly for strategic reasons since, frustratingly, in common parlance the word 'mystery' is often taken to mean something opaque, like the dénouement of a detective story, unknown merely *in practice*. The argument I advance turns on the understanding of 'mystery' as what is *in principle* unknowable – I therefore generally avoid the term.[26] So my main reason for going no further with the theological conception is that its articulation does not involve the concept that is of interest to me. There is, however, some more recent philosophical work that articulates the logic of this conception and attempts to defend it.

In a recent paper, Steven D. Boyer attempts to provide a logical analysis of the senses of mystery.[27] He draws a distinction between the above New Testament sense of mystery, which he labels a 'revelational' mystery, and mysteries of what he calls the 'investigative' kind. Whereas the former, revelational kind of mystery, likely inherited from the ancient Greek mystery religions, somehow remains mysterious in its revelation, the latter, investigative kind is like those found in detective fiction, where investigation and revelation dispel the mystery.[28] He articulates the logic of the New Testament's 'revelational', theological conception of mystery, in contrast to this, as follows:

> It remains incomprehensible even to those who know it.[29]

> This kind of mystery involves real knowledge, and yet a knowledge that is always reflexively aware of its own incompleteness or inadequacy. The reality known is always known as enigmatically larger or deeper than our knowledge of it. In other words, revelational mystery is revealed precisely *as* mystery. The defining feature of mystery in this sense is that its mysterious character is not undercut by being made known.[30]

The defence of the revelational kind of mystery (the explanation of '*why* a revelational mystery is a mystery ... [i]f it has been revealed or made known, then how can it continue to "defy reason", in some sense?') which Boyer appears to think the most promising proceeds with the aid of a mathematical analogy. The precise extent to which this analogy is inspired by Edwin A. Abbott's famous novel, *Flatland*,[31] is unclear, though Boyer does refer to it and admits, in a footnote, that he cannot help being reminded of it in the context of the present argument.[32]

He asks us to consider a circle, an example of a two-dimensional shape, and the way in which geometry allows us to reason about it.[33] If the figure were in fact a three-dimensional cylinder being investigated by a mathematician limited to two dimensions, the mathematician could reason geometrically and thus know everything that is two-dimensional about the cylinder. She would reach the same conclusions about the circular end of the cylinder, and with the same accuracy, as in the case of the two-dimensional circle. But, for this mathematician, there is always more of the cylinder to be discovered: a 'more' which transcends what geometry can understand and describe of the figure but which does not cease to be geometrical in character.[34] Such a mystery transcends the normal workings of human reason 'dimensionally': even when the object is known (as a two-dimensional circle) it remains unknown (as a cylinder). It is with this notion of dimensional revelational mystery that Boyer wishes to challenge the assumption made by what he disparagingly calls the Cartesian 'philosophy of clarity' that every piece of reality is either knowable or unknowable absolutely. It strikes him as a more sensible and fruitful possibility that 'the mystery of God' should normally be construed in the dimensional revelational sense that steers a course between these two options set out by the philosophy of clarity.[35] On this approach, the religious mystery

> is one in which reason is appropriate and is legitimately exercised, just as two-dimensional geometry is legitimately applied to the cylinder – yet no ultimate 'clearing up' is expected or hoped for. A dimensional mystery welcomes rational investigation, but expects reason to testify to an unfathomable depth or dimension that it can perhaps investigate or even illuminate but never explain or make clear.[36]

These arguments reinforce the initial sense I noted earlier that the concept involved in the theological conception of mystery is not the same as my notion of ineffability. Given the latter notion, revelation, or the possibility of experiencing the ineffable, is a philosophical problem and, if this problem were solved and a place found for religious experience or revelation, it should be possible to rehabilitate some version of the theological conception or of 'revelational' mystery once this conceptual work has been done. Boyer, by contrast, starts with a weaker sense of mystery (one which immediately allows it to be in some sense known) in order to build in the idea of revelation straight away. But there is another relevant distinction that cuts deeper than that made by the 'philosophy of clarity' as Boyer represents it. Recall Toland's thought that the mysteries involved in (what I am calling) the theological conception are unknown in practice but in principle knowable: 'things in their own Nature intelligible enough, but call'd Mysteries by reason of the Vail under which they were formerly hid'. We should, I think, apply a similar distinction to Boyer's mathematical analogy. We need not assume, with the 'philosophy of clarity', that everything is knowable or unknowable *absolutely*, but I suggest that the related distinction between that which is knowable or unknowable in principle and that which is so merely in practice has a more helpful bearing on the notion of ineffability.

Boyer's cylinder is unknown in practice (since the nature of two-dimensional geometry happens to be such that it cannot describe solids) but is in principle knowable (were two-dimensional geometry capable of describing solids, or if we used three-dimensional geometry, it would be apparent that there had always been a solid object there to describe). But he also claims that the cylinder's nature is not, like an investigative mystery, something which investigation could ever uncover. Now, this must be true also in practice, rather than in principle, since the cylinder is unknown only in practice (the relevant meaning of 'unknown' here is just 'resistant to being uncovered by investigation'). For Boyer, the religious realities are unknown because our rational faculties and our sense organs are such that we cannot reason about them or directly perceive them. In order to determine whether our notion of ineffability (the unknowable in principle) is involved, the key question is therefore 'Does the way our minds and bodies are constituted determine in practice or in principle whether something is knowable?' Boyer's implicit answer to this question is 'in practice' since his argument allows that, if our faculties of reason or our sense organs were different, we could experience and describe the objects of higher dimensions just as the three-dimensional mathematician could experience and describe the cylinder. In this respect, we resemble the inhabitants of Abbott's two-dimensional *Flatland* who lament that their inability to experience or comprehend the third dimension is owing to the contingent fact that 'we have no eye in our stomachs'.[37] But if the objects which this argument defends are *unknown in practice* and not *in principle unknowable*, it is not clear just how they are distinct from Boyer's first category of 'investigative' mystery or what is not really a mystery at all.[38] It seems that they are just 'investigative' mysteries or puzzles that we humans simply happen to lack the relevant powers to solve, powers which, in principle, we could have had and powers which we might conceivably develop in the future.

My notion of ineffability, by contrast, would have to be defended along different lines, according to which 'unknowable by the human mind' is taken simply to mean 'unknowable in principle'. To anticipate briefly the arguments of the next chapter, the existential phenomenological perspective seems more helpful in this connection.[39] From this perspective, 'the world' just is that which is constituted by the mental and bodily possibilities of the human way of being, that with which these possibilities are always already engaged. There is no possibility of considering potential ways in which the world might be 'if our minds and bodies were differently constructed', or 'if our geometrical reasoning were different', since, if they were, we would not be the kind of beings we are and the world constituted by our way of being would not be the same, human world. Since, for the existential phenomenologist, reality owes crucially to the human contribution, the concepts and values with which human beings invest it, the ineffable cannot be located within those structures of human conceptualization and evaluation. As we shall see in the following chapter, 'the ineffable' cannot be taken to refer to a part of the world, or to another, transcendent world, for the experience and description of which our faculties merely happen, in practice, to be inadequate. What Boyer's argument has been trying to defend is a movement by analogy from our conceptualizable world to a supposedly non-conceptualizable world. But when we reach *this* world, we cannot avoid investing it with concepts. If we refrain from so investing it, then it loses its significance as a 'world' or 'dimension' or as anything at all and the point of invoking it as such is lost. But if we do invest it with our concepts, then we turn it into part of our finite, human world like any other.

The Apophatic Premise and the Problem of Answerability

I now want briefly to draw attention to the central claim of the apophatic tradition, which continues to be popular in the twentieth century (and into the twenty-first), for it is here that our notion of ineffability *can* clearly be seen to be operating. For example, Christos Yannaras finds that Pseudo-Dionysius the Areopagite adopts the notion of divine ineffability (as opposed to absence) as the starting point for his apophatic theology;[40] Denys Turner draws attention to one definition of apophaticism as theology 'done against the background of [acquired] human ignorance of the nature of God'[41] and Anthony Kenny describes the tradition of negative theology (whose founder he takes, according to common perception, to be Pseudo-Dionysius the Areopagite) in terms of the writings of theologians who have 'maintained that God was ineffable and indeed inconceivable ... [and that w]e humans ... cannot speak appropriately about God, and ... cannot even think coherently about him'.[42] Leaving aside for the moment the question of the immediate connection of the concept of ineffability with the language of God which, it seems to me, still requires philosophical defence, I have a great deal of sympathy with the idea being articulated here, which I call the 'apophatic premise'. The idea, that is, that the word 'God' refers to the concept of ineffability. The popularity of versions of this claim both in the history of the Christian tradition, notably in the apophatic tradition, and its continued popularity perhaps indicate the presence of an intuition that God could only be of thoroughgoing religious significance (could only be God) if he is identified with what is philosophically ultimate.[43] It is only if considered beyond the created world that God can be regarded to be responsible for the meaning and existence of that world; if God created time and space (and everything else) he cannot himself be coherently thought of as bound by time and space. Dionysius gives voice to such an intuition when he writes, for example, that God 'is the Cause of all things. The sources and goals of all things are in him and are anticipated in him. But he is also superior to them all because he precedes them and is transcendentally above them.'[44] In my view, this intuition captures the important philosophical insight, which is defended in the following chapter, that only that which is ineffably beyond the human life-world can serve to explain the meaning of human life.

But, this being the case, a tension exists between the concept of ineffability and the reason that the concept is appealed to and the use to which it is put in theological discourse. There is a tension, in other words, between the work that the concept is required to do in order to be worth invoking and the concept itself. If God is held to be ineffable, that is because it is only as such that he can be appealed to in explanations of the meaning of life and of our human world. In religious terms this tension manifests as the philosophical problem of the possibility of religious experience. This tension, which is created by the use (in this case, the religious use) of the concept of ineffability, I call the tension between 'ineffability and answerability'. The problem of answerability to which this tension leads is nicely summarized by John Hick in connection with Dionysius, whom he thinks is

> caught in the dilemma which faces everyone who affirms the ultimate divine ineffability but who is also required, by the practice of worship and the religious life generally, to think of God as a personal being with whom a personal relationship is possible. For how could we worship the totally transcategorial [*sic*]? And how could Denys, as a faithful Christian monk, allow the scriptures, liturgies and theologies of the church to be undercut by an unqualified divine ineffability?[45]

It is obviously philosophically problematic, in this apophatic context, to affirm the concept of (in this case, divine) ineffability and also to insist that there are ways in which human beings are answerable to the ineffable in, say, various kinds of experience and in religious practices. But, perhaps less obviously, the same problem exists in its opposite formulation for one whose aim is to trace a route to the ineffable from the starting point of revelation. In the case of Casel, as we saw earlier, one could, with Toland's help, accuse him of not *really* employing the concept of ineffability, whatever the language he uses. However, more recently (and I think more defensibly), David Brown has sought to approach divine 'mystery' *via* revelation.[46] Here, he takes revelation for granted but argues for its inevitable inexhaustibility and locates mystery in that inexhaustibility, in the fact that our understanding can never be complete, our utterances never exhaustive and that there is always more to be said. However, this approach, no less than the apophatic one, cannot but acknowledge the tension which, Brown admits, 'exists in almost all forms of religion ... that between explanation and mystery, between the conviction that something has been communicated by the divine (revelation) and the feeling that none the less God is infinitely beyond all our imaginings'.[47]

Thus, the notion of ineffability, at work in religion and theology, requires long-overdue philosophical treatment, not least because of this potentially crippling philosophical tension.[48] Although this tension is of particular importance in religious uses of ineffability, on which I focus here, it obviously applies in any other instance of the concept's use. Why invoke the concept of ineffability in *any* context, and thus pretend to present it for human evaluation, when its content, or rather its lack of content, entails that it cannot do any work and thus in principle precludes such evaluation? As Gabriel Marcel eloquently expresses this last thought, 'when all is said and done, what I am unable to evaluate is for me as if it were not.'[49] A philosophical resolution to this tension is set out in the following chapter, while some options for applying it in a theological context are explored in chapters 3 and 4. Very little philosophical material exists which explicitly deals with the notion of ineffability from the period of present interest. And even if we allow, for the sake of argument, that the concepts involved in the theological and apophatic lines of thought *are* the same, it is mainly from the latter (importantly religious) line of thought that the existing philosophical analysis has taken its cue.[50] It is therefore to representative examples of this analysis that I now turn.

Philosophical Analysis

A rare recent study of ineffability *per se* describes William James's 1901–2 set of Gifford Lectures, which famously assigns a key role to ineffability,[51] as the '*locus classicus*' for philosophical discussion of mysticism.[52] Since James's lectures were delivered and published as *The Varieties of Religious Experience*, such discussions have typically been the context in which the notion of ineffability has been addressed by philosophers. I want to draw attention to two closely related problems arising from these discussions which, if insoluble, would do considerable damage to the notion of ineffability: namely, the problem of self-stultification (which, in the discussions in question, problematizes the possibility of securing reference to an *ineffable* God) and the problem of the possibility of mystical experience, a version of the problem of answerability mentioned above.

The first and most obvious claim to be considered in this context is discussed in what Kukla describes as a 'nearly definitive analysis' carried out by William Alston.[53] Alston quotes several versions of the claim, from various religious and philosophical traditions, that God (Brahman, the Soul, the One) is ineffable.[54] Following W. T. Stace, he interprets the meaning of this claim as follows: 'To say that God is ineffable is to say that no concepts apply to Him, and that he is without qualities ... Thus to the intellect He is blank, void, nothing.'[55] Alston's aim seems to be to point out the self-stultification of the unqualified claim 'God is ineffable' since the statement's content, the assertion that God cannot be described, is contradicted by its logical form which entails that it asserts something about God, namely, his ineffability.[56] In other words, the very idea of securing reference to an ineffable God (as the statement appears to be doing) makes no sense. In apparent reaction to this problem, generally agreed to be insoluble, later discussions, including Alston's own,[57] have applied the concept of ineffability to objects other than God. Kellenburger, for instance, suggests that the mystical literature allows for ineffability to be variously applied to (1) a being but also to (2) a truth, (3) the self and, most importantly and in a return to William James, (4) mystical experience.[58]

Kukla takes up this line of thought, identifying two reasons behind the claim that God is ineffable. The first, found in Stace, is that God has no properties; the second is that God does have properties but which are so extraordinary that they cannot be understood or spoken of.[59] Kukla wants to say that the first possibility has nothing to do with ineffability since he agrees with the charge of self-stultification[60] and it is also his 'inclination … to use "ineffability" to refer to the thesis that there are facts that defy expression'.[61] With Kukla's sympathy for the second reason, the possibility is opened up for the argument for such ineffable facts from mysticism, that is, from the view that some humans have ineffable knowledge about, or experience of, some religious state(s) of affairs, perhaps involving God.[62]

This line of argument, which I take to be a reaction to the charge of self-stultification, has been perceptively summarized and developed in an important paper by David E. Cooper. This summary brings out the inseparability of the problem of the possibility of securing reference to an ineffable God (which stems from the charge of self-stultification) from that of the possibility of experiencing such a God:

> Let us grant that a totally ineffable God is an absurdity. What we are assuming to be ineffable is not God himself, but experiences of him. Clearly there is much we can say about him. He is one, perfect, omniscient, and so on. This is enough to support the claim that it is experiential encounters with him, and not something else, which are ineffable.[63]

According to the argument so far, enough can be said about God as the object of reason to identify that it is *he* who is encountered in the ineffable state of knowledge or experience. But, as Cooper argues, it is not clear that the God of reason is quite as effable as the argument requires. The terms describing him are either unhelpfully obscure ones like 'One' or 'Absolute' or admitted by theologians to be 'irredeemably analogical or figurative'.[64] Some theologians claim that if God can be described at all, then it must be analogically, metaphorically or symbolically. But, as Cooper suggests, it is not immediately clear that the idea of a being who can *only* be described in these ways is a viable concept since we apparently 'need a straight description of something before we can identify it as that which can be analogically or figuratively depicted'.[65] Thus, since the God of natural theology also turns out to be ineffable and irreducibly analogical (we can provide no such 'straight description' which would enable us to secure reference), a common response is to return to the God of experience: 'if we can directly experience God, then the fact (if it is one) that reason can capture him only figuratively is not devastating'.[66] But this will not do either:

> The problem assumed earlier was precisely the ineffability of God as object of experience. The idea, a short while ago, was to blunt the edge of this problem by appeal to the God of natural theology [i.e. reason], a being about whom we could say enough to explain his experiential ineffability. Clearly that idea falls apart once we concede that sense can be made of this being only via experiences of him. The circle would be complete: we can allow an ineffable God of experience only if we can identify an effable God of reason, but we can do the latter only if we can first make sense of, and therefore communicate, the former.[67]

More recently, Alston has been in danger of falling into this circle in some later work in which, contrary to his earlier position, he defends divine ineffability. In his Taylor Lectures delivered at Yale, he defends what he calls the 'Divine Mystery Thesis (DMT)', which he initially formulates in the following terms: 'No concepts in the human repertoire can be truly applied to God as he is in himself'.[68] He makes the qualification that this cannot be true of negative concepts: 'However mysterious God may be in the DMT sense, we can still be sure that he is not identical with the pizza I had for lunch today and true that he does not (literally) have arms and legs'.[69] But Alston thinks the problem of securing reference to an ineffable God constitutes a reason to qualify the DMT and to concede that it cannot hold for absolutely all our concepts for '[i]f it did, we would leave ourselves with no way of directing our denials to God rather than to someone or something else'.[70] Alston considers the 'descriptivist' view of reference, according to which it depends on one having in mind, either explicitly or implicitly, a uniquely applicable description of the referent, which obviously requires the application of concepts, and a Kripkean alternative, according to which reference depends on an ongoing practice of using a particular name to refer to a particular thing. While the alternative does not require a uniquely applicable description, it suggests that one refers to something by attaching oneself to a chain of communication, an ongoing practice of reference. When it comes to the origin of this chain, Alston reads Kripke as implying that it results not from the application of a uniquely applicable description but from an initial experience or perception of the referent (and Alston defends this possibility in the case of God by appeal to the arguments in his earlier book, *Perceiving God*). But even this view of reference requires *some* concepts to be applicable to God

> [f]or how could it be the case that I directly perceive a baby, God, or anything else without thereby being able to use some of my concepts to characterize what is perceived? If it is a baby, I could say that it is chubby or emaciated, awake or asleep, and so on. If it is God, I could say that he is powerful or loving or good or communicating a certain message to me, or whatever.[71]

The possibility of experiencing God (on which, on this account, the possibility of referring to him depends) requires the weakening of the DMT to the extent that some concepts *are* applicable to God. (However Alston does not think that this implies that a uniquely applicable description is truly applicable to God nor does it require any specification of just which concepts are applicable to God.) Thus Alston reformulates the DMT such that it allows for the application of the smallest set of concepts whose true application has to be assumed in order to enable reference to God. If there is more than one equally small set of concepts that fulfils this role, then the reformulated version of the DMT is compatible with only one such set being truly applicable to God.[72]

So Alston only avoids falling into the circle described by Cooper by weakening his initial thesis that God is ineffable. He at first posits an ineffable God but, to secure reference and thus ensure that it is God, and not something else, which is claimed to be ineffable, he appeals to the God of direct experience. But this very idea cancels out the original claim of ineffability since concepts can clearly be applied to such an object of direct experience. And if they cannot, and the *experience* of God is ineffable, God must be rationally effable to ensure that it is experiential encounters with him, and not something else, which are ineffable. Either way, the claim that God is ineffable does not survive. Since the purpose of his third and final lecture is to make the DMT give ground to its antithesis and to reconcile both into a synthesis, this strategy no doubt suits Alston's argument very well. But, less helpfully for the present purposes, the philosophical analysis so far suggests that we are not entitled to claim ineffability either for God or for experiences of him. And if this applies in particular to the religious or mystical case, it presumably holds for claims of ineffability in general. This conclusion is suggested, firstly, by the rejection of statements of the form 'X is ineffable' on the grounds of their alleged self-stultification and, secondly, by the rejection of an inadequate and closely related proposed alternative where ineffability is instead attributed to the *experience* of X (it so happens that the X in most of the discussions has been God). Further, both of these problems with the notion of ineffability, as Cooper pointed out, reinforce each other. Even if the notion of ineffability can be made sense of, the possibility of human answerability to the ineffable, especially in some kind of experience, remains problematic. Perhaps, then, Richard Mason was right to state that 'Ineffability has to be taken with a pinch of salt'.[73]

However, there is, I think, a way of philosophically rehabilitating both the concept of ineffability and that of an experience somehow connected to the ineffable. Although the detail of this rehabilitation, and the consequent philosophical resolution of the tension between ineffability and answerability, will be a major concern of the following chapter, I do want to make some initial remarks straight away.

The first rehabilitation is straightforward. The alleged contradiction, between the function of the assertion '*x* is ineffable' (asserting that nothing can be said of *x*) and the act of making that assertion (and thereby stating something about *x*), can be dissolved by distinguishing between levels of language: that which talks about things and that which talks about talk.[74] To apply the distinction to our mystical example, the statement 'God is ineffable' can be interpreted as being about the sense, rather than the referent, of the word 'God', which evokes the ineffable by referring to the concept of ineffability. Although Alston had in fact been aware of this possibility, he did not appear to think that it constituted a robust enough defence of the mystical claims that were his main concern.[75] But A. W. Moore has advanced an interesting argument for the idea that some religious language results from the attempt (doomed to failure) to put ineffable knowledge into words.[76] In what follows it is not my intention to register agreement with Moore's conception of ineffable knowledge[77] but merely to draw attention to one interesting way in which religious language can be interpreted as resulting from the ineffable. What is ineffable, according to Moore's argument, so happens to be specifically delineated as certain states of knowledge.

Moore does not think that there are ineffable truths since a truth must be either expressible linguistically or a kind of representation with content that answers to the way the world is. But he thinks that some states of knowledge are ineffable: they lack content, are not representations, do not answer to reality and are thus things as which nothing counts as their linguistic expression. He gives as an example of such knowledge that of how to exercise concepts. Our knowledge how to exercise the concept of greenness, for instance, can be governed by the rule 'Whatever is green is coloured'. Such knowledge does not depend on knowing *that* anything is the case and is governed by contingencies: we would not know how to exercise the concept of greenness had we not the faculty of sight. As we reflect on our ineffable knowledge of what it is for something to be green, Moore continues, we become aware of the same contingency in that to which the knowledge answers. We become aware that the link between being green and being coloured might not have been imposed upon the world and are led to entertain other possibilities, that of green colourless things, for instance. These possibilities obviously cannot be 'real' so we think of them as 'transcendent', as going beyond everything of which we can make sense. We then attribute to this transcendent level the reason why what we *can* make sense of has the structure it does. We think of it as what prevents the other, unrealized possibilities from being realized and call it divine *fiat*, or whatever. It is in this sense that in 'attempting to put our ineffable knowledge into words involves talking as though there is a supernatural reality that both surpasses and shapes all that we can make sense of'.[78] Had we resisted the temptation to put this ineffable knowledge into words, we should have simply affirmed both the necessity of the link between something's being green and its being coloured and the contingency of our having the concept of greenness at all (thanks to the faculty of sight). But, having succumbed, we instead seek assurance against these latter contingencies that ground the former necessities. It is not that we fear that the necessity of the link between greenness and colouredness might one day no longer obtain but that we might no longer be able to think in these terms. This possibility, if realized, would have some rather disturbing ramifications. As Moore writes, 'the possibility that we shall cease to be able to make good narrative sense of our lives is one to which we are constantly and frighteningly exposed'.[79] We thus apply to the contingencies that allow us to make sense of things the language of transcendence and necessity. Thus, in some cases, 'attempting to put our ineffable knowledge into words ... involves talking as though God exists'.[80] Moore is keen to stress that his project is not necessarily a deflationary one since it does not follow from the claim that religious sentences often result from the attempt to put ineffable knowledge into words either that such sentences are true or that they are false. He does admit, though, that it perhaps compounds the sense of 'dissatisfaction' to which the religious person is condemned; for '[h]ow can there be ultimate satisfaction where attempting to do the impossible is concerned?'[81] Whatever we may think of the detail of Moore's argument, it does show, with specific reference to its religious manifestation, that the idea that language can result from what is ineffable is not necessarily contradictory, nor does it necessarily entail a contradiction. Cooper takes up this point by summarizing Moore's 'suggestion that "A is shown that x" means "A has ineffable knowledge, and when the attempt is made to put what A knows into words, the result is x"'.[82] The implication of this suggestion, for Cooper, is that that the speaker's uttering x, which may just be a nonsensical sentence, does not violate the claim that the knowledge or experience is ineffable.[83]

The detail of our second rehabilitation, that of religious experience, must wait until the next chapter, which sets out this book's philosophical background in Cooper's distinctive defence both of the notion of ineffability and of the possibility of human experiential connection with, and answerability to, the ineffable. It is, however, worth making here some initial remarks on the relation of Cooper's ideas, in this second connection, to the existing philosophical reflection on the notion of ineffability that I have been discussing in the present chapter. Cooper's strategy has its closest parallel in what Kukla calls the argument from epistemic boundedness: 'human minds have limitations on what they can think; and what we can't think, we can't say.'[84] Cooper's defence of the notion of ineffability, we shall see, appeals to the related notion that explanations of meaning must always be given in terms of something's place against a background of human practices (the life-world of the existential phenomenologists) whose role, precisely as background to what is grasped as meaningful, entails that it cannot itself be grasped in its totality. It *may* be that there is also here a point of contact with Moore's argument. The background of which Cooper speaks is certainly what enables us to know how to apply concepts to things insofar as it 'obtrudes and penetrates in its role as the condition of meaningful talk and experience'.[85]

However, the originality of Cooper's argument can be seen at the point at which it departs from the arguments of the thinkers I have been discussing in this section. For Kukla, the argument from epistemic boundedness runs in the opposite direction to the argument from mysticism discussed by Alston, Stace and James but shares with it a dependence on the idea that there are ineffable facts or states of affairs. Whereas the argument from mysticism argues from the mind's capacity to grasp these ineffable states of affairs, the argument from epistemic boundedness argues from its incapacity to do so.[86] Thus in, Stace, Alston, Kukla and Moore (and in the shift from the claim that God is ineffable to the Jamesian claim that the *experience* of God is ineffable), we repeatedly come up against the idea that there is, if not some ineffable object, then a state of affairs which, if not itself ineffable, is at least the 'object' of an ineffable state of knowledge or experience. It is not immediately obvious what phrases like 'ineffable object' or 'ineffable state of affairs' might mean or what precisely would make an experience ineffable if it had a (presumably) perfectly effable object like any ordinary experience. It seems that, insofar as the ineffable object or state of affairs is an object or state of affairs it is, to that extent, perfectly conceptualizable. Whatever the apparent similarities between Cooper's argument and Kukla's argument from epistemic boundedness, we may here observe two differences. First, we shall soon see that, given the importance of his rejection of 'absolutism', Cooper's argument turns precisely on ruling out the idea of ineffable facts which Kukla takes to underlie both opposing lines of argument (from epistemic boundedness and from mysticism). Second, his focus is not, with Moore, on cognition in a narrow sense of knowing how to exercise concepts but, which includes this sense of cognition, on the broader notion of meaning and its inescapably interpretative and lived experience.[87]

For both these reasons, it is Cooper's suggestion that the distinction between subjective and objective dimensions to the notion of experience is 'badly drawn',[88] and it is this move in his argument that resolves the difficulty, noted above, of making sense of the possibility of experiencing an ineffable God (we can have an ineffable God of experience only if we allow an effable God of reason and *vice versa*). The distinction between these two dimensions entails the vagueness and ambiguity in the phrase 'what I experienced', which could equally refer to the object of meaningful experience as to the experience itself. Cooper likens the observation of this distinction to the absurd suggestion, rejected by some of Wittgenstein's remarks on art, that the sense of a piece of music is detachable from the work itself.[89] In that case, Cooper asks, 'why not just have the sense and forget the work? Two works having the same sense should be interchangeable, like identical tins on a supermarket shelf.'[90] In the mystical case, then, the challenge to the mystic to describe the objects of mystical experience is illicit. The mystic will not talk about the object experienced (if the notion of object is even intelligible here)[91] but may evoke it 'by the way he speaks his lines, and tells his story'.[92] He does not so much secure reference to God as make meaningful use of religious language. We should not bemoan the mystic's failure to describe his experience, or to refer to its supposed object, for that would be 'like complaining that a musical performance has not conveyed the sense of the piece because it was not punctuated by statements about that sense'.[93] As we shall shortly see in much more detail, Cooper's suggestion, based on his existential phenomenological conception of meaning, is that, when it comes to ineffability (and even in general), we should attempt to dissolve the distinction between the subjective and objective dimensions to experience, between the experience itself and that of which it is an experience. This alternative conception of experience avoids the difficulty, faced by a philosophical account of (mystical) religious experience, that the ineffable cannot, by definition, be experienced if the notion of experience necessarily requires, as it does for some philosophers, the application of concepts.[94] Cooper is not convinced that this requirement, dependent on the subject–object dualism, is a reasonable one. His alternative strategy of dissolving this dualism serves, in the specific case of experience, to broaden this notion such that Wordsworthian 'Tintern Abbey moments' are not required to involve the application of concepts but neither are they 'debarred from counting as, strictly speaking, *experiences*'.[95]

Donald MacKinnon makes a similar suggestion with characteristic eloquence and I end this chapter with some of his well-chosen words:

> We have to reckon with a state of awareness which claims that the opposition of subjective and objective is overcome and the separation of an investigator's biography from the yield of his investigation obliterated without damage to either.[96]

> [I]t must also be characterized as an experience in which the object is so totally transparent that one must speak of the subject as reduced to the near locus of its transparency ... to use the metaphor favoured by Paul ... the earthen vessel in which the treasure is contained and through which it is mediated is broken in pieces. All we sometimes see is the breaking.[97]

2 PHILOSOPHICAL DEFENCE OF THE CONCEPT OF INEFFABILITY

A Philosophical Defence of Ineffability: David E. Cooper

David Cooper sees the notion of ineffability (which he refers to as 'mystery') as the only escape route from a philosophical tension between what he takes to be two major potential responses to the philosophical question of the meaning of life: 'uncompensated humanism' and 'absolutism'.[1] Cooper, as will become clear, takes 'mystery' to refer to concept of ineffability. He takes it to refer to the concept of what is 'beyond the human' and therefore 'undiscursable', 'since any discourse inevitably captures only a "human world"'.[2] It is appropriate, briefly, to rehearse his argument since the notion of ineffability that it defends is central to what follows in later chapters of this book. Cooper's way of arriving at the notion of ineffability, and his suggestions about the appropriate human response, form the philosophical background to my own arguments.

Cooper accepts the philosophical background to humanism, a conception of meaning reflected in what he calls the 'humanist thesis', which is taken up by existential phenomenology. According to this thesis, an explanation of the meaning of anything must be given in terms of its place in some broader context, in terms of its relation to something external to or beyond itself.[3] A word's meaning owes to its place in a sentence just as the meaning of a hammer must be explained in terms of its place in the practices and projects of, for instance, carpentry or the hanging of pictures. Anything's meaning is thus explained in terms of its relation to the other things in which those practices to which it contributes consist. The meaning of such human practices, taken as meaningful 'referential totalities' of the things that constitute them, is in turn explained in terms of the place of these practices in human (forms of) 'Life', a human world.[4] The early Heidegger, for instance, whose existential phenomenological approach made him an exponent of the humanist thesis, clearly recognized the implication that the meaning of any item ultimately implies a human world, a world of human purposes, practices and projects:

> *with* this thing, for instance, which is ready-to-hand, and which we accordingly call a 'hammer', there is an involvement with hammering; with hammering, there is an

involvement in making something fast; with making something fast, there is an involvement in protection against bad weather; and this protection 'is' for the sake of providing shelter for Dasein – that is to say, for the sake of a possibility of Dasein's Being.[5]

Cooper defines 'meaning' in this way as 'appropriateness to Life'.[6]

Cooper accepts the humanist thesis but recognizes its inadequacy in its 'raw' or 'uncompensated' form. Uncompensated humanism (or what he also calls 'the dis-encumbenced posture') accepts the humanist thesis but denies that human Life as a whole has meaning or that it even makes sense to ask for the meaning of Life as a whole.[7] 'Roughly, the "dis-encumbenced" person', the uncompensated humanist, 'is one who, without abandoning beliefs and commitments, accepts that there can be no [ultimate] "foundations" or independent "grounding" for these'.[8] Uncompensated humanism denies that Life as a whole, with all its constituent practices and projects, has measure, that it is answerable to anything beyond itself and therefore meaningful.[9] The inadequacy of uncompensated humanism, for Cooper, is shown by its unendurability, the fact that it is unliveable – a fact to which Heidegger's phenomenological analysis of *Angst* testifies.[10] For Cooper, what is revealed in this mood, as Heidegger describes it, is the human awareness of the existential freedom and responsibility to interpret the world but a freedom that is not answerable to anything beyond the human.[11] It is possible, as Heidegger says, to delegate this responsibility inauthentically or authentically by losing oneself in 'the way things have been publicly interpreted' by *das Man* or by appropriating a 'heritage';[12] but these are, in their own ways, parts of that of which one is ultimately trying to make sense – the human world, *Dasein*, human Life itself. For the uncompensated humanist, anything we can rely on to make an existential choice is human but, in the *Angst* which testifies to this viewpoint, the human world, taken as a whole, is itself revealed to be 'without grounds' – without, at any rate, grounds which do not appeal to the sense of that very world whose meaning is in question.[13]

Cooper's interpretation of Heidegger's *Angst*, I think, helps to make sense of some more literary descriptions of this mood by Sartre and Beckett, which throw into relief the unendurability of the uncompensated humanism they reflect. Perhaps Roquentin's disturbing experience while looking at a chestnut root in the park can be understood as a function of uncompensated humanism: 'I no longer remembered that it was a root. Words had disappeared, and with them the meaning of things, the methods of using them, the feeble landmarks which men have traced on their surface.'[14] This passage reflects an experience of the arbitrary nature of the world's meaning if this is dictated by nothing beyond the human. If Life as a whole is meaningless, the things that contribute to it are also meaningless and words can be no more than feeble landmarks arbitrarily traced on their surface. Similarly, the major philosophical theme of Samuel

Beckett's work has been taken (notably by his English publisher, John Calder) to be the absurdity and meaninglessness of human existence. Beckett's plays celebrate individual human practices (especially habits and daily rituals), which have meaning in virtue of their contribution to Life. But this celebration just serves to soften the blow of their inherited meaningless from Life as a whole. As Cooper puts it, '[a]n activity whose point is to contribute to something that itself turns out to be pointless retrospectively inherits this pointlessness'.[15] Thus, for Beckett, human projects are meaningful only *provisionally*: 'it is the norm of the Western world to live ... through habit and a disciplined timetable, pushing what is unpleasant outside consciousness', 'what is unpleasant' being, of course, the *ultimate* pointlessness of any human action.[16] It is Beckett's dramatic calling, Calder says, to draw our attention to the provisional nature of the meaning of human habits, to their ultimate absurdity, which we are all too wont to brush under the carpet. This ultimate pointlessness is dramatically hinted at in *Act Without Words II* when A and B engage in such apparently meaningful rituals such as hair-brushing and time-keeping.[17] But the characters never meet, each one carrying out his rituals in isolation while the other is asleep in a sack! This renders the practices ultimately meaningless in the context of the play since the meaning of such habits derives from their place in a specifically social context. And the only potential context of this kind *in the play* is intercourse with the other character, which is never realized. It is of course hoped by actors, audiences, drama critics and so on that the point made in the somewhat confined context of this play will tell us something about Life as a whole – that, considered on its own terms (and here I agree with Calder's interpretation of Beckett's oeuvre) it, too, is *ultimately* pointless. The meaninglessness of the habits in the context of Beckett's play strengthens the humanist conception of meaning as the connection of something to what is beyond itself. This is because that conception can be defended, as it is by Cooper, by appeal to the psychological fact that 'an activity is typically regarded as devoid of significance when perceived as so limited and enclosed as to fail appropriately to connect up with anything beyond itself'.[18] Thus Beckett's play not only affirms the humanist thesis but also dramatically shows that, in its uncompensated form, that thesis entails the ultimate absurdity of any human action. Calder's justification for Beckett's own practice of writing plays which convey uncompensated humanism (a practice which is itself presumably absurd) is the contention that '[h]opelessness discussed *seems* a little better'.[19]

But this position is practically, if not logically, inconsistent – it is, for Cooper, unliveable. If the claim being made in our interpretation of Sartre's novel and Beckett's play is true, that human endeavour is pointless and words arbitrary landmarks traced on the surface of things, it is not clear how the words expressing this attitude itself (which, together, constitute plays and novels) could convey this in a sense that was of any ultimate significance, that is, in a way that was not purely trivial. Surely, when one chooses to spend one's life writing plays and novels that communicate the pointlessness of human Life, the writing of such works is tacitly and implicitly regarded to be more worthwhile than other activities which do not. It would take a stronger claim than Calder's ('hopelessness discussed seems a little better') to resolve this apparent inconsistency. Our worry that what we have invested time and effort in might turn out to be pointless, as Cooper points out, will not be abated either by the claim that *everything* is ultimately pointless or by a circular appeal to the fact that we have invested time and effort in it.[20] At least insofar as Sartre and Beckett invest time and energy in writing literary works they cannot, in fact, *always* be of this unliveable, uncompensated humanist stance, though some of the content of their work might misleadingly suggest that they are.[21]

Given, as has been suggested, that an explanation of something's meaning relates it to something beyond itself, given the persistence of the question of the meaning of Life and that the answer that Life is simply absurd really is inconsistent or unliveable, Cooper argues, any explanation of Life's meaning (any compensation for the humanist thesis in its hitherto raw form) can be given only by relating human Life to some measure beyond the human to which it is answerable. The attempt of absolutism to find this measure in a discursable realm of independent facts, *the* way in which the world is independently of the human contribution, is wrong-headed since our provisional acceptance of the humanist thesis that meaning is appropriateness to Life entails that 'there is no such way'.[22] The humanist thesis entails that any set of independent facts about the world or a realm (like a cosmos or god) that contains or transcends Life would itself be invested with the very concepts whose meaning it is supposed to explain:

> any world – physical and/or divine – that we could articulate and conceptualize is a 'human world': one that is the way it is only in relation to human perspective, purpose and preference, and not one, therefore, which is that way 'in itself' or 'anyway' independently of such human factors.[23]

It is illegitimate, Cooper claims, thus to provide a measure for human practices and perspectives by appeal to a realm which is invested with any of those very values – and any conceptualizable realm would necessarily be so invested. We are now in a position that is strikingly similar to that of existential phenomenologists such as Heidegger and Merleau-Ponty; we are able to see how the existential phenomenological conception of meaning (basically the humanist one) entails a doctrine of engagement (intimacy or logical interdependence) of 'self' and 'world' – a doctrine of what Heidegger calls 'Being-in-the-world'.

Cooper also rejects a position labelled the 'two-levels' position, which is attributed to thinkers like Kant and Schopenhauer on some interpretations of their work. The two-levels position is characterized by the 'conjunction of a "humanist" ... view of the discursable world with the idea of an ineffable realm "beyond the world"'.[24] In such a view, he says, one finds

> the thought of an 'absolute' or 'in itself' reality that is to be distinguished from a 'phenomenal' or empirical world that crucially owes to what William James called 'the human contribution'. And ... one also finds the thought that, undiscursable as the former is, it can nevertheless provide some sort of measure for this human contribution.[25]

Cooper thinks that the incoherence of this view comes to light when consideration is given to the one major exception to the general rule that 'the discursable world depends for what it is on human beings' (or on the *a priori* structures of the mind), namely, human existence itself. The two-levels view cannot adequately explain how 'we, so to speak, are already there, up and running, as the filters ... responsible for our world taking on the contours it does'.[26] This incoherence is best avoided by the existential phenomenological doctrine of engagement towards which Cooper's argument has been gesturing: 'Our existence is "Being-in-the-world": it is the existence of creatures, that is, whose being – whose practices, moods, structures of thought, "form of life" – cannot be even notionally separated from the world in which we are engaged'.[27]

The only escape from the tension which is entailed by acceptance of both the humanist thesis and its required compensation in the notion of a measure beyond the human to which human Life is answerable (but an idea of measure that entails neither an unbelievable absolutism nor an incoherent two-levels doctrine) – between humanism and absolutism – is, for Cooper, a doctrine of mystery.[28] 'Mystery', here, is taken in the strong sense of not what, as a matter of fact, we will never know (and, in principle, *could* know) but what is in principle unknowable and ineffable, by definition resistant to conceptual formulation and linguistic articulation.[29] There must, given the unendurability of uncompensated humanism, be a measure for human Life but it would be inconsistent to think of this measure as conceptualizable or discursable. Therefore the measure must be *un*discursable, ineffable: in short, a *mystery*. A view which recognizes this fact, and regards human existence as answerable to an ineffable measure, may be described as a 'doctrine of mystery' or, in my terminology, a 'doctrine of ineffability'.

I am persuaded by Cooper's suggestion that a doctrine of ineffability underwrites the rhetoric of Heidegger's later philosophy, the purpose of which he construes as being to attune us to, or to evoke (but obviously not to describe), the ineffable.[30] But it is a premise of this book (which I have referred to as the apophatic premise), that some part, at least, of the Christian tradition, which Cooper largely neglects,[31] is underwritten by a doctrine of ineffability, understood in the above sense, and that the two are compatible. As I suggested in the previous chapter, the dimension to the Christian tradition which consists in the mystical or apophatic writings can be seen to be underwritten by such a doctrine, a system in which the concept of ineffability has a place.[32] In the case of the Christian mystical tradition, it appears, the word 'God' (or 'Godhead') is supposed, at the very least, to evoke this concept of ineffability.[33]

The final stage in Cooper's argument follows the implications of the notion of ineffability to their logical conclusion. Recall that any world that can be articulated and conceptualized is a human world, intimately related to, and logically inseparable from, human perspectives, values and concerns. It is for this reason that the notion of ineffability, whilst necessarily evoking what is beyond the human, should not be held to refer to a transcendent thing or realm (a god or a cosmos) set over against the human world. Such a transcendent conception of mystery would, illegitimately, invest the ineffable with the very human meanings and values for which it is invoked to provide measure precisely by not being so invested.[34] The task of the philosopher or the poet is not, for Cooper, to describe mystery (for then, as we have seen, it would not be ineffable in the relevant sense) nor is it a Wittgensteinian silence; it is, rather, to devise a vocabulary of 'attunement to mystery'.[35] The vision or rhetoric that this latter stage of the argument calls for, he concludes, is not one of 'the human world ... as disjoined from what is beyond the human ... [but] one of their entire intimacy'.[36] A vocabulary of the right sort would cultivate at once an experience of the human world as 'presencing' or 'epiphanizing' from mystery *and*, simultaneously, of mystery 'sending' or 'giving' the human world.[37] To be meaningful, 'Life [*itself*] needs to be viewed as ... a "gift", as the coming to presence of what is mysterious'.[38] Perhaps the language closest to doing justice to this vision is the ancient rhetoric of epiphany: the human world, we might say, is to be viewed as an epiphany of the ineffable. But even this is inadequate to the extent that the phrase 'epiphany of ... ' fails adequately to capture the required view of intimacy between the ineffable that shows up and its showing up *as* the human world, between subjective and objective dimensions of the experience of the ineffable. It would be better, Cooper suggests, to think of the phrase as less akin to 'flash of a knife' than to 'flash of lightning' – the kind of expression in which it would be 'obviously ... mistaken to imagine a divide between what shows and its showing'.[39] The right kind of rhetoric, then, will attune us to what Cooper calls this 'vision of intimacy' of the human world and its ineffable measure, a vision in which the human world is viewed as itself mysterious. In the next section I want to show, in detail, that Cooper is right to read the later Heidegger as a practitioner of a rhetoric of attunement to mystery whose work after about 1935 is underwritten by precisely the kind of doctrine of ineffability for which Cooper has provided a sophisticated philosophical defence.

Ineffability in Heidegger's Later Philosophy

It would seem, owing to Heidegger's consistent description of his philosophical project as the posing, if not the addressing or answering, of the *Seinsfrage* (the question of Being), that examination of Heidegger's use of the word '*Sein*' in a given period of his work provides us with a pretty reliable guide as to his central philosophical concern in that period. Julian Young believes that the meaning of '*Sein*', in the period of *Being and Time*, denotes what Cooper calls the human world, the widest 'referential totality' within which anything, partly in virtue of its connections with other things, can be said to be meaningful and thus apprehended and encountered by us.[40] In the *Being and Time* period, Young argues, Heidegger used the word '*Sein*' (translated into English by Young as the lower-case 'being') to refer to this human world. (The world, it should be noted, is here taken not in the ontical sense of (even the sum total of) experienceable entities, the German for which is usually '*das Seiende*', but rather in the ontological sense of the non-optional, transcendental horizon, the foundational referential totality, within which those entities can be encountered and experienced.) I extrapolate that this sense of 'world' was, in this early period, Heidegger's central philosophical concern.

But there is a distinct shift, which might perhaps be identified with at least one instance of what, following Heidegger himself, commentators have labelled the 'turning (*die Kehre*)' in his thought and which I locate at around 1935 with the appearance of 'The Origin of the Work of Art'.[41] In that essay, Heidegger uses the familiar term 'world' to refer to the ontological horizon just mentioned, that which is familiar and intelligible, but pairs it off with the new and eccentric term 'earth' with which he clearly means to denote that which is concealed and opaque but which also makes such a horizon possible: the mysterious condition for 'world' which is at once 'self secluding', 'unexplained', 'that which is essentially undisclosable', and yet also that on which the 'world grounds itself', 'that on which and in which man bases his dwelling'.[42] It is my argument that the notion of 'earth' is the added dimension to *Sein* on the basis of which Heidegger's early and late interpretations of his cardinal concern, the *Seinsfrage*, may be distinguished. 'The Origin of the Work of Art', I think, constitutes a useful marker of Heidegger's shift of philosophical emphasis from the human world to its mysterious 'source'. Young glosses Heidegger's revised understanding of Being in the terminology of that essay:

> while in one sense *Sein* is just 'world' (in the ontological sense), in a different and, in the end, much more important sense its heart lies in 'earth'. More accurately, *Sein* in this second sense is 'world' (in the ontic sense) and 'earth' taken together.[43]

It will be surmised from the foregoing remarks that I am in wholehearted agreement with Cooper's reading of the later Heidegger that leads to his statement that 'Heidegger is an unequivocal proponent of a doctrine of mystery'.[44] I agree, too, with Young's view that Heidegger sometimes evokes this concept of ineffability with the word '*Sein*'[45] (which, in these uses, Young translates with the capitalized English word 'Being') and I think that the ineffable is the fundamental philosophical concern of his later works; however, I am less certain than Young of the extent to which, in this context, it is appropriate, straight away, to listen for the religious overtones of the concept of ineffability as expressed in these uses of '*Sein*'.[46] Although 'Being' is perhaps the most common, it, together with 'earth', is not the only word that Heidegger uses to evoke the concept of ineffability. The terms he uses, Cooper observes,

> range from mere place-holders, like 'Being' and 'It', to ones indicative of the dependence of the world on mystery, such as 'wellspring' and 'source', to a bewildering array of apparently bizarre terms – 'the Enowning' or 'Appropriating event' (*Ereignis*), 'that-which-regions', 'the Giving', 'the nearing nearness', and so on.[47]

Young's suggestion that, in the terminology of 'The Origin of the Work of Art', 'Being' refers, in one sense, to 'world' (in the ontological sense) and, in another, to 'world' (in the ontic sense) and 'earth' taken together may be supported by appeal to the fact that Heidegger thinks of Being as possessing a concealing-revealing 'rhythm'. For Heidegger, 'Being' refers to the self-secluding condition for there being a world within which entities can be meaningfully encountered and thus experienced. In 'On the Essence of Truth', he calls that worldly encounter the 'letting-be' that, as it reveals entities, flags up the nature of being 'as a whole' as 'incalculable and incomprehensible'.[48] He writes: 'Precisely because letting be always lets beings be in a particular comportment that relates to them and thus discloses them, it conceals beings as a whole'; it is this concealment which Heidegger, in this essay at least, terms 'the mystery'.[49] He speaks, here in 1930, of 'forgottenness of the mystery', of the essentially concealed and concealing dimension to *Sein* which, as the *Kehre* develops through the 1930s and beyond, modulates into the notion of *Seinsvergessenheit*, the 'forgetfulness' or 'oblivion' of Being itself or Being 'as a whole' as he incorporates the notion referred to by the words 'mystery' and 'earth' into the meaning of the word '*Sein*'.[50] He seems to express this notion in embryonic form when he writes, in 'On the Essence of Truth', that Being (capitalized) 'appears primordially in the light of a concealing withdrawal'.[51] In later works, with the *Kehre* further advanced, Heidegger clearly thinks of 'Being' as containing at once the revealing significance of 'world' and the concealing meaning of 'earth', 'withdrawal' and 'mystery'. One commentator summarizes the tension I have in mind in terms of the 'tension between Being as self-revealing and Being as self-concealing, between some concrete world-disclosure which we can experience and the ground of a world-disclosure which "withdraws" as the disclosure occurs'.[52] In 'Letter on Humanism', for instance, Heidegger quotes an earlier passage in which he wrote 'only so long as Dasein *is* ... "is there" Being'.[53] Here, he insists that he was using the German for 'there is' – '*es gibt*' – quite literally to evoke the phrase 'it gives'.[54] He identifies 'It' with the mystery of Being but it is this mystery that 'gives' the world; it is the condition for world as the ultimate ontological horizon.[55]

Thus, in his later work, Heidegger espouses a position in which Being is, although ineffable, that to which human beings, and with them the world with which they are interdependent, are answerable. Heidegger claims that Being is itself responsible for its withdrawal; Being is, in other words, self-concealing.[56] But he speaks, in the same breath, of a 'draft' created by the withdrawal of Being into which man is drawn and towards which man points as, in Hölderlin's word, a 'sign'.[57] Man's essential nature, whereby 'man first *is* man', lies in being drawn into the mysterious 'draft' and, as a sign, pointing into it towards Being.[58] One step towards resolving this tension between what I have called 'ineffability' and 'answerability' is by incorporating both poles of the tension into the single notion of 'transcendence', a notion which I take to be Heidegger's first step towards the 'vision of intimacy' (of the ineffable and the human world which answers to it) that Cooper advocates.

Heidegger, firstly, applies the term 'transcendence' to Being in order to evoke its ineffability. He states that 'Being is the *transcendens* pure and simple' with the self-professed intention of making the claim that 'man' 'does not decide whether and how' Being comes to presence, how, in other words, Being 'gives' the world and provides us with that horizon within which entities can be experienced.[59] This statement of the transcendence of Being not only designates Being as 'the mystery' but also states Being's independence, in one provisional sense, of the human contribution. But, secondly, transcendence also applies to man who 'ek-sists' (this bizarre spelling is meant to draw attention to the word's Latin etymology, '*extare*' – 'to stand out'). The term is meant to express the way in which Being concerns man, namely, in and through the meaningful structures of the world ('Being-in-the-world').[60] Man apprehends Being, in all its ineffability, in terms of the world with which he is essentially interdependent, the 'clearing' of meaning onto which he stands out. The non-optional and transcendental horizon of world limits the ways in which beings (on the basis of which Being must be thought) can show up for us. It is in this sense that Being *does* need a human world in order to come to presence *as* anything.[61] This second point, thirdly and finally, implies man's answerability to Being, the requirement that he 'think' Being 'on the basis of beings', which show up within the world's horizon, whilst remaining sensitive to the 'ontological difference' between the two.[62] To think in this way is, in Heidegger's vocabulary, to experience beings, the world, as 'transparent' to Being or 'in the light of Being'; it is to accept the 'nearness of Being', its 'coming to presence' and to recognize that it is 'nearer to man than every being'.[63] It is, in my terminology, to accept man's answerability to the ineffable by accepting the possibility of an, albeit indirect, *experience* of mystery. One (if not *the*) way in which man is answerable to the ineffable is in that he can, in some sense, *experience* it.[64]

What Heidegger means by 'thinking', I suggest, might be put in the more straightforward terms of 'the experience of the ineffable' or 'the experience of Being' but with the understanding that 'Being' refers less to an object of which an experience may be had than to what pervades the experience itself and is inseparable from it. It is certainly the case that thinking is that with which Heidegger sometimes identifies the practice of philosophy, rightly viewed, and that he sees it as a (if not *the*) way in which human beings are answerable to the ineffable.[65] This can be seen in the terms he uses to describe thinking: 'co-respondence (*Ent-sprechung*)' with or 'attunement (*Gestimmtheit*)' to Being; further, Steiner's gloss on these terms (possibly mindful of Heidegger's comment that the 'path of our discussion must, therefore, be of such a kind and direction that that of which philosophy treats concerns us personally, affects us and, indeed, touches us in our very nature') brings out with even greater clarity the sense of answerability which they capture.[66] He describes correspondence as 'a response, a vital echo, a "re-sponsion" in the liturgical sense of participatory engagement'.[67] The notion of correspondence, he suggests, evokes both the idea of a 'response' and a 'responsibility, custodianship, answerability to and for' while the notion of 'attunement', in which we are told by Heidegger that correspondence consists, captures the idea, which Steiner claims is at least as old as Pythagoras, of 'tuning the soul' to Being.[68] Both of these terms used to describe thinking, on Steiner's interpretation, capture Heidegger's central idea that the thinker is answerable to the *Seinsfrage*.[69] This answerability, I suggest, takes the form of a certain sort of experience of that to which the thinker is answerable, an experience of 'the Being of being' or 'being with respect to Being', of which sense is best made in the terms of correspondence and attunement.[70]

Thinking, as Heidegger further describes it, has two main required elements: Bartky makes the point that the dual or divided nature of thinking echoes the rhythm of Being to which thinking must respond, both revealing and concealing.[71] Heidegger tells us that thinking firstly comprises (and this aspect stresses ineffability) 'openness to the mystery', the mystery, I have suggested, that is Being (the 'essential trait' of the mystery is that it is '[t]hat which shows itself and at the same time withdraws').[72] If the thinker is to be open or answerable to the *mystery*, if she is to experience it, she will be unable to think in the ordinary manner of employing concepts in order to represent objects since, as Heidegger incessantly reminds us, Being is not an object: there is an important sense in which Being, in its mysterious 'earth' dimension, 'shows itself only when it remains undisclosed and unexplained'.[73] Thus the experience of Being cannot, without serious error, dispel the mystery of Being by objectifying it, by admitting it 'only as an object for man's estimation'; in short, ('meditative') thinking, as the experience of or attunement to Being, cannot proceed in the same way as does what Heidegger, with disparaging intentions, calls 'calculative thinking'.[74] It is this dissatisfaction with the subject–object dichotomy that makes Heidegger's relationship with the language of 'experience' in this connection ambiguous,[75] tied up as that kind of language has mostly been with that of representational or conceptual thought. In what may be interpreted as an attempt, like Cooper's, to dissolve the dualism between experience's subjective and objective dimensions, Heidegger sometimes prefers to speak not in terms of man's 'experience of Being' but instead in those of man's being 'appropriated by' Being.[76] However, he continues to use the term throughout the 'Conversation on a Country Path about Thinking' and even states that the way of thinking *derives from* the 'representational thinking' which is grounded by 'experience', construed as a relation of a subject to an object. He writes that the way of thinking 'remains necessarily bound to a dialogue with traditional thinking' and this may be compared with his suggestion that thinking, as correspondence, must be 'in conversation with [*im Gespräch mit*]' the history of 'philosophy', whatever the extent to which that history has been bound up with, even responsible for, *Seinsvergessenheit*, the oblivion of Being.[77] Thus, although I shall, with Heidegger, continue to speak of an 'experience of' Being, of mystery or of the ineffable, this language should be heard with care. Perhaps 'experience' should be heard in the context of the early Heidegger's remarks on 'mood', referring less to an experience 'of' something than to a value-laden attitude towards one's experience *as a whole*. Such an understanding is at least a step in the direction of the dissolution of subjective and objective dimensions to the concept of experience, which Cooper suggests. Following on from this, as we shall see towards the end of this section, 'experience' in this context is inseparably bound to other practices, both linguistic and non-linguistic, which, for Heidegger, constitute 'dwelling'. This kind of experience, it is worth noting, is not hermetically sealed with neat boundaries but is inseparable from a whole way of comporting oneself, from a way of Life.

    The structure of Heidegger's dialogue, 'Conversation on a Country Path about Thinking', may serve to give us some idea of what this non-objectifying thought might involve.[78] The participants are discussing how best to attain attunement to, experience of, Being (the conversation is, after all, 'about thinking') but the narrative context for the participants' conversation is a walk along a path. In their introductory remarks, the translators make a suggestion as to the significance of this fact as follows: 'We might think of it, metaphorically, as the activity of walking along a path which leads to Being. Certainly metaphorically, the conversation along the path referred to in the Conversation symbolizes such an activity and in such a direction.'[79] As the character of the 'Scientist' is having trouble letting go of representational thought, the 'Scholar' and the 'Teacher' (Heidegger's *persona*?) try to teach him to employ the rhetoric of thinking. When he finally believes he has been able to do this, he claims, significantly, that what allowed him to do so was connected less with the conceptual representation of certain objects than with the course of the conversation itself.[80] It is my view that this remark represents Heidegger's view of his own work, some of which is 'about thinking', as itself partially constitutive of thinking or of the expression which arises from thinking. As Timothy Clark puts it, some of Heidegger's work 'cannot be read as being "about" something in the familiar sense of making a conceptual model of it. They strive towards the status of thinking-in-action.'[81] The nature of the non-representational, non-objectifying thinking involved in an experience of the ineffable, and how this is possible, are best brought out in Heidegger's second requirement for thinking which emphasizes answerability – 'releasement toward things (*die Gelassenheit zu den Dingen*)'.[82]

Thinking, in its dimension of 'releasement towards things', Heidegger states, goes beyond the experience of the appearance of objects. A 'horizon' within which objects ('beings') can be encountered and which can, in principle, be transcended (such as a referential totality or, ultimately, the human world) is only experienced relative to the objects themselves and our conceptual representations of them. The condition for there being a 'horizon' at all ('Being', 'the mystery', Heidegger's main concern) has not yet been encountered in such conceptual thought. Properly thought, therefore, a 'horizon', in the Teacher's (and Heidegger's own?) words, is 'but the side facing us of an openness that surrounds us'.[83] Heidegger calls this openness (by which I take him to mean the human world) the 'region' and its condition (which I take to be 'Being') 'that-which-regions'.[84] It is nothing other than Being into which we are 'released', to which we correspond or are answerable, when we think.[85] But releasement, we were told, is releasement 'towards *things*' – the world of things (the 'horizon', the 'region') 'is but the side of that-which-regions turned towards our re-presenting'.[86] The recognition has been made that the meaningful world of entities is but the side facing us of the ineffable condition for there being a meaningful human world at all, that is, of Being. To be released towards entities in thinking *is*, in other words, to be open to the mystery of Being and *vice versa*. 'Releasement toward things and openness to the mystery belong together'.[87] They are part of the unified whole that is thinking. It is my argument that Heidegger is here trying to encourage the picture advocated by Cooper whereby the ineffable and the human world of things are seen as being in a condition of total intimacy.

In order to arrive at a clearer idea of what effect the identification of these two dimensions with one another has upon the 'shape' of thinking, it is worth contrasting thinking, so understood, with Heidegger's 'letting-be (*Sein-lassen*)' mentioned above with reference to his early conception of 'world'. 'Letting-be', as we saw, is a meaningful encounter that reveals beings and is, in this sense, connected with man's transcendence or ek-sistence.[88] However, letting-be at the same time conceals the mystery in a way that leads to *Seinsvergessenheit*. Releasement, on the other hand, also ecstatically reveals beings but in a way that is, at the same time, 'open to the mystery' of Being. It is perhaps this idea that led Heidegger to state that every 'thoughtful' doctrine of man is itself a doctrine of Being and *vice versa*.[89] This point, together with the fact that releasement *towards Being* just *is* releasement *towards things*, entails the nature of thinking as expressed in the third and final point of my description of Heidegger's notion of 'transcendence' above, namely, the requirement that man, as the thinker, think 'Being on the basis of beings'.[90] As Bartky expresses the necessity of thought of this kind, 'Being is always the Being *of* beings just as *Dasein* is never without a world'.[91]

The kind of experience which is involved in Heidegger's 'thinking', then, is one of the intimacy of Being, the ineffable with the human world itself. It is as though, in Cooper's language, the world is an epiphany of Being. But, as we saw in Cooper's work, Being is not an entity *of* which the world is an epiphany but rather an 'epiphanizing', entirely intimate with the world itself.[92] It is perhaps this notion that Heidegger is trying to capture in his talk of *Ereignis* or *Seyn* – a seamless 'event' or 'flow' from Being to beings.[93] The point of Heidegger's talk of 'presencing', '*Ereignis*' and 'the worlding of the world', it seems, is to discourage the idea of a dichotomy between the ineffable which shows up and the world *as which* it shows up. The task of the thinker, construed as that of experiencing the world as an epiphany of mystery or a gift from Being, is to see the world itself as intimate with its ineffable source, to see the world *as itself mysterious*. In his essay 'The Thing', Heidegger describes this experience in more specific detail in the form of a meditation on an earthenware jug. In thinking, we experience the fourfold (which is just the later Heidegger's interpretation of the concept of 'world',[94] arguably in the ontical sense) 'gathered' in the thing, the jug in this case.[95] It is this 'gathering' that is 'the jug's presencing' *as* a jug; as Heidegger obliquely (as ever) puts it, 'The thing things. Thinging gathers.'[96] Not only do we see through the thing to the world, or fourfold, gathered in it ('thinging') but we also see through the world *as a whole* to Being ('worlding'), 'the region from which it presences', we 'inhabit the nearness' and, in some sense, experience Being, the ineffable mystery.[97] Cooper sees two 'double-exposures' at work here. There is, firstly,

> that of 'seeing through' something – a tree, say – to the network of relations, the 'relational totality of significance', on which that depends, whilst also 'seeing' that whole 'gathered', 'con-centrated', in the tree. Then, second ... the experience of seeing things as ordinary particulars, while also 'seeing through' the world as a whole, a sense of which is cultivated in the first experience, to [mystery].[98]

Thinking, it must be stressed, is both receptive and creative. In Cooper's terms, it is to 'experience ourselves as at once "world-makers" and "world-receivers"' in dissolution of the subject–object dualism; in Heidegger's terms, it is 'beyond the distinction between activity and passivity'.[99]

Crucially, thinking, for Heidegger, already implies language: 'only when man speaks, does he think'.[100] Thinking as 'correspondence (*ent-sprechung*)' appears to contain the idea of speaking and, controversially, this signifies, for Heidegger, that thinking is a linguistic phenomenon and is 'in the service of language'.[101] He writes in his characteristically etymologizing manner, '*Dieses Ent-sprechen ist ein Sprechen*'.[102] But the linguistic experience in which thinking as correspondence consists is, Heidegger tells us, 'not of our own making'.[103] It is not man who speaks language but rather language that speaks man. As Heidegger suggests, speaking is a hearing 'in advance'; we can only speak because we have already 'listened to language. What do we hear there? We hear *language speaking*.'[104] The source of the 'saying' to which we are exhorted to listen is Being itself but the intimate 'relation' between reality and its source is analogous to that between speech and language. Language, Heidegger tells us, is the 'language of Being' as clouds are the 'clouds of the sky'.[105] The 'relation' is one of total intimacy such that it is possible to say that Being, for Heidegger just '*is* a "Saying"'.[106] 'Poetry', then, is a listening to and 'reiteration' of Being's saying.[107] It is the poet's active duty to bring Being to language through this reiteration and to guard the truth of Being in that poetic language. But language is not wholly a human product; it is also a 'mittence' of Being. To put it in these more passive terms 'language ... is appropriated by Being and pervaded by Being'.[108] As Cooper puts it, '[i]t is *as if*, when speaking, we are hearkening to and translating signs which have been given us'.[109] Strictly speaking, poetry, too, is beyond the active and passive distinction: it reveals man as 'the shepherd of Being', an image which nicely brings out the interdependence of activity and passivity, creativity and receptivity, which Heidegger thinks essential to 'thinking' and 'poeticizing'.[110] For Heidegger, language is the primary way in which human beings have a world – Steiner calls this the 'language-condition' for human existence.[111] For Heidegger, it is partly owing to language that anything can be meaningfully, that is interpretatively, encountered *as* this or that; as he writes, '[o]nly where there is language, is there world'.[112] It is unsurprising, then, that Heidegger thinks poetry necessary in order to cultivate the experience, involved in thinking, of the world as mysterious or (as some commentators like to emphasize) 'holy'. Heidegger believes that it is, in fact, poetic language that first makes language possible: thus he can claim that 'the essence of language must be understood through the essence of poetry'.[113]

It ought to be noted that, owing to this view of language as constitutive of the world of beings (on the basis of which Being must be thought) and as derivative from poetry, poetic language does not so much *express* the experience of the mystery of Being as create that experience. For Heidegger, 'Poetry is the *establishing* of [B]eing by means of the word'.[114] Even Being requires establishment, 'opening out', since it is its nature to withdraw: 'Being must be opened out, so that the existent may appear'.[115] Reflecting on Wittgenstein's question whether Shakespeare was a *Sprachschöpfer* ('creator of language', 'wordsmith') rather than a *Dichter*, Steiner argues that 'poet' does not fully translate the meaning of the latter German term.[116] The *Dichter*'s task, Steiner suggests, is comparable to Adam's primordial and essentially creative act of nomination: '[l]ike Adam, the *Dichter* names that which is, and his naming embodies its veritable being'.[117] In this way, the *Dichter* operates 'in the neighbourhood to blasphemy inherent in the exercise of fictional invention, of counter-creation to the divine or the unknown'.[118] Steiner, I think, has in mind the Romantic notion of the poem as a heterocosm and thus of the poet as 'another God' creating a whole universe.[119] These ideas, Steiner argues, chime in with those of Heidegger who, we have seen, accords a creative function to poetic language and who thinks of the poet as the apotheosis of human potential. For Heidegger, as Cooper summarizes, the distinction between 'thinking (*Denken*)' and 'poeticizing (*dichten*)' is, at best, provisional: 'thinking ... is inseparable from a certain form of "saying", of seeking the appropriate language of mystery. Hence his frequent use of the compound "thinking / saying"'.[120]

I now want to show that, although our reading of Heidegger's argument depends to a great extent upon a view of experience and expression of the ineffable that is within the limits of language, that argument does not leave things there but rather undercuts the distinction between linguistic and non-linguistic by way of a broad conception of the poetic which embraces them both. It would indeed be a strange account of the experience and expression of the ineffable that could not cope with transcendence of the linguistic sphere! Heidegger appears to absorb non-linguistic meaningful practices into his understanding of the linguistic phenomenon of poetry. The title of one of his essays reiterates a line from Hölderlin, '... poetically man dwells ...'.[121] In that essay, he suggests that humanity's 'dwelling' ('the manner in which we humans *are* on the earth'[122]) is itself, when attuned to Being, poetic. He suggests that the measure for dwelling, that against which human conduct is measured, is taken from another order, the mysterious order of Being, and that this measure is provided by the poet's linguistic establishment of (and the thinker's correspondence to) that order. The unity that, I have argued, is thinking/poeticizing, he writes elsewhere, 'grant[s] us the possibility of dwelling in the world in a totally different way'.[123] As Cooper glosses the idea of dwelling, 'to experience the mystery and to comport oneself in a certain way towards it are two sides of the same coin'.[124] In other words, thinking/saying gives rise to a certain experience/comportment towards the ineffable insofar as the ineffable is thought of as intimate with the world. A certain kind of comportment towards *the world itself* (viewed as mysterious) is ultimately implied by the experience and expression of the ineffable and Heidegger calls this comportment 'dwelling'. We might describe his position as the incorporation of non-linguistic practices into language (in Heidegger's broad, poetic sense) or, alternatively, as absorbing language into non-linguistic meaningful practices. Strictly though, I think Heidegger visualizes a constellation of experience, speaking and comportment (or, in his rhetoric, 'thinking (*Denken*)', 'poeticizing (*dichten*)' and 'dwelling (*Wohnen*)'), none of which can be separated from the others in anything but a provisional manner, for the purposes, say, of Heidegger's own elucidations (or mine). It is not that poeticizing presupposes thinking or that dwelling presupposes poeticizing but rather that each implies the others. Heidegger is evoking a broad notion of the poetic which includes, but is not limited to, the linguistic dimension (narrowly construed) and which undercuts the traditional linguistic/non-linguistic distinction by embracing phenomena of both kinds.

In this first part of the book, I have set out both the theological problem of ineffability and a contemporary philosophical defence of the concept, drawing attention to the Heideggerian roots of that defence. But some twentieth-century theologians have attempted to apply this Heideggerian line of thought in an attempt to resolve the tension between ineffability and answerability and thus to solve the theological problem of ineffability. They have advocated an understanding of religion as a means of attunement to the ineffable God and have attempted to articulate a specifically theological vision of the intimacy of the human world and its ineffable source. Moving into the book's second part, which is concerned with some existing theological and philosophical attempts to solve the problem of ineffability, I take a detailed critical look, in the next chapter, at examples of these attempted theological solutions to the problem of ineffability and examine their strengths as well as their shortcomings.

3 TWO ATTEMPTS AT THEOLOGICAL APPROPRIATION

As we have seen with Cooper's philosophical defence of the idea, the concept of ineffability provides the measure for human concepts precisely by evoking that which is *not* invested with those concepts, including that of existence and cannot therefore be construed as an entity or object, bound by the finite conditions of time and space. When we consider the concept of ineffability, we must, in Heidegger's language, be mindful of the ontological difference. The philosophical analysis considered in Chapter 1 revealed the need for this in the form of the objection that claims of ineffability are self-stultifying. The way round this was to deny that the idea of 'ineffable objects' makes sense and to claim, instead, that the meaning of the claim '*x* is ineffable' should be interpreted as 'the word "*x*" refers to the concept of ineffability'. Concomitantly, when it comes to the experience of the ineffable, it was suggested with the help of Cooper and Heidegger that we should think not so much of the experience of some object by a subject but rather of a situation in which subjective and objective dimensions to experience are undifferentiated.

The idea of self-stultification recurs in a religious connection with, for example, Boyer's conception of the 'elusive objects' of religion, the supreme example of which is God. But, as we saw, no object, however elusive, can be regarded to be ineffable in my sense. One problem with the idea of God as an ineffable entity is that it requires us to posit the existence of an entity in connection with which all our concepts are inaccurate, including the concept of what it is to be an entity, a concept which is itself closely related to other concepts such as time and space. We saw with the later Alston in Chapter 1 that if a particular entity can, in principle, be identified as the referent of 'God', enough concepts must, in principle, be applicable to this entity to secure that reference. If God were conceived as an object, his ineffability (if it could be claimed at all) could be claimed only in a weak or trivial sense and his religious significance would, at the very least, be attenuated.[1] The alternative, to deny that the word 'God' refers to an object and to affirm instead that it refers to the concept of ineffability, is theologically attractive in the light of the implication of Cooper's argument that only this concept can serve as the measure for human life. It is precisely because of this unique role that the concept of ineffability can be religiously significant in a way that the concept of any particular entity could not. This alternative strategy is implied by our existential phenomenological approach inherited from Heidegger and Cooper. On this approach, any entity that is conceptualizable and discursable (and there is no other kind) is part of the human world, not logically independent of the human contribution in the form of concepts, meanings and so forth. God, construed as an entity in this context, is robbed of his ineffability since, as Alston points out, 'if what God is like is, at least partly, shaped by how we conceptualize him, then those concepts that do the shaping must in the nature of the case truly apply to him'.[2] To say that God is ineffable, by contrast, is precisely to deny that the word 'God' has *any* conceptual content (save the negative, positively and determinately *contentless* concept of ineffability) and this must include the concept of being or existence. If the referent of 'God' were thought of as determined, conditioned or limited by being (and thus were conceived as a contingent entity, conditioned by time and space),[3] it would be invested with *at least one* of the very concepts for which the concept of ineffability provides measure and would therefore not be ineffable. Indeed, the arguments of classical and contemporary pragmatist thinkers like William James and Hilary Putnam support this point by advancing the view that the meanings of even very general ontological terms like 'object' and 'exists' are at least partly dependent on our conceptual schemes and ultimately, therefore, on the practical interest and purposes that those schemes serve.[4] But if, on the other hand, 'God' is taken to refer to the concept of ineffability and thereby to be in some way evocative of the ineffable (the only acceptable sense to the statement 'God is ineffable', as we saw), it is inconsistent also to think of the referent as conditioned by any human concepts, including that of existence. It is therefore inconsistent to think of there literally being a referent at all. It follows that, once this latter idea is given up, the problem of securing reference to an ineffable God is no longer a problem because, when the claim of God's ineffability is in play, use of the word 'God' is no longer interpreted as being a matter of referring to some entity, an *object* of language or experience. In this chapter, I want to defend this idea that ontotheology is inconsistent with our acceptable version of the claim of God's ineffability. I critically examine some existing attempts to explain how religious experience and, by implication, its expression may be justified after the rejection of ontotheology, how the tension between ineffability and answerability may be resolved in a specifically theological vision of intimacy and how the problem of ineffability can be solved. In other words, I address the question how religious experience is possible given the anti-ontotheological implications of the notion of ineffability. It is hoped that this resolution will prepare the ground for a philosophical account of religious practice in the final section. I embark on this task with the aid of two existentialist theologians: Paul Tillich and John Macquarrie.

The Rejection of Ontotheology (and Objections)

Ontotheology is defined by the *OED* as 'a branch or system of theology in which God is regarded as a being, esp. the supreme being'.[5] If he was not the first thinker to consider or to criticize ontotheology,[6] Heidegger has certainly been the most influential, especially in the twentieth and twenty-first centuries.[7] As Iain Thomson has pointed out, Heidegger's original use of the term was broader and more complex than the use to which it has subsequently been put by theologians;[8] it is significant that, in *Identity and Difference* (regarded by many theologians as the *locus classicus* for its critique), ontotheology is introduced in the context of a discussion of the general nature of the history of metaphysics, which is the main target of Heidegger's critique.[9] So, while he notes that there is no general agreement among theologians over just what the error of ontotheology is, Denys Turner interprets it in accordance with the *OED*'s definition as the specifically theological ramification of the metaphysical 'forgetfulness' of the ontological difference (which, for Heidegger, is endemic to the history of Western thought) that involves thinking of the referent of 'God' as '*a* being'.[10] We considered Heidegger's notion of the ontological difference in Chapter 2 by way of which he tries to ensure that (ineffable) Being is not confused with the entities for whose being it is the prior condition. Heidegger's own application of this crucial distinction to theological themes in *Identity and Difference* famously takes the form of a thoroughgoing critique of theology as inescapably bound to what he calls 'metaphysics' and *its* forgetfulness of the ontological difference. Heidegger writes of God, conceived as the highest being and *causa sui*, as the 'god of philosophy' and, in a remark that theologians are fond of quoting,[11] writes, 'Man can neither pray nor sacrifice to this god. Before the *causa sui*, man can neither fall to his knees in awe nor can he play music and dance before this god.'[12] Turner describes the way in which ontotheological error occurs in a way that brings out the close relationship that Heidegger describes (and Thomson recognizes) between the history of metaphysics and the history of theology:

> Heidegger insists that what he calls 'metaphysics' can represent to itself only beings; and it follows that any attempt 'metaphysically' to represent Being can result only in the misrepresentation of Being as *a* being. The onto-theologian [sic], therefore, in making Being into God, makes Being, and so God, into *a* being, hence into the supreme object of metaphysics ... [a]nd this is aptly named 'onto-theology [sic]' because it both makes 'Being' into God and, thereby, reduces God to *a* being.[13]

As Heidegger continues, it is this 'god of philosophy' with which theology deals; he writes, 'The god-less thinking which must abandon the god of philosophy, god as *causa sui*, is thus perhaps closer to the divine God. Here this means only: god-less thinking is more open to Him than onto-theo-logic would like to admit.'[14] Theologians have long been frustrated by the fact that Heidegger immediately turns away from theology towards 'god-less thinking' and does not consider that a kind of theology ('God-ly thinking', I suppose) may be possible that does not fall into ontotheological error. Indeed, many theologians believe, like Turner, that such non-ontotheological thought may be found to a greater or lesser degree throughout the history of the Christian tradition. To their further annoyance, no doubt, George Steiner equates Heidegger's stated project of the overcoming of metaphysics to an overcoming of theology which he thinks explains the increasingly ironic nature of Heidegger's allusions to theology and to the uses that theologians were making of his ontology.[15] Nonetheless, taking their cue from Heidegger's notion of Being, some theologians have sought to renew the meaning of 'God' in the light of this notion of the ineffable source of reality beyond the human, which takes proper account of its ontological differentiation from (Young's lower case) 'being' and from entities. Calvin Schrag alludes to a well-known passage in 'Letter on Humanism' in which Heidegger writes:

> Only from the truth of Being can the essence of the holy be thought. Only from the essence of the holy is the essence of divinity to be thought. Only in the light of the essence of divinity can it be thought or said what the word 'God' is to signify.[16]

With this, and presumably similar remarks,[17] in mind (rather than Heidegger's more negative ones), Schrag comments:

> It would seem that in Heidegger's 'Letter on Humanism' an invitation to link the elucidation of the truth of Being to the question about the Deity is extended ... It were as though Paul Tillich, Heidegger's colleague at Marburg University in the 1920s, accepted the invitation to appropriate Heidegger's fundamental ontology in designing his *Systematic Theology*.[18]

I have suggested that ontotheology is inconsistent with our notion of ineffability, a notion that we have found at work, *inter alia*, in Heidegger's later philosophy of Being. This is the notion in terms of which, with our Heideggerian theologians, I want to interpret the meaning of 'God' and in the light of which I want to consider the possibility of justifying religious language and practice on the grounds that, unlike the ontotheological conception of God as an entity (which has its well-rehearsed philosophical problems), this notion has greater mileage for religious significance. In the remainder of this section, therefore, I give some consideration to the work of two of the theologians whose ideas have been most directly influenced by Heidegger's thought. I show that the rejection of ontotheology is central to the ideas of both theologians and that, whether it was intended to or not, this safeguards in both cases a version of the claim of divine ineffability and thus the religious significance of 'God'.

Paul Tillich appears to share the Heideggerian suspicion of 'metaphysics'. Towards the beginning of his *Systematic Theology*, he describes the philosophy on which his system is based as ontology, 'analysis of those structures of being which we encounter in every meeting with reality'.[19] Such analysis, he observes, has traditionally been termed 'metaphysics' but he prefers the less misleading term 'ontology' since the prefix 'meta-' in 'metaphysics', far from its original Aristotelian, bibliographical meaning, has been taken to mean something he is very keen to avoid, namely 'a duplication of this world by a transcendent realm of beings'.[20] As is well known, Tillich's ontology is heavily influenced by Heidegger and he has well understood that it is to the ineffable that Heidegger's notion and language of Being are meant to attune one. Tillich uses the word 'mystery' in my sense of 'ineffability' to refer to the concept of what 'would lose its very nature if it lost its mysterious character',[21] what is in principle unknowable,[22] and to point to a 'dimension which "precedes" the subject–object relationship ... It is impossible to express the experience of mystery in ordinary language because this language has grown out of, and is bound to, the subject–object scheme.'[23] For Tillich, ontological terms, and the word 'God', express the mystery that alone can make possible and provide measure for the structure of subject and object since it is not itself part of that structure; these terms constitute that structure, 'they are not controlled by it'.[24] Therefore, the meaning of 'God', Tillich says, is 'being-itself',[25] the 'ground of being',[26] the unconditional and the unconditioned. To put it in congenial terms borrowed from Gabriel Marcel, the word 'God' evokes the ontological mystery.[27]

The main and perhaps the most important implication of this Heideggerian interpretation of the meaning of 'God' is the critique of ontotheology.[28] God, as ineffable being-itself, must be thought of as outside the subject–object structure of reality, as the prior condition and measure for that structure but '[i]f God is *brought into* the subject–object structure of being, he ceases to be the ground of being and becomes a being among others (first of all, a being beside the subject who looks at him as an object)'.[29] It is this view, that ineffability is inconsistent with ontotheology, which leads Tillich to make these (in)famous statements in rejection of ontotheology:

> God does not exist. He is being-itself beyond essence and existence. Therefore, to argue that God exists is to deny him.[30]

> the question of the existence of God can neither be asked nor answered. If asked, it is a question about that which by its very nature is above existence, and therefore the answer – whether negative or affirmative – implicitly denies the nature of God. It is as atheistic to affirm the existence of God as it is to deny it.[31]

> Ultimately, it is an insult to the divine holiness to talk about God as we do of objects whose existence or non-existence can be discussed.[32]

In the context of a discussion of the 'so-called ontological argument' for God's existence (to which we shall return), Tillich states that, however it is defined, the idea of the existence of God flatly contradicts his idea of 'a creative ground of essence and existence'.[33] The ground of being, he argues, is not within or among beings and the ground of essence and existence cannot participate in the tensions and disruptions involved in the transition from essence to existence. As he elaborates:

> The scholastics were right when they asserted that in God there is no difference between essence and existence. But they perverted their insight when in spite of this assertion they spoke of the existence of God and tried to argue in favour of it. Actually they did not mean 'existence'. They meant the reality, the validity, the truth of the idea of God, an idea which did not carry the connotation of some*thing* or some*one* who might or might not exist.[34]

The tone of Tillich's remarks is designed to be critical and corrective of religion and especially of theology, which he thinks almost inevitably does create the misleading impression that the word 'God' refers to an existent person or thing. Towards the end of *The Courage to Be*, in a section entitled 'Theism Transcended' (of which Tillich is reported to have said that 'he let the conclusion "come to a point like a needle" which was "meant to prick"')[35] he writes that God is often wrongly seen as part of reality. The Heideggerian notion of Being with which he is working implies that God instead be thought of as beyond the 'ontological categories which constitute reality. But every statement subjects him to them.'[36] He points out elsewhere that anything towards which a cognitive act is directed becomes an object in the *logical* sense (the sense in which the theologian cannot avoid making an object of God) but, beyond this, the notion of object carries *ontological* assumptions and limitations which theological discourse must do its best to avoid. Tillich writes:

> Theology always must remember that in speaking of God it makes an object of that which precedes the subject–object structure and that, therefore, it must include in its speaking of God the acknowledgement that it cannot make God an object.[37]

Tillich's critique of ontotheology has led some writers to accuse him of atheism,[38] but it is clear that his critique, which develops from the assimilation of Heidegger's notion of Being into his theology, is consistently geared towards *preserving* the religious significance and import of the idea of God by identifying it with the notion of ineffability in terms of which, alone (for Tillich, Heidegger and Cooper), the meaning and significance of human life and any part of the human world can be explained. Tillich sees this criticism of ontotheology as a powerful weapon against what he believes to be the true atheism, the denial of the reality, validity and truth of the idea of the ground of being, of that which both precedes and makes possible the duality between subject and object and which therefore resists human conceptualization and articulation – riven as such thought and language is, in his opinion, by this pervasive dualism.

Like Tillich,[39] John Macquarrie, an important pioneer of 'existentialist theology', is dissatisfied with what he calls Classical Theism, a conception of God closely linked to the methods of 'natural theology in the old style' whose aim he construes as being 'to supply rational proof of the reality of those matters with which theology deals'.[40] He believes that classical theism has wrongly had a monopoly on the term 'theism' and so develops an alternative and, he feels more satisfactory,[41] conception, dialectical theism, whose history he traces from Plotinus to the twentieth century and central to which are the dialectical oppositions within the concept of God which Macquarrie thinks have been left out by its one-sided Classical counterpart.[42] He wishes to avoid the attenuation of the religious significance of 'God' which natural theology's attempted inference of God from the observable facts of the world is wont to perpetuate:

> A God whose existence is deduced from the existence of the objects we perceive within the world ... must be regarded himself as another object; or a God who is posited as a hypothesis to account for the observed phenomena must be considered as himself part of the phenomenal nexus.[43]

'The God who is the conclusion of an argument' such as this, he writes, 'is not the God who is worshipped in religion'.[44] Macquarrie wishes to avoid the idea of a god that can be used to account causally for the phenomena which constitute reality only by making God a part of that reality, by investing him with its concepts. Macquarrie believes that such a god is religiously insignificant such that, even if it does exist, it is worshipped by no actual religion. His alternative view is that 'God' refers to the ineffable, to that which is resistant to human thought and expression, such that '[w]hatever we say about [God], it seems we are bound to correct it by saying something of opposite tendency'.[45] This view is reflected in the most fundamental dialectical opposition in his dialectical concept of God, that of being and nothing. On the one hand, Macquarrie wants to say that God is real, he wants, in Tillich's terms, to assert the reality, validity and truth of the idea of God but, on the other hand, this affirmation must be taken together with the rejection of ontotheology: God

> is not an item within the world, so that in the ordinary sense of the word 'exist', God does not exist, he is nothing.[46]

> I have insisted again and again that God is not an object or a being of any kind. He comes before all existence, as the ultimate mystery of whom we cannot properly say that he is, but must rather say that he lets be.[47]

The reason for Macquarrie's rejection of ontotheology, then, is to preserve the claim of God's ineffability and thus his religious significance. It is only as ineffable, and therefore not as an entity necessarily invested with the concepts of the human world, that 'God' can be religiously significant, that God can appropriately be thought of as the prior condition, the source of or measure for, the meaningful human world rather than just another bit of that world. For both Tillich and Macquarrie, God is identified with the later Heidegger's Being as they understand it. Since Being (in one sense) is for all three thinkers clearly situated on the ontological, rather than the ontic, side of the ontological difference, it is by way of this identification that Tillich's and Macquarrie's theological systems strive to avoid ontotheological error. As Macquarrie puts it, making use of Heideggerian language, 'If the truth of being is finally uncovered as the "It gives", then surely this ultimate giving, this original event of donation, deserves the name of "God".'[48]

Macquarrie is clear that God implies not *just* Being but also an attitude towards Being such that 'God' is synonymous with 'holy being' and, although Heidegger remained agnostic or ambiguous as to whether religion and theology could avoid ontotheology (as Macquarrie thinks they can, indeed must), even he spoke of Being, Macquarrie rightly observes, in 'religious or quasi-religious language'.[49] The point of the rejection of ontotheology, for both thinkers, is to preserve the religiously significant status of the concept of God as, analogous with Heidegger's Being and Cooper's mystery, measure-providing for the inescapably meaningful human world. (As Tillich intimates with his talk of the schema of subject and object, this world is often subsequently carved up into such dualistic categories.[50]) Whereas natural theology can explain the world of facts causally only by drawing God into the chain of causation, an ineffable God can be measure-providing for a world of conceptual meanings (with which human being is inseparably engaged) precisely by not being thought of as another part of that meaningful structure or invested with the concepts that constitute it, including that of existence.[51] This is so whether or not the notion of meaning in general, and the meaning of the notion of existence in particular, are explained in terms of the subject–object dichotomy.

I now want briefly to pre-empt two objections to the argument made by Tillich and Macquarrie that could be advanced at the stage it has reached in our discussion so far. The first objection concerns the validity of the whole project of appropriating Heidegger's notion of Being for theology in the way that Tillich and Macquarrie undeniably do. W. J. Richardson identified two stages in Heidegger's thought which he famously labelled 'Heidegger I' and 'Heidegger II'.[52] There is much debate about the 'turning (*die Kehre*)' or shift in Heidegger's thinking, when it occurs and how it should be interpreted, but most commentators follow something like Richardson's scheme and talk, as I have done, about the 'early' and 'later' Heidegger. Schrag follows the consensus up to a point, describing 'Heidegger II' in similar terms as I understand the later Heidegger, but identifies a third 'Heidegger' ('Heidegger III') who is distinguished from Heidegger II by the former's practice of the 'erasure of Being' and the replacement of Being with *Ereignis*, his transformation of 'language (*Sprache*)' into 'Saying

(*Sagen*)' and his announcement of the 'end of philosophy', heralded by a 'radical deconstruction' which is taken to be an intensification of the deconstruction of the history of ontology advocated by at least one of the other 'Heideggers'.[53]

Although the unelaborated point about language is of least relevance to a criticism of the projects of Tillich and Macquarrie (though, interestingly, it is of most relevance to Schrag's case for the existence of Heidegger III),[54] I still think it worth disputing. I have suggested elsewhere that the invocation of 'Saying' is a clarification of Heidegger's view in the 1940s and 1950s (for Schrag, this view belongs to Heidegger II, although he refuses to be bound to dates) that 'Language is the house of Being' and that it is not we who speak language but language which speaks.[55] It is supposed to clarify the intimacy of language and Being in the context of 'poetic saying'. I mentioned earlier that Heidegger claims that, far from being a quasi-technological manipulator of language, the poet can only speak after listening to 'language speaking'.[56] This is, of course, because it issues from Being, the source which is beyond the human and which makes possible any human speech. 'We are trying to listen to the voice of Being',[57] where the word 'of' is used with care owing to the intimacy of language and Being – language is, Heidegger tells us, the 'language of Being' as clouds are the 'clouds of the sky'.[58] As Cooper summarizes, the source of the 'saying' to which Heidegger exhorts us to listen is Being but Being is not considered distinct from this 'saying'. It would be more accurate, he suggests, to say that Being '*is* a "Saying"', which, in Heidegger's view, it is the poet's calling to reiterate.[59] Far from being evidence for a 'third Heidegger', then, the very touchstone of Schrag's argument turns out to be mere commentary on Heidegger's later work of the 1940s and 1950s.

The two other related points about Heidegger III's erasure of 'Being', his replacement of the language of Being with that of *Ereignis* and about the 'deconstruction of the history of ontology' are the real weapons for the attack on thinkers like Tillich and Macquarrie. Schrag sets the scene as follows:

> Being suffers an erasure, a 'crossing out', a radical deconstruction. At the end of the destruction of the history of ontology, at the end of philosophy, there is an appropriation of a concernful [*sic*] dwelling that is beyond and otherwise than Being.[60]

He refers to Tillich's 'hurried embrace of the ontological grammar of Heidegger II' and suggests that Tillich has unduly neglected the shift from Heidegger II to Heidegger III.[61] He rightly acknowledges Tillich's rejection of ontotheology but apparently thinks him inconsistent in his rejection while he holds the other view ascribed to him, that 'the grammar of being [lower case] can still be utilized in our discourse about God'.[62] Schrag intimates that the most interesting insights of Heidegger's (those of Heidegger III, that is) have been ignored by Tillich but taken up by theologians like Jean-Luc Marion who try to think of God 'otherwise than Being'.

The first response to this argument must be to contest the idea that the use of *'Ereignis'* is some indication that Heidegger decided to give up the idea of Being and replace it with something different. As I suggested earlier, the point of the *'Ereignis'* language was an attempt to capture the intimacy of Being with entities and to discourage the idea that Being is a transcendent thing from which entities epiphanize. The point of Heidegger's talk of the 'event of appropriation' is not to invent *another* notion aside from that of Being but rather to stress the importance of its meaning as a present participle rather than as a noun. Since the word *'Ereignis'* occurs in (and even in the subtitle of) Heidegger's relatively early *Contributions to Philosophy*,[63] it is unlikely that its use represents an *abandonment* of the idea of Being since, arguably, that idea did not reach fruition until the essays on language and thinking of the 1950s.

Secondly, Heidegger's relationship with the history of philosophy is not as straightforward as a project of deconstruction. He believes that, although often distorted, the voice of Being can be heard in the history of philosophy. If Being deigns to speak through the tradition, and with the correct mode of human receptivity, Being's voice can be transmitted even in the language of the 'metaphysicians'. Thus Heidegger tells us that we must be 'in conversation with' the history of philosophy in order to attain correspondence to Being through it.[64] The following passage suggests that, at least at times, Heidegger thinks the best strategy with regard to philosophy's distortion or oblivion of the question of Being to be not 'deconstruction', still less 'destruction', but rather patience. 'Should we not rather suffer a little while longer those inevitable misinterpretations to which the path of thinking in the element of Being and time has hitherto been exposed and let them slowly dissipate?'[65] It is surely more consistent with passages like this to read his remarks on the 'end of philosophy' as an articulation of the envisioned point where philosophy, conceived as correspondence to Being,[66] bleeds into the 'poetic dwelling' in the light of Being and where the boundaries of philosophy (or 'metaphysics' considered solely as a set of academic exercises concerned with entities) are thus transcended.

Finally, and most importantly, there is the issue of the erasure of Being which Schrag interprets as Heidegger's admission that the notion of Being was no longer adequate to the task which he had set it and thus as a move to push beyond and otherwise than Being. Marion reads Heidegger in a similar way and posits a God beyond Heidegger's Being, a God under erasure.[67] I cannot here go into the detail of Marion's argument,[68] but I want to question his implicit interpretation, on which his argument turns, of the point of Heidegger's practice of putting Being under erasure which Schrag draws out: that for both writers it signifies a desire to push beyond even the ontological difference. But (and here I agree with Julian Young) this is a misinterpretation. The point of writing 'Being' under erasure is precisely to *reinforce* the notion of the ontological difference, to create a 'radically disruptive device' to remind the reader that being is not an entity or object, that the word should not be read as a noun and that Being 'is', in Heidegger's word, 'nothing'.[69] Not only that but, as Heidegger says, each point of the cross is meant to point to a region of the fourfold 'and their being gathered in the locale of this crossing through'.[70] I suggested earlier, following Young, that the fourfold is the later Heidegger's notion of the human world and registered agreement with Cooper that the vision of intimacy that he advocates is meant to cultivate the experience of Being 'gathered' in the world and of the world similarly gathered in individual things. So much for the idea that Being under erasure is meant to push beyond the ontological difference (or beyond Heidegger's Being) and to think 'outside' of it. Rather it is a device designed to discourage the objectification of Being, to remind us not only of the ontological difference, the radical alterity of Being from entities, but also of the seamless intimacy *within* it (which, for Heidegger, the ontological difference also implies) between Being, the human world and entities.[71] The practice of putting Being under erasure is a further way of trying to articulate the same notion of Being, which was the consistent concern of the later Heidegger. Thus, at least at this point, that practice gives us no substantial reason to object to the theological appropriation of the idea of Being by Tillich and Macquarrie.

The second potential objection specifically concerns the critique of ontotheology and involves the idea of necessary existence. That critique certainly shows the idea of God as a *contingent* being to be unattractive. Ontotheology fails because it conceives God as a causal metaphysical ground. It can do this only by drawing God into the causal chain, thinking of God as just another contingent entity and thus compromising God's religious status as ground *and* his ineffability. But could not God's religious significance be preserved if God were thought of as a *necessary* being, as in the conclusion of the ontological argument? As Le Poidevin describes this possible cosmological application of the ontological argument, a necessary being could perhaps explain the existence of the (contingent) universe. Since such a being is not itself caused, it could serve as a causal explanation for the universe which itself does not call for further explanation.[72] The kind of explanation that concerns Le Poidevin is also causal, in contrast to the explanations of meaning which concern Cooper in his defence of the notion of ineffability. Thus, if God could be conceived as a *necessary* being, appeal to ineffability (and the rejection of ontotheology which that implies) might not be necessary to safeguard his religious significance. In that case, it might derive from our ability to appeal to him in causal explanations of the existence of the world without also drawing him into the causal chain. However, Le Poidevin persuasively criticizes the modal version of the ontological argument:

(1) If it is possible for God to exist, then, necessarily, God exists.
(2) It is possible for God to exist.
Therefore: Necessarily, God exists.[73]

He identifies as crucial for this argument the question whether necessary truth (where the statement is not possibly false) is the same as analytic truth (where the statement's falsehood implies a contradiction).[74] If they are not the same and there are necessary truths that are not analytic, Le Poidevin argues, there can be no justification for choosing between premise (2) of the modal ontological argument and the equivalent premise of its atheistic counterpart (It is possible that God does not exist.[75]) The modal ontological argument fails to establish the analytic truth of 'God exists', a claim that we would need other reasons for making, thus rendering the argument itself redundant. If, on the other hand, necessary truth is the *same* as analytic truth, the proposition "'God is either necessary or impossible" is equivalent to "The proposition 'God exists' is either analytically true or analytically false'".[76] The ontological argument, if sound, would establish whether 'God exists' is analytically true but its soundness is what is at issue, so, unless there are other grounds for establishing this (in which case the argument is redundant), we cannot say whether 'God exists' is analytically true or analytically false. This being the case, either premise (1) is false or, as already shown, there can be necessary truths which are not analytic and the argument is redundant; it is in this way that we can rule out the idea that the modal ontological argument is *both* sound *and* non-redundant. As Le Poidevin summarizes the two equally unsatisfactory potential responses to his central question (whether necessary truth is the same as analytic truth), 'If it is, then this creates problems for the first premise. If it is not, then we have no way of establishing the truth of the premise that God's existence is at least possible.'[77]

Le Poidevin also criticizes the notion of necessary existence itself. He takes the relevant kind of necessity to be logical necessity, the strongest kind, since it is arguable that 'only a logically necessary being requires no explanation for its existence ... since it is not true that it might not have existed'.[78] Distinguishing the idea of necessarily true propositions from that of a necessary being, he observes that according to the linguistic theory of necessity, which lies behind the former idea, all necessary truths are analytic but that their necessity owes to features of language rather than to those of reality. The idea of God as a necessary being, by contrast, does not require this commitment to the analycity of the statement 'God exists' since the relevant kind of necessity is conferred on the statement by something in reality, not by a property of language. On this basis, Le Poidevin argues from the perspective of modal realism, appealing to the idea of possible worlds, i.e. worlds that are equally real though temporally and spatially unrelated.[79] It follows from this perspective that nothing can exist in more than one world since if A is temporally and spatially unrelated to B, A and B cannot be the same object – but if A is in one world and B in another, they *are* spatially and temporally unrelated. Since the definition of a necessary being is one that exists in *all* possible worlds, and nothing can exist in more than one possible world, there can be no such thing as a necessary being. One possibility could be to reject the assumption that everything that exists does so in space and time (perhaps a necessary being exists 'outside' of space and time). But here there are difficulties with the conception of what it is for something to be in a world, i.e. to exist. A necessary being, in this sense, exists in no possible worlds and since possible reality just is the sum total of possible worlds, such a being is unreal. 'Worse, it is an impossible being'.[80] The only possibility left for the modal realist is to claim that there is *a* god in every possible world, beings very like each other in some respects but not so in others. Perhaps, in this sense, God exists in all possible worlds and thus confers necessary truth on the statement 'God exists'. But this is far from satisfactory from a religious point of view. The object of worship is then either a contingent being, the god who just happens to exist in *this* possible world, the real world, or a fragmentary 'collection of God-counterparts in all possible worlds'.[81] Further, the religious person wants to say that God is responsible for reality but, on this view, each god could be responsible, at most, for the world in which that god existed, not for the sum of all possible worlds. The final nail in the coffin for the idea of a necessary being, for Le Poidevin, is that, even if we could make sense of the idea of a necessary being, necessary facts cannot explain contingent ones in the way that the ontotheologian requires God to do when applying the modal ontological argument cosmologically. This is because 'we cannot make sense of [necessary facts] not being the case, whereas causal explanation requires us to make sense of causally explanatory facts not being the case'.[82] As Le Poidevin illustrates, if A causes B, if A had not occurred, B would not occur either (or its probability of occurring would be weakened). To make sense of this, we have to entertain the possibility that both A and B might not have occurred and thus are both contingent. Therefore, even if the idea of a necessarily existent being makes sense (and we have seen reason to doubt this), such a being cannot be both necessary and causally explanatory in the way that ontotheology, the object of Heideggerian critique, requires it to be.

Not only is the ontological argument, as interpreted by Le Poidevin, of no help in defending ontotheology against the critique advanced by Heideggerian theology but Mulhall has suggested that, in its Wittgensteinian variations, it could actually be recruited to the cause of ineffability, which I want to suggest is the more attractive alternative to ontotheology.[83] Starting with Norman Malcolm's reading of Anselm's argument, in which Malcolm compares it with other non-religious modes of discourse on existence and necessity, Mulhall suggests that this reading 'appears on closer examination, to tell us far more about what religious discourse is not than about what it is'.[84] Although Malcolm's emphasis is on the distinction between claims about God's existence and existential claims of an empirical nature, Mulhall observes that he wants to clarify the grammatical link between the perfection of God and his necessary existence 'by invoking a chain of grammatical links (between imperfection, dependence and limitation, on the one hand, and perfection, independence and absence of limitation on the other) which have their home in empirical contexts'.[85] However, for Mulhall, although a less limited empirical object might be greater than a more limited one, it could never wholly lack the possibility of limitation, the lack of which is an integral element to Anselm's characterization of God. The relevant comparisons, which turn out to be more like contrasts, therefore establish what cannot be said of God (e.g. that he is contingent) and give only negative or 'exclusionary' sense to talk of God's necessary existence. Such expressions, Mulhall claims, 'ward off mistaken or irreligious talk of God as if he were a being amongst beings; but they do not tell us what genuinely religious talk of God – talk that is properly directed towards its target – might amount to'.[86]

Malcolm tries to separate the grammar from the sense of religious concepts, their logical structure from their point or purpose but, for Mulhall, this is puzzling from the Wittgensteinian perspective. From this point of view, meaning is manifest in use and it is not clear how, even in principle, one could grasp the grammar of a concept while simultaneously failing to grasp the point of using it. For Malcolm, the concept's grammar might be clarified while the concept still appears arbitrary and absurd and, if it appears so, we surely have not appreciated the point of its use. Mulhall wants to read this apparent weakness in Malcolm's reading of Wittgenstein as a strength by exploiting the link between it and apophatic theology. He suggests that Malcolm's presentation of the ontological argument as a way of ruling out ways of speaking of God 'simply reflect[s] the fact that any attempts positively to characterize God's nature are doomed to failure'.[87] Mulhall appeals to Denys Turner's suggestion that, in this context, negation is inextricable from affirmation to defend the idea that Malcolm's propensity to use terms familiar in non-theological contexts, apparently in tension with it, does not in fact subvert that apophatic insight. If God is understood as the source of all reality, everything must be seen as a potential source of imagery for the divine. Using language in all these ways would inevitably lead to contradiction (images of male and female contribute to our understanding of God, the source of both, but we end up saying, more or less explicitly, that God is both male and female). But Mulhall thinks (and he finds Aquinas agreeing with him on this) that it is precisely in these contradictions that divine ineffability is acknowledged. We know that no person can be both male and female and thus, in the case of God, are led to appreciate that our idea of God as a person, for example, 'is itself a misrepresentation – a necessarily unsuccessful attempt to delineate that which is beyond delineation'.[88] Mulhall wants, with Turner, to see theological language as essentially self-subverting and also interprets the idea of *creatio ex nihilo* in these terms. This form of words points not to 'a uniquely peculiar kind of antecedent condition for making, but rather negates the very idea of an antecedent condition'.[89] The phrase is saying, as it were, 'There is a making here but no "out of"'.[90] On the cataphatic side, then, we are able to appreciate *that* God is the answer to the cosmological question but, on the apophatic side, we can come to no understanding of *how* he is. And it is in this way, Mulhall suggests, that the ontological argument might be recruited 'to point towards the mystery underlying the world's comprehensibility'.[91]

Despite this last direct allusion to Wittgenstein, Mulhall feels the need to discourage the idea that his approach goes against the Wittgensteinian grain in that the grammar of religious language turns out to be its lack of grammar, its status as nonsense. To do so he appeals to Cora Diamond's exploitation, in a Wittgensteinian context, of a comparison between religious language and riddles. To answer a riddle question, one has to know both *what* that form of words describes and *how* it does so. Until we come to an understanding of both these things, Diamond argues, we lack an understanding of the riddle phrase employed by the question and thus of the question itself. To solve the riddle we must apply our imagination, keeping in mind existing patterns of language use, in order to establish both the conditions under which a potential answer makes sense and what answer, if any, fits those conditions. For Diamond, Anselm's 'that than which no greater can be conceived' should be seen as an example of just such a riddle question and as based on the existing pattern of 'great, greater, greatest, greatest conceivable'. For Diamond, Mulhall reports, Anselm's riddle phrase embodies the great riddle of the meaning of life to which there is no conceivable solution and in which the question can only be dissolved as a question. We can know *that* something is the answer to this riddle question but not *how* it is. There is an allusion here, Mulhall suggests, to 'a "language" we cannot even conceive of speaking before actually finding ourselves in a position to speak it'.[92] The answer to Anselm's riddle question, however, does not consist in religious language-games since, for Diamond, the answer cannot come from us human beings but from that to which this form of words applies. But this is not to seek cover in the fideism which Mulhall is keen to deny as being characteristic of a Wittgensteinian approach to the philosophy of religion since, for Wittgenstein, language-games are susceptible to 'deep confusion':

> we cannot show that people who wish to think the God of the Old Testament as a genocidal maniac are conceptually or philosophically confused simply because language-games are played in which such things cannot be said of God (because he is conceived of as perfect).[93]

The riddle question thus holds for all human beings, not just those who play the religious language-games. And it is here that Mulhall sees Diamond's work meeting that of Denys Turner: they share the idea that the cataphatic uses of religious language (as imaginative engagement with riddle phrases, perhaps) cannot be severed from their apophatic uses (in which it must be admitted that we cannot know how the answer to Anselm's 'great' riddle question is the answer) without compromising their religious significance. As Mulhall summarizes his argument,

> For Diamond, our love of riddles exemplifies the interplay of what comes naturally with our capacity for imaginative play ... and Anselm's way with [that that which no greater can be conceived] shows how, at its fullest extent, that interplay can acknowledge the possibility that reality might utterly overturn our best efforts to imagine what might lie beyond our wildest imaginings.[94]

So the ontological argument, and its notion of God as a necessarily existent being, can not only be seen to be of no help in salvaging ontotheology but, with Mulhall's help, can actually be read as gesturing in the opposite direction, towards the idea which I have argued is inconsistent with ontotheology, that the word 'God' refers to the concept of ineffability and thus evokes, or attunes us to, the ineffable and is, on this interpretation, supportive of apophatic theology. As Wittgenstein rather more succinctly put it in 1949, 'God's essence is supposed to guarantee his existence – what this really means is that what is here at issue is not the existence of something'.[95]

Macquarrie, too (I shall come back to Tillich), reads the ontological argument's formulation '*necessary* being' as 'such a radical qualification that God is removed by it from the series of items among which he appears'.[96] It is in this way that Macquarrie also reads the other classical theistic 'proofs'. While they apparently try to argue from the existence of certain entities to the existence of another (albeit exalted) entity conceived in essentially the same way,

> [t]he subsequent amendments of the arguments, as, for instance, the insistence that a 'first cause' must be of a different order from any subsequent or phenomenal causes, is basically an attempt to get away from the notion of *a* being to the notion of being. But ... this is happening only confusedly, and to recognize what is happening would demand giving the 'proof' a whole new look altogether.[97]

What the relevant variations of the ontological argument point towards is the anti-ontotheological idea of Simone Weil, that of 'the necessary *non*-existence of God'. Rowan Williams quotes what he takes to be Weil's 'most concise crystallization' of this theme (echoes of which are mainly to be found in her notebooks), which has received very little systematic discussion:[98]

> Of two men who have no experience of God, he who denies him is perhaps nearer to him than the other.
> The false God is like the true one in everything, except that we do not touch him, prevents us from coming to the true one [*sic*].
> The 100 possible thalers in Kant. The same applies to God.
> We have to believe in a God who is like the true God in everything, except that he does not exist, for we have not yet reached the point where God exists.[99]

As Williams elaborates Weil's point: 'There is no thing in the world's reality to which the name "God" applies. I cannot but conceive God as some sort of object, because I cannot (logically) conceive what is not in the world.'[100]

Our two theologians can hardly leave matters here. If they did, they would perhaps not properly be called theologians. In the next section, therefore, I want to look at what they do once they have given up ontotheology. To facilitate critical engagement with their views on the possibility of religious experience, I then return to the ontological argument. Before criticizing Tillich's view, I consider the suggestion of one commentator that he actually, more or less implicitly, endorses a version of it during the next stage of his argument.

A Theological Vision of Intimacy? The Possibility of Religious Experience

The fact that our two theologians were most directly influenced by Heidegger makes it unsurprising that their attempts to account for the possibility of religious experience are carried out in close connection with Heidegger's notion of Being. Since they believe that this Heideggerian evocation of the ineffable designates what is philosophically and religiously ultimate, their attempts to argue that such experience is possible must relate back to the same notion that led to their rejection of ontotheology and thus made the possibility of such experience philosophically problematic. It is because of the tension created by this fact that the so-called problem of ontotheology is a problem. It is an especially urgent problem if, as our two Heideggerian thinkers believe, the only way of rescuing religious experience, language and praxis after the rejection of ontotheology is in connection with a conception of God influenced by the same Heideggerian notion of Being as the ultimate, ineffable 'source' of reality which necessitated that rejection. Since it is not a foregone conclusion that this is the only way, their assumption requires some defence.

Marion, for example, denies that (upper-case) Being is associated with God in the way that it is associated with finite creatures. He claims that whereas finite creatures 'must first be in order to love, God loves "before Being"'.[101] This, for Marion, is the implication of what he takes to be the fundamental designation 'God is love': 'If, to begin with, "God is love", then God loves before being.'[102] While I disagree with Marion's exegesis of Heidegger's notion of Being and therefore with the reasoning behind his assertion, I do recognize his challenge that Being might not be the most ultimate category or 'name' and might therefore not be the most appropriate one for God. And it is a challenge that has to be answered. If, as he claims, the relevant issue is not whether God attains to Being but *vice versa*, there might (or perhaps must) be other philosophical terms or 'names',[103] more ultimate than Being, which are more appropriately associated with him. For Marion, 'love' is such a name, which, unlike Being, has the advantage of not making so urgent a philosophical problem of the possibility of religious experience. According to our existential phenomenological approach, however, Marion's objection that thinking of God in terms of Heidegger's Being indirectly subjects God to human categories (because Being is in the last analysis inseparable from *Dasein*, the being for whom Being is an issue)[104] applies no less to Marion's own suggestion that the God who 'is' beyond even (upper-case) Being should be imagined instead in terms of 'love'. This is nicely pointed out by Karl Jaspers in the context of a more general critique of the application of the categories of personality to the ineffable 'transcendent', which in his view properly deserves the name 'God'. As Jaspers expresses it, the reciprocity implied by the concept of love refers us back to the human world for its meaning (in this case the specific sphere of interpersonal relations) in just the way that we would expect with an existential phenomenological analysis.[105]

> I quickly shrink from the impulse that would make the deity a thou for me, because I feel I am profaning transcendence. The very idea entangles me in delusions. After all, personality is the mode of self-being that is by nature unable to be alone; relations are its essence; it must have other things, persons and nature, besides itself. The deity would need us, would need mankind, to communicate with. In the idea of God's personality, transcendence would be diminished into an existence.[106]

It therefore follows that

> [t]he love I bear the deity as a person can only metaphorically be called love; it truly becomes love only in the world, as love of an individual human being, and it becomes enthusiasm for the beauty of existence. Worldless love is love of nothing, an unfounded bliss. I really love transcendence only as my love transfigures the world.[107]

Whatever our opinion of Marion's exegesis of the later Heidegger, then, his alternative philosophical term for God turns out, according to the kind of existential phenomenological analysis pioneered by the early Heidegger, to be no more adequate a philosophical concept with which to associate the meaning of 'God' than that of Being. To be sure, it is fairly intuitively true that the content of the concept of love resists exhaustive rational elucidation but it is also no less of a concept for that. But if, as I have argued, the Heideggerian concept of Being is designed to evoke the ineffable, these facts are no less true of that concept of Being. The fact that Heidegger's term *does* refer to a concept does not in any way compromise its ability to evoke what is beyond conceptualization, provided that Cooper's distinction is observed between the ineffable and the concept of ineffability. It was only by way of this distinction, moreover, that the otherwise devastating self-stultification of statements connected with the ineffable could be avoided. In order to justify the idea that, between the concepts of love and

Being, the former is the more fundamental, Marion would have to show that the concept of Being depended on that of love. Not only does he provide no argument for this but Jaspers's existential phenomenological analysis points us in the opposite direction. So Marion's suggestion does not attenuate the urgency of justifying religious experience, language and praxis in connection with the notion of Being, in Heidegger's sense of the ineffable source of reality, which I have been arguing evokes what is ultimately real for both philosophy and religion. Admittedly, this is most likely because he does not see that Heidegger *is* using the concept of Being to evoke the ineffable but, crucially, he does not show us that his own alternative concept has the advantage of evoking it any more effectively, less still that it does so in such a way that overcomes the attendant philosophical difficulties concerning the possibility of religious experience.

Of course, as with Tillich,[108] the source of Macquarrie's notion of God is Heidegger's Being, which explains this forthright rejection of ontotheology.[109] But according to Macquarrie, as some remarks in the previous section intimate, Heidegger's notion is 'dialectical' and implies more than the simple rejection of ontotheology. As Macquarrie describes Heidegger's Being as the *transcendens* above all categories,

> Being... must remain mysterious, and yet it is not just a blank incomprehensible. The very fact that it is the condition that there may be any beings or properties of beings is an indication that although we cannot say of being that it 'is', and might even say that it is 'nothing that is', being 'is' nevertheless more beingful [*sic*] than anything that is, for it is the prior condition that anything may be.[110]

In the identification of God with (holy) Being, Macquarrie draws the distinction between Being's primordial mode, 'the ineffable and incomprehensible superexistence which does not itself exist but is the creative source and condition of everything that does exist' and its expressive mode, the sense in which the same God is also simultaneously held responsible for the intelligibility of the cosmos, a responsibility which is expressed in theological terms like that of creation.[111]

For Macquarrie, one of the most valuable consequences of the rejection of ontotheology, after his first dialectical opposition of being and nothing in connection with God (the conception of God as 'Being' rather than '*a* being'), is a second dialectical opposition: 'we are then compelled to think of him as both transcendent and immanent'.[112] This second opposition is Macquarrie's theological appropriation of the vision of intimacy between the human world and its source which we have seen to be an important aspect of Heidegger's notion of Being as Cooper and Young interpret it and the other part of the point of Heidegger's designation of Being as the *transcendens*. It is in terms of this vision that Macquarrie understands the meaning of 'revelation', that to which religious experience may correspond, the paradigm for which he takes to be Heidegger's 'meditative thinking'.[113] To say that religious experience corresponds to revelation, as Macquarrie and Tillich tend to, would be to emphasize, in theological terms, the passivity involved in the experience of what is beyond, and independent of, the human, phenomenal world. To speak of human beings attuning themselves to the ineffable (God), as, following Heidegger and Cooper, I tend to, would be to stress, more philosophically, the active possibilities of one strand of natural theology. But, of course, both are required since, as I have suggested, the kind of experience involved is beyond the distinction between activity and passivity. In Marcel's term, it consists in 'creative receptivity'. As Macquarrie suggests, the distinction between 'natural' and 'revealed' theology is in any case a blurred one. In one sense, all theology is revealed because God is the source of everything, our knowledge of him included, such that there is no unaided knowledge of God with which 'revealed' theology might be contrasted. In addition, however, even all 'revealed' theology must be considered 'natural' in Macquarrie's broad sense since it comes to us through persons, things and events in the phenomenal world and is thus appropriated by universal human faculties.[114] Elsewhere, Macquarrie suggests that the 'old' distinction between 'natural' and 'revealed' theology be abandoned in favour of a rational and existential appeal, incorporating both, to a 'general possibility of revelation'.[115] It is important to note, then, that what is said about 'revelation', in what follows, could equally be said about human beings' more active experiential attunement to the ineffable. The main question I want to address in this way is one that applies to both models: that of how religious experience has to be understood once it has been accepted, on both philosophical and theological grounds, that such experience is directed necessarily towards the ineffable and ontotheology has consequently been jettisoned.

According to Macquarrie, the person who receives revelation (who undergoes religious experience) perceives no more than anyone else would in the situation since it is not *another* being that is revealed. Rather, the person who receives the revelation perceives 'the same things *in a different way*'.[116] That Being is the prior condition for anything (that it 'is', as Macquarrie says, 'letting-be'),[117] implies that God is not only essentially mysterious but also, at least insofar as he reveals himself, present and manifest in and through every entity.[118] One consequence for Macquarrie is that it is 'misleading and inappropriate' to say that God exists any more than Being does.[119] However, he also believes that God's status as the prior condition for the existence of anything makes it less inappropriate to say that God exists than that he does not exist, insofar as God is conceived as in some way 'above' existence rather than 'below' it. Macquarrie cites the Psalms in support of this suggestion: 'He who planted the ear, does he not / hear? / He who formed the eye, does he / not see?'[120] and interprets the claim 'God exists' as an assertion of the holiness of Being,[121] adamant that it is 'not to be taken as meaning that there is to be found a being possessing such and such characteristics'.[122] But it seems to me that, as a tactical suggestion, this could be improved upon since it is quite likely that this, at best 'oblique',[123] sense in which Macquarrie thinks existence applicable to God will remain unheard. After all, he claims that the move from God as *a* being to God as Being is happening even in the relatively precise philosophical demesne of traditional (or old-style) philosophy of religion 'only confusedly'.[124] *A fortiori*, how much more so with the ordinary religious believer? A better option might be the one taken by Eckhart (a thinker whom Macquarrie reads as an early exponent of dialectical theism),[125] that is, the continued oscillation between the claim that God does not exist and that *only* God truly exists. Arguably this strategy is not only more in the spirit of dialectic than Macquarrie's but also better avoids the confusion he mentions by refusing to refer to God and entities in the same terms, to place them, as it were, on the same level, at any one time. The oscillation between these claims indicates that neither is wholly adequate, each needing the corrective function of the other. It undermines the supposed legitimacy of the question 'Does God exist?' and could be seen to evoke the vision of intimacy, which is also required. We might say that Eckhart's strategy is a rigorous linguistic observance of the ontological difference to which Macquarrie prefers a more traditional and less controversial form of religious language.

This terminological point aside, Macquarrie's identification of God with Being in dialectical theism, especially in the opposition between transcendence and immanence, appears to express the vision of intimacy which Cooper finds in Heidegger's later thought. On the philosophical side, in the language of Being, the two poles of this particular dialectical opposition are bound together in the Heideggerian notion of *Ereignis* and in Macquarrie's conception of God as the event of 'letting-be': 'Being always includes becoming, and … the essence of Being is the dynamic act of letting-be'.[126] Theologically, on the other hand, the poles are bound together in the other symbolic language of doctrines like that of creation ('making' and 'emanation' models respectively emphasizing the 'transcendent' and 'immanent' poles of the dialectical conception of God) and of the Incarnation which

> is highly compatible with dialectical theism. It implies an ultimate source, in itself hidden and incomprehensible, whether we call this source the Father or Being or Beyond-being or whatever. But we could know nothing about this source and it would not rightly be called … 'source' … if it did not come out to relate itself to what is other than itself.[127]

It is worth contrasting Macquarrie's and Alston's ways of reconciling the tension between ineffability and answerability, between divine ineffability and the possibility, if not necessity, of 'revelation' and religious experience, language and practice, since they both use the language of dialectic while addressing this issue.

Alston's strategy was to weaken each antithesis and merge both into a synthesis. Ineffability was weakened to the point where *some* concepts are applicable to God and answerability was weakened to the point where none of the concepts can be said to be truly accurate. The synthesis was that statements *can* be made about God but which enjoy only a 'close approximation to truth'.[128] Macquarrie, by contrast, explicitly resists the strategy of weakening either pole of any of the dialectical oppositions in his concept of God and any resultant 'half-way position':[129] for him, God is both Being and nothing, both transcendent and immanent.

Similarly, Tillich's identification of God with being-itself rejects ontotheology and preserves the ineffability of God whilst also apparently emphasizing God's intimacy with the meaningful human world in a manner similar to Macquarrie's dialectical conception. God, as being-itself (this identification is the only non-symbolic thing that can be said about God),[130] is beyond finitude and infinity, unconditioned and *infinitely* transcends every entity. But, on the other hand, everything finite participates in being-itself and its unconditioned nature. As Tillich expresses it:

> This double relation of all beings to being-itself gives being-itself a double characteristic. In calling it creative we point to the fact that everything participates in the infinite power of being. In calling it abysmal we point to the fact that everything participates in the power of being in a finite way, that all beings are infinitely transcended by their creative ground.[131]

Tillich gives an affirmative answer to the important question whether some part of finite reality can be the basis for a statement about the unconditioned, because the unconditioned is being-itself and because everything participates in it.[132] It is this intimacy which, for Tillich, makes religious experience possible and which entails the apparently paradoxical affirmation by religion and theology that an ineffable God can remain ineffable even in his experienced revelation. However, the paradox is only apparent since the 'revelation of mystery' means, for Tillich, 'the manifestation of something within the context of ordinary experience which transcends the ordinary context of experience'; the ineffable God becomes, in some sense, a matter of experience but is not dissolved into knowledge and adds nothing to our knowledge of the subject–object structure of reality.[133] Tillich stresses that mystery is beyond the limits of reason and must be conceived in relation to it both positively as its 'ground' and negatively as its 'abyss'. In the functions of reason, conditioned by the schema of subject and object, mystery is always present as abyss (since it would otherwise cease to be mysterious) but it is also present as ground, which includes the sense of 'abyss'. It is perhaps precisely *as* mysterious abyss, unconditioned by concepts, that the divine grounds those rational functions of the mind that make their application possible. God, the mystery of Being, is manifest in revelatory experience and is our 'ultimate concern', that to which faith is directed.[134] Tillich thus conceives revelation or religious experience as the 'depth of reason and its mystery'.[135] His notion of what constitutes a revelatory event reflects this general conception of the nature of revelation in that the subjective and objective dimensions are inseparable and in strict interdependence: on the subjective side, someone is always grasped by the manifestation of mystery but, objectively, something always occurs through which that person is grasped by that revelation.[136] It is thus that the notion of an 'objective miracle' is a contradiction in terms and that scientific research on the objective side cannot dissolve miracles, though it can and should undermine supernatural interpretations;[137] miracles, rather, concern 'the depth of reason and the ground of being', they point to 'the mystery of existence and to our ultimate concern'.[138] Revelation does not destroy reason any more than reason 'empties' revelation.[139] The vision of intimacy that we have found Tillich encouraging implies that nothing, no entity, cannot become the bearer of the mystery of being. Reason raises the question of mystery in terms of the question of its own ground and abyss but cannot answer it since, bound to the duality of subject and object, it cannot pass beyond a bare analysis of the objective situation. Revelation, on the other hand, passes into the realm of the non-differentiation of subject from object and thus makes the situation 'transparent for the ground of being and meaning', turning it into a revelatory situation.[140]

Therefore all revelation, albeit 'of' the unconditioned, is itself conditioned by the finite conditions of the medium *via* which it appears. The resultant danger is idolatry, the elevation of the medium of revelation to the unconditioned status of the revelation itself.[141] Tillich states, 'The claim of anything finite to be final in its own right is demonic' since he takes the demonic to be 'the elevation of something conditional to unconditional significance'.[142] The antidote to such idolatry is the self-negation of the revelation's medium: the conditioned medium of revelation must overcome its finite conditions 'and itself with them'.[143] Tillich sees the crucifixion, Christianity's 'final' revelation, as the supreme example of such self-negation in which the symbol of Christ (the medium of revelation) must overcome itself in its conditioned nature.[144] He believes that the mystical tradition avoids the danger of idolatry by devaluing every possible medium but at the cost of removing revelation's concrete character and its relevance to the human situation. Mysticism is therefore viewed as a useful corrective to revelation, which helps it to transcend its own finite symbols. It is mysticism's 'permanent function', Tillich writes, 'to point to the abysmal character of the ground of being and to reject the demonic identification of anything finite with that which transcends everything finite'.[145]

But this is not to say that what transcends everything finite is not also intimate with everything finite. Interpreting (dialectically) the meaning of negative theology's 'non-being', Tillich states his view of it as 'not being anything special', as not only beyond all concrete predicates but also as embracing everything: 'it means being everything; it is being-itself'.[146]

Revelation thus creates what Tillich calls 'theonomy', to be distinguished from autonomy (where reason is not alive to its own depth, the ineffable 'abyss' and 'ground' on which it depends) and heteronomy (where the authority of the infinite and unconditioned is claimed for the finite and conditioned). If the medium of revelation is transparent to the ground of being, autonomous reason is prevented from losing its depth and rational man from being thought the measure of reality. And if the self-sacrifice of the medium of revelation to its content comes about, heteronomy's subjection of man to a higher law (in Greek, '*nomos*') of objective 'religious facts' (the very meaning of 'metaphysics' from which Tillich wants to get away) is also overcome.[147] Tillich sees theonomy as a resolution of the conflict between absolutism and relativism.[148] Autonomy as the law of reason, structured by the subjective–objective distinction, affirms this structure without regarding its depth, and heteronomy issues external commands about the way in which reason should grasp and shape reality. Heteronomy is the claim of the conditioned to speak in the name of the ground of being, i.e. in an unconditional way. Theonomy, however, is that in which both have their basis, where 'autonomous reason is united with its own depth' such that reason is applied to reality according to its 'inexhaustible ground'.[149] Thus the 'depth of reason' is identified with the 'ground of autonomy' and God is identified as the law for reason's structure and ground which are united in him. Tillich claims that 'there is no complete theonomy under the conditions of existence' since, under these conditions, autonomy and heteronomy struggle to destroy each other, a struggle which tends to destroy reason: 'Therefore, the quest for a reunion of what is always split in time and space arises out of reason and not in opposition to reason. This is the quest for revelation.'[150]

There are parallels between Tillich's schema and Cooper's humanism, absolutism and mystery. We might see Tillich's autonomy as comparable to Cooper's uncompensated humanism where human concepts are alone responsible for the world taking on the contours it does and according to which their application has no measure beyond the human. We could think of heteronomy as analogous to Cooper's absolutism in which the application of human concepts to the world, and resultant experience of the world, is ruled by the way in which the world is independently of those concepts, an objective set of contingent facts which are independent of the human. And finally, mystery is comparable to theonomy, providing a middle way between the other unattractive apparent alternatives. It is what governs the application of concepts to the world without itself being representable in those concepts. It grounds the structures of lived experience, conceptualization and practice, precisely by being an inexhaustible 'abyss'. Whereas Tillich's discussion is always in terms of the subjective–objective structure of reason, Cooper's is cast in the mould of the existential phenomenological ones of meaningful, lived experience and practice. I shall return to this dissimilarity later on.

For Tillich, further, revelation is characterized by the drawing together of the absolute and the concrete. In the Christian symbol of Jesus as the Christ, for example, 'the most concrete of all possible forms of concreteness, a personal life, is the bearer of that which is absolute without condition and restriction'.[151] The logical form of this unity of the absolute and concrete is the paradox that cannot be expressed in terms of the structure of reason but only in those of its depth. It is for this reason that revelation does not constitute 'logical nonsense': it arises out of, and not in opposition to, reason and occurs as 'a concrete event which on the level of rationality must be expressed in contradictory terms'.[152] For Tillich, the absolute and concrete elements, which are unified in revelation, are mirrored in the nature of faith as ultimate concern. Human beings can only be concerned about the concrete but, if idolatry is to be avoided, this concern is properly directed only towards the ultimate, beyond finitude. Similarly to Macquarrie's dialectical theism, Tillich sees this tension as inescapably integral to the idea of God. He writes, 'The conflict between the concreteness and the ultimacy of the religious concern is actual wherever God is experienced and this experience is expressed'.[153] This is because the ultimacy of the religious concern represents the universality of value and meaning in which religion properly deals and the concreteness of the concern represents the particular meanings and values through which human experience and expression are necessarily channelled. As he summarizes this last point, 'Man can speak of the gods only on the basis of his relation to them'.[154] But this relation, Tillich claims, is unavoidably expressed in the supernaturalistic terms of the finite actions of God, understood as an interventionist highest being, interfering with and transforming the course of finite events. But these terms and concepts, like all which are used to describe divine self-revelation, are symbolic so the theologian must 'try to use terms which indicate that their meaning is not categorical', an example of which is 'ground'.[155]

It is here that the importance of the role of paradox in religious discourse becomes apparent. If two strictly contradictory terms are used together, which result in a statement that is, literally, nonsense, then symbolic interpretations are implicitly encouraged. Significantly, it is in the case of one example of this that Tillich thinks there might, in fact, be a case for applying the term 'existence' to God. He believes that it would be better if the terms 'God' and 'existence' (which he takes to be mutually exclusive) were entirely separated except in the case of the 'Christological paradox', which symbolically represents 'the paradox of God becoming manifest under the conditions of existence'.[156] In other words, Christological claims symbolically express 'the mystery that appears in revelation and which remains a mystery in its appearance'.[157] Such claims are specifically Christian examples of symbols which, famously for Tillich, *participate in the reality which they symbolize* and, to that extent, are affirmed but are simultaneously negated insofar as they *point beyond themselves* to the ultimate with which, on pain of idolatry, they must not be confused. The religious symbol's 'proper' meaning is paradoxically negated by the ultimate reality to which it points.[158] It follows that any statement about God being in relation (to *anything*) is symbolic and therefore must similarly be affirmed and denied at the same time: affirmed because man, for Tillich, is the intentional kind of being for whom every relation involves an object and denied because God can never become an object for human knowledge or action.[159] It is for similar reasons that Macquarrie rejects Buber's interpersonal model for revelation, since he believes the terms of personal existential thinking to be no more adequate to the subject than the impersonal language of calculative thinking.[160]

Reflection of this kind on Tillich's theory of symbols highlights the symbolic status of Macquarrie's dialectical use of theological terms. The terms he applies, like 'transcendent' and 'immanent', though theologically orthodox, are not being applied literally but symbolically. The dialectical relationship between them, their mutually correcting function, cannot therefore be metaphysical or ontological but must be symbolic. If the terms were being applied literally, the dialectic would result in logical paradox and nonsense rather than mutual correction. Nothing can be both transcendent and immanent at the same time *and* be the same thing in both cases. But the symbolic dialectic involved in dialectical theism concerns meaning rather than being.[161] Two opposing meanings enter into a dialectical relationship that results in mutual correction rather than the paradoxical nonsense that would result from the simultaneous assertion of two opposing facts. And, if God is indeed ineffable, no facts can be known about him in any case. The dialectical application of opposing terms demands a symbolic, rather than a literal, interpretation. And it is only under the sufferance of Macquarrie's dialectical application, which implicitly recognizes their inevitable inadequacy and allows for their self-negation, that symbolic meanings can be applied to an ineffable God at all.

In the next section but one, I want to engage critically with some issues arising from the material on revelation (one 'take' on religious experience, emphasizing passivity) covered in this section, especially Tillich's idea of symbolic revelation implicitly endorsed by Macquarrie. First, however, I want to consider whether Tillich's argument about the possibility of revelation implicitly involves or implies a version of the ontological argument since consideration of this question brings those issues into clearer focus.

Tillich's Implicit Ontological Argument?

Duane Olson takes up Tillich's idea of God as the unconditioned depth of reason, in terms of which, as we have just seen, Tillich articulates the possibility of revelation.[162] Olson focusses especially on Tillich's vision of intimacy, which is an important part of that idea. He concentrates on Tillich's suggestion that God is present in our practical and, more importantly, theoretical acts which involve the division between subject and object (at least according to the correspondence theory of truth which Olson thinks Tillich is working). It is as reason's ground and abyss that God makes possible this division precisely by being unconditioned by it. Olson takes Tillich's claim to be that, if we have eyes to see, we shall come to the awareness that an ineffable, unconditioned God is therefore implied by the fact that we have the capacity to make judgements about reality (regardless of whether we deny, affirm or remain agnostic about whether some particular judgement does, in fact, apply). God, as the depth of reason, the measure of our judgements about the world, cannot be wholly subjective (since the subject uses such a measure to assess the correspondence between a subjective impression and an object) nor objective (since the subject 'bears' this measure: God is not an object of which the subject can have knowledge but is that by which the subject may judge all possible contents of knowledge). If God is to enable judgements about correspondence between subject and object, he cannot himself fall on either side of the division but must be seen as the identity of subject and object or their 'shared unity'. As Olson summarizes this way of thinking about Tillich's vision of intimacy: 'Something that transcends the difference between subject and object, but is not another object, appears in knowing and enables the determination of correspondence despite difference'.[163]

This capacity to make judgements about reality, which Olson calls the 'norm of truth', is not conditioned by the subject but the subject is conditioned by it. And (here the parallel with the ontological argument begins to show) whereas the subject can doubt the veracity of concrete truths, she cannot doubt her own ability to apply the norm of truth. This is something about which she can, in Tillich's phrase, have 'unconditional certainty' in stark contrast to the contents of knowledge, which are always dubitable. The acknowledgement of this idea, says Olson, is the subject's recognition of the necessary ground by which she is herself conditioned, the depth of the unconditioned which appears in every field of knowledge and which bears the capacity to negate, doubt and question as well as to affirm. Olson interprets this capacity as the presence of the unconditioned in theoretical acts and in the process of knowing as a whole. By way of a conclusion to his positive suggestion that Tillich makes use of a similar logic to the ontological argument, Olson draws attention to Tillich's praise of Anselm's recognition of an unconditioned element beyond the subject–object dichotomy that makes truth possible. But he points out that Anselm's obvious fault, for Tillich, is that he still regards God as *a* being.[164] Moving on to defend Tillich from some critics of this supposed use of the ontological argument, Olson cites J. M. Russell who claims that the move that Tillich inherits from the ontological argument is its most criticized one, 'that transition from the ideational to the extra-ideational'.[165] In my own opinion Russell is mistaken when he discerns a paradox in Tillich's position in that '[h]e concomitantly denies God's existence and affirms God's reality'.[166] Russell claims that the distinction of reality from existence will not remove this paradox because '[i]f the logical intension of the term "God" denotes the objective reality of being-itself, then, minimally, Tillich must concede that God, as being-itself, is'. But, for Tillich, the claim that God has reality is distinct from the claim that God exists to the point where the logical intension of 'God' is *not any* objective reality. Recall the passage where he glosses the meaning of 'the reality of God' as 'the validity, the truth of the idea of God, an idea which [does] not carry the connotation of some*thing* or some*one* who might or might not exist'.[167] It is in this way that Olson interprets Tillich as making use of a version of the ontological argument whilst simultaneously rejecting ontotheology: 'Tillich's argument', he writes, 'purports to reveal the implicit awareness of the unconditioned in agnosticism about the existence of God'.[168] I leave open the question whether this can properly be called an 'ontological argument', and I have reservations about the strength of the connection between this and the styles of argument of traditional philosophy of religion. But I agree with Olson's interpretation of Tillich on this point: that there is for him something undeniable about the 'reality of God' as Tillich interprets this.

Olson's suggestion also shows up a further parallel between Tillich and Cooper: both present a kind of rational demonstration of the validity of the concept of ineffability with which they are both working. As just suggested, Tillich starts with the subject–object schema, which he believes conditions all human thought and practice. His search for a truly satisfactory ground for these leads him to the idea of God as ineffable being-itself, the ground and abyss of reason. The reality, validity or truth of the idea of a God who at once transcends and embraces the subject–object dichotomy can consequently be demonstrated by appeal to the fact that human beings do in fact engage in acts of reason and practices apparently conditioned by that dichotomy. Similarly, Cooper's notion of ineffability grounds the concepts, meanings and practices which constitute the human world, by not being itself invested with those concepts and meanings. As long as the existence of a meaningful world of experience, an ultimate field of significance, is acknowledged (as it is implicitly acknowledged for as long as we continue to engage in meaningful thought and activity), the validity of the concept of ineffability must also be accepted. Using reason to demonstrate the limits of reason,[169] this kind of argument demonstrates the validity of the concept of ineffability and, in Tillich's case, it is to this concept that the word 'God' refers. If, as Olson believes, this can reasonably be called an 'ontological argument', then Cooper, as much as Tillich, must be said implicitly to make use of one.

Despite the parallels, however, there is a significant difference between the arguments with which Cooper on the one hand and Tillich and Macquarrie on the other argue for the validity of the concept of ineffability or of God. Aside from the difference in their relationships to the Christian tradition, this former difference has an important bearing on the issue of the possibility of revelation and religious experience as the two theologians conceive it, i.e. symbolically.

Critical Remarks: The Subject–Object Dichotomy and the Self-Denial of Symbols

We have seen that commitment to the subject–object dichotomy is an important stage in Tillich's argument for the validity of the idea of God. However this is not a commitment that Cooper explicitly shares. He sees the major contribution of the existential phenomenologists as being the dissolution of this dualism, the various modes of which they view as the source of the sense of alienation and 'homelessness' which came to a crisis in the twentieth century.[170] Unlike Tillich's argument for the idea of God, Cooper's argument for the validity of the notion of ineffability does not assume the thoroughgoing validity of the subject–object dualism. It depends rather, as we have seen, on meaningful human experience as articulated by the existential phenomenologists from which this dualism is regarded to be a misleading abstraction. The concept of ineffability, for Cooper, is the ultimate measure (beyond life) for our constitution of the world in concepts, meanings and values because it is not itself invested with those values, meanings and concepts. Since, as Merleau-Ponty strikingly claimed, 'the world is nothing but "world-as-meaning"', Cooper allows no logical gap between meaning and being as is made possible by the subject–object dualism.[171] For Tillich, meaning, as a 'thick' concept, can in principle be explained by objective features of that which is judged to have meaning. The relation between subject and object that this way of explaining meaning requires is made possible by their underlying identity in being-itself, God. Meaning is always mediated through some object even when, as is particularly obvious in a religious context, this is in practice inseparable from the subjective response of an individual or group. A miracle is always grasped by *someone* (Jesus, Tillich tells us, refuses to perform purely 'objective' miracles) but there is always also an objective happening by which someone is grasped. For the existential phenomenologists and Cooper, by contrast, human beings are just the kind of things that always already have a meaningful world and the human world is just what human beings always already find meaningful. Meaning, for them, is not a thick concept but something more akin to the 'thickness' of concepts, the condition for the application of concepts and for the carving up of experience into subjects and objects. The world *is* nothing but 'world-as-meaning', meaning as apprehended, experienced, interpreted by us human beings. Meaning is not logically distinct from, or independent of, being and involves neither a dualistic distinction nor a problematic relation between subjective and objective spheres. If the terms 'subject' and 'object' are meant to refer to distinct entities or substances that are thinkable in isolation from each other, there is no subject and object, only the human world. Elaborating a point made by Dewey, we might say that the *distinction* between subject and object may sometimes be useful but that the insistence on a *dualistic* understanding of the distinction or on a *dichotomy* between them, which renders the potential relationship between the distinguished items unintelligible, is a 'vicious affair'.[172] When I speak critically, throughout this book, of a subject–object dichotomy or dualism, it is Dewey's philosophically 'vicious affair', rather than the pragmatic, provisional (and therefore potentially more virtuous) distinction, that I have in mind.[173]

Tillich's contrasting view of reality implies that symbolic revelation and religious experience, as necessarily meaningful, are always mediated through an object, even where this is inseparable from a subjective response. The inseparability of a subjective reaction to Jesus's miracles from whatever objective event took place just points to the underlying identity of subject and object which makes possible what is superficially, but necessarily, interpreted as a philosophically problematic relation, or correlation, between them. We cannot but think in terms of the subject–object dichotomy; as Tillich writes, 'everything which becomes real to us enters the subject–object correlation'.[174] Therefore, on Tillich's view of meaning, our subjective evaluation (i.e. the meaning) of a symbol must also be at least partly explicable in terms of features of the object which has become a medium of the divine revelation and its human experience: symbols *participate in that which they symbolize*. But unlike symbolic objects, the God to which they *point beyond themselves* is not an object and is unconditioned by the subject–object dichotomy – hence the requirement that symbols deny themselves if they are to avoid occluding that which it is their purpose to reveal. In this section, I argue that Tillich's view of reality, unlike that of the existential phenomenologists and Cooper, is in tension with this requirement to the extent that it prevents him from honouring it.

Tillich's reaction to the views of the practitioners of 'existential' philosophy is instructive here. Interpreting the early Heidegger, Tillich rightly observes that he locates the meaning of Being in *Dasein*. But Tillich confuses Heidegger's claim about that which is ultimate (the place where the dichotomy between subject and object is overcome, namely human existence) with a claim about what is of religious significance. The early Heidegger did not claim, as Tillich writes, 'that immediate experience is the door to the creative "Source" of Being'.[175] This is because it had most likely not yet occurred to him that it could make sense to speak of such a source. The 'Source' which Heidegger begins, in his later works, to evoke by means of the notion of Being as ineffable, does have a quasi-religious significance and is something like what Tillich regards as ultimate, 'being-itself'. But *Dasein* for the early Heidegger was not ineffable but articulable in terms of the meanings and modes of meaning (where meaning is understood not as a 'thick' concept but more like the 'thickness' of concepts) that he set out in *Being and Time*. It was what Heidegger, in his early existential humanism, thought to be ultimate. But it does not follow from this that he thought that being-itself (in Tillich's sense of the religiously significant 'Source' of reality) should be identified with human existence, or that human existence consequently had any kind of religious significance. This leap, made by Tillich, owes to his own assumptions about what is the *locus* of ultimacy (the place where the subject–object dichotomy is overcome) and about what is the appropriate response when it is encountered ('ultimate concern', religious faith). Tillich's concept of ultimate reality has religious overtones to which the early Heidegger, as an existential humanist, is simply deaf. Neither does the early Heidegger share these assumptions of Tillich's about what is ultimate and in what sense. He would vehemently disagree with the idea that the sphere where the subject–object dichotomy is overcome is the religious one. It is just the sphere of *Dasein*, of the human world.

The gap between meaning and being is something else to which Heidegger, unlike Tillich, does not subscribe. For the early Heidegger, *Dasein* is what is ultimate, it is where the subject–object dichotomy is overcome but it is not an object and not ineffable. Whereas, for the later Heidegger, Being is ultimate, evokes the ineffable and is of (at least quasi-) religious significance. But the subject–object dichotomy is still dissolved in *Dasein* (although his terminology changes), rather than in Being. Being 'is' beyond even this dissolution, beyond the human world. For Tillich, on the other hand, what is ultimate is ineffable *because* beyond the subject–object dichotomy which otherwise accurately represents the nature of reality and of our ordinary experience. If, as I suggest, we accept the Heideggerian notion of meaning rather than the concept of meaning as a thick concept, dependent on the subject–object dichotomy, then Tillich's ultimate cannot be regarded as an object (for in it subject and object are overcome). But neither can it be claimed to be ineffable because, as Heidegger showed in *Being and Time*, the nature of the place where the subject–object dichotomy is overcome is still articulable by way of the meanings revealed by existential phenomenological analysis. This is because, for Heidegger, explanations of meaning do not have to be given in terms of objective features of what is judged to be meaningful, indeed they cannot, because there are no such objective features isolable from the subjective. The subject–object dichotomy does not accurately reflect the nature of our primordial, pre-reflective experience of reality. Meaning cannot therefore be accurately thought of as a thick concept, a thought dependent on that dichotomy. The most that could be claimed, therefore, is that Tillich's ultimate is ineffable with regard to being (it is not an object) but not with regard to meaning (it is still in principle articulable).[176] This logical gap between being and meaning is entailed by Tillich's view of reality as conditioned by the subject–object dichotomy, a view that it is the whole point of Heidegger's early phenomenological work to jettison. However all this does not prevent Tillich from speaking of being and meaning in the same breath, from writing as if there were no such gap: 'The measure of [the] … truth [of religious symbols] is the measure of their self-negation with respect to what they point to, the Holy-Itself, the ultimate power of *being and meaning*'.[177] It seems to me that this gap compromises the ineffability of being-itself, preventing it from being regarded as ineffable with regard to both being and meaning, which, rooted in existential phenomenology, my understanding of the notion of ineffability implies. Even if a separation is accepted, it is only as ineffable with regard to both that being-itself can, as Tillich requires, properly be the source or measure of both and thus be worthy of the religious response.

It is my view that it is this gulf, too, which compromises the possibility of the self-denial of symbols. The previous quotation from Tillich is one among many pieces of evidence that this is something which he has not properly recognized. The example Tillich gives as the pre-eminent case of the self-denial of symbols is the crucifixion of Christ.[178] It is easy to see how this symbol denies its own meaning: Christ's death is a negation of the very life that is the bearer of divine revelation for a group of human subjects (the Christian community). But it is harder to see how it could negate its own being; even the death of Christ presupposes Christ's existence. And it is not the symbol's meaning which creates the risk of idolatry but its status as an object such that a symbol must overcome the finite conditions in which it appears, 'sacrificing them, and itself with them'.[179] Tillich claims that the negative quality 'which determines the truth of a religious symbol is its self-negation and transparency to the referent for which it stands', the positive quality being the value of the symbolic material.[180] It follows that the criterion of truth is 'the degree to which the concreteness of the concern is in unity with its ultimacy'.[181] Tillich's account of the self-denial of symbols, then, is supposed to explain to us how this unity is possible, how an object that is within the subject–object dichotomy (which in his view conditions all reality) can represent, or otherwise embody, the ineffable beyond all objects. As he writes, 'A real symbol points to an object which can never become an object'.[182] He uses the example of the symbol 'God' to show how this happens. Religious symbols, Tillich says, fall into two categories: objective symbols (for example, the notion of God as the highest being) and self-transcending religious symbols (in which, for example, 'God' is taken to refer to the unconditioned transcendent which goes beyond any conception of a being, even the Supreme Being). The symbol 'God' is used in both ways so that the latter self-transcending function brings about the 'annihilation' of the former 'objective' idea of God as a being.[183] It makes explicit its necessarily inadequate nature, such that the use of this single symbolic term involves the 'oscillation between the setting-up and destruction of the religious object'.[184] It is thus that the word 'God', like other religious symbols 'has the peculiarity of transcending its own conceptual content'[185] and, in my view, this is what Tillich is getting at when he makes his rather cryptic statement that 'God is the symbol of God'.[186] So the way in which symbols are able to bridge the gap between the objectivity of the medium in which they appear and the non-objectivity of the ineffable is by way of this double meaning, by having (1) a symbolic-objective dimension of meaning and (2) a literal-non-objective one.[187] The meaning of 'God' as (1*) the Supreme Being is symbolic, for it is not literally true that 'God' refers to a being of any kind. It is also objective because it creates a conception of a specific object.[188] The meaning of 'God' as (2*) the unconditioned transcendent is literal, for it is literally true that 'God' intends the unconditioned ineffable. It is also non-objective because it is obviously incorrect to think of the ineffable as an object. The symbolic term 'God' thus represents something figurative but objective (the notion of God as an object) which itself evokes something literal but non-objective (God as the unconditioned ineffable) through the destruction of the former idea. It is in this way that something objective, and perceivable by us within the subject–object dichotomy, can nonetheless deny or overcome its own objectivity and thereby evoke the ineffable.

But this distinction between dimensions of symbolic meaning leaves Tillich open to attack. He writes, 'The criterion of the truth of a symbol naturally cannot be the comparison of it with the reality to which it refers, just because this reality is absolutely beyond human comprehension'.[189] While this might be defensible with regard to the literal-non-objective dimension of symbolic meaning, with regard to the symbolic–objective dimension it is not true. We *can* compare the God-object, or the concept of it, to the concept of ineffability and judge that the object always infinitely falls short because ineffability and objectivity are mutually exclusive. Tillich writes, 'The only criterion that is at all relevant is this: that the Unconditioned is clearly grasped in its unconditionedness. A symbol that does not meet this requirement ... is demonic.'[190] This must mean that, at least in their symbolic–objective dimension of meaning, symbols *always* fail. This is all well and good, so long as the literal-non-objective dimension can always take over. But Tillich makes the further claim that, in symbols, 'both aspects, the empirical and the transcendent, are manifested ... and their symbolic power depends upon this fact'.[191] It follows that if symbols fail in one dimension of their meaning, they fail as symbols in their entirety. One dimension cannot be negated without also negating the other. If symbols are to evoke the ineffable for Tillich, he must dispense with the notion of objectivity. Given that he views all experience as conditioned by the subject–object dichotomy, a symbol would in that case cease to be a perceptible object in the world as soon as it began to symbolize and would thus be unable to symbolize. The potential success of a symbol would then depend on its non-existence, the impossibility of its success! If, on the other hand, symbols do remain objects, they will never be able to evoke the ineffable, only other objects. Tillichian symbolic objects are at best non-existent and at worst idolatrous. Having been devised to bridge the gap between ineffability and objectivity, which was created by Tillich's rejection of ontotheology, they can succeed only by reinstating ontotheology on the symbolic level and thereby undermining the point of invoking them.

In any case, Tillich hammers the final nail into his argument's coffin when he conflates the two dimensions of meaning which he carefully distinguished earlier on. He writes: 'The real religious symbol is the objective symbol, which ... represents the unconditioned transcendent'.[192] But his entire argument depends upon the idea that it is the non-objective (and literal) dimension of symbolic meaning which evokes the unconditioned precisely by annihilating the symbolic–objective dimension. In the light of this argument, it is hard to understand the import of Tillich's complaint that the idea of God has been misused by objectification and has therefore lost its symbolic power, now serving to conceal, rather than to symbolize, the unconditioned.[193] The objectification is surely an essential stage in a symbol's symbolic function – were there no dimension of objectification in the symbol, there would be nothing within the subject–object dichotomy to 'annihilate' and therefore no way to evoke the unconditioned to us human beings, whose experience is, for Tillich, inescapably conditioned by that dichotomy. Tillich only compounds his conflation when he claims that the 'unobjective, symbolic character' of the 'God' symbol only has a chance of influence insofar as the 'ring' of the unconditioned can also be heard in the word 'God'.[194] The symbolic dimension of symbolic meaning, according to his own argument, is objective, not 'unobjective'. It was only as such that the notion of a religious symbol had a chance of bridging the gap between ineffability and objectivity.

So Tillich's argument fails on account of the view of reality on which he bases it, his insistence that the subject–object dichotomy accurately reflects the nature of ordinary, lived experience. He does not acknowledge that, according to his argument, idolatry is the inevitable result of the religious use of symbolic material that is thought to be appropriately described in the terms of the subject–object dichotomy. However, he does admit that the situation with symbols is 'fraught with great danger' on account of the possibility of idolatry.[195] He considers one possible way of avoiding it, which involves what he calls 'an emancipation from the burden of ... symbolism':[196]

> Undoubtedly, it might well be the highest aim of theology to find the point where reality speaks simultaneously of itself and of the Unconditioned in an unsymbolic fashion, to find the point where the unsymbolic reality itself becomes a symbol, where the contrast between reality and symbol is suspended. If this were really possible, the deepest demand of the religious consciousness would be fulfilled; religion would no longer be a separate thing. This ... signifies ... an immediate concern with things insofar as they confront us unconditionally, that is, insofar as they stand in the transcendent.[197]

This possibility, as he describes it here, sounds very like the relatively unelaborated notion of *Grundoffenbarung* ('fundamental divine revelation') which Werner Schüßler finds in only three places in Tillich's oeuvre and which is the content of 'absolute faith',[198] faith 'which has been deprived by doubt of any concrete content'.[199] *Grundoffenbarung* refers to an immediate awareness of the divine, which is without form or determinate content, is non-symbolic and is the basis for any symbolic apprehension.[200] The absolute faith of which this is the content transcends the notion of a divine–human encounter that is conditioned by the subject–object dichotomy (even if the encounter is, as for Buber, better conceived as a subject–subject one). '[R]adical doubt undercuts and prevents this encounter, leaving nothing but absolute faith'.[201] But Tillich believes that, absolute faith, with *Grundoffenbarung* as its contentless 'content',[202]

> is not a place where one can live, it is without the safety of words and concepts, it is without a name, a church, a cult, a theology. But it is moving in the depth of all of them. It is the power of being, in which they participate and of which they are fragmentary expressions.[203]

Because born of radical doubt, absolute faith admits of no further doubt because the unconditioned, of which it is an immediate awareness, cannot be doubted, only its symbolic representations. Tillich does not think that one can live without symbols because he believes that there is a gap between the way in which reality is and the way it ought to be. He thinks that reality is not ordinarily transparent to its ultimate meaning and that, if it were, we should not tend to place realities with symbolic power on a higher level than those without. The idea that reality could have a specifically symbolic significance should never have occurred to us. (This tendency lies behind Tillich's own distaste for the phrase 'only a symbol'.) Only if reality were so transparent, he argues, 'would reality itself acquire symbolic power and thus the realm of "special" [i.e. determinate] symbols would become unnecessary: reality and symbol would become identical'.[204] The counterargument must be, of course, 'What if reality *is* as it ought to be?' And even if it is not, it seems an odd strategy to *reinforce* the division with the suggestion that the idea that reality 'stands in God' should be interpreted eschatologically and not with regard to the way things are in the present.[205] Heidegger's and Cooper's views, which do not constrain human experience to the subject–object dichotomy, again come to mind. For Heidegger there is no need even for reality to become a symbol in any determinate sense, since it is regarded as wholly intimate with its 'Source' in Being itself. On this view, objectifying tendencies may, to be sure, still be a problem but one only needs to think of Heidegger's thoroughgoing critiques of technology to be reassured that his view is not an absurdly optimistic alternative. It does not follow from the idea that reality is what it ought to be that views to the contrary are impossible. And one can, as Heidegger does, acknowledge and criticize such deep-rooted objectifying views without buying into their own supposition that they are at all based on an accurate picture of reality.

The real reason for Tillich's unwillingness to dispense with symbols, I suspect, is that he wants to separate the religious from the everyday encounter with reality and to think of them as being qualitatively different. 'The presupposition of theology is that there is a special encounter with reality – or a special way in which reality imposes itself on us – which is ordinarily called "religious"'.[206]

A kind of philosophical mysticism, like Heidegger's, or Tillich's own 'absolute faith', need not necessarily dispute the idea that there is a specifically religious way in which reality imposes itself, which is qualitatively different from other kinds of experience. But it turns out that it is not just the distinctiveness of the specifically 'religious' experience that Tillich wants to protect but the specifically *Christian* religious experience. This is shown by his resistance to a wholehearted embrace of philosophical mysticism of the kind represented by the later Heidegger, or his own concept of absolute faith. He claims that it is necessary to be within the theological circle of a concrete religion in order to be able to interpret it existentially. The theological circle could only be denied, he thinks, 'in the name of an assumedly higher ultimate, which immediately would establish the same circle'.[207] Now there seems no good reason to choose Christianity as the *highest* circle rather than absolute faith or another form of philosophical mysticism. Nonetheless, Tillich resists the latter, declaring: 'I am convinced that Christianity is able to take all possible elements of religious truth into itself without ceasing to be Christianity'.[208] This may indeed be true. One is immediately reminded of the project, popular at various points in the history of the Christian tradition, of identifying 'Christians before Christ'. If figures like Moses, Abraham or Socrates were inspirational in a religious way, one could claim that they are saved because of Christ's harrowing of Hell. But I do not think that this view avoids a *cultural* arrogance of a particularly distasteful kind. Leaving aside the unanswerable question of how it is possible to judge which concrete theological circle is the highest, in order to avoid such arrogance, one would have not only to measure other religions by the standard of the Christian theological circle but also to measure Christianity by the standard of other theological circles. One would have to accept equivalent religious challenges to the notion of what constitutes Christianity. True humility, on a cultural as well as on a religious level, implies that the truth of Oscar Wilde's aphorism is a genuine possibility: 'there were Christians before Christ. For that we should be grateful. The unfortunate thing is that there have been none since.'[209] I accept the point of Tillich's statement that faith is always 'subjective and objective in a strict interdependence', namely, the importance of highlighting its existential quality.[210] But I dispute the idea that this is what marks off religious from everyday experience. If the existential phenomenologists have taught us anything, it is surely that *all* truth is existential, Kierkegaard's *truth for me*, and not merely objective. Tillich is right to argue that the polarity of objective statements and subjective emotions desperately needs to be overcome in theology in order that both (reductive) naturalism and supernaturalism can be avoided. However, it is harder to see why this needs to be overcome if the subject–object dichotomy, and thus the model of objective truth, is to some degree generally defensible, i.e. as a description of ordinary everyday experience. If, with the existential phenomenologists, it is regarded to be always a misrepresentation, then the urgency of jettisoning it becomes all the more palpable.[211]

We have found that Tillich's symbolic account of revelation, and therefore of religious experience, has the advantage of articulating, in explicit philosophical terms, the symbolic understanding involved, more implicitly, in Macquarrie's dialectical theism. But we have also found Tillich's account to be an inadequate answer to the notion of God as ineffable, incapable of reconciling ineffability and answerability into a specifically theological vision of intimacy that philosophically accounts for the possibility of religious experience. Owing to his view of reality, his commitment to the subject–object dichotomy and his construal of (revelatory) religious experience in these terms, Tillich's attempted reconciliation tended to compromise ineffability by refusing to abandon the notion of pure objectivity when this abandonment was a crucially important implication of the notion of ineffability. Having initially rejected ontotheology, Tillich reinstates it on the level of symbolic meaning. Consequently, his account of religious experience fails to move beyond the terms of the subject–object dualism. We have found these terms to be an unsatisfactory mould in which to cast our conception of experience, especially in connection with the concept of ineffability, since the brief discussion of the relation between these concepts at the end of Chapter 1. The symbolic account of answerability endorsed by both Macquarrie and Tillich is therefore not a viable theological solution to the problem of ineffability described in the first part of this book. As I have been intimating, a theological application of the Heidegger–Cooper line of argument, with its more immediate vision of intimacy, seems an obviously attractive alternative. But before embracing it too hurriedly, it is appropriate to acknowledge that there is another, rather subtle and unjustly neglected, philosophical position whose contribution to the discussion warrants detailed consideration. It is this stance, that of Karl Jaspers, that is the subject of the next chapter.

4 KARL JASPERS'S PHILOSOPHICAL POSITION

The philosophical system of Karl Jaspers, which he called a 'periechontology',[1] is complex and idiosyncratic. It involves the identification and analysis not of a world of objective definitions, as he believes ontology does, but of realms or modes of the Encompassing (or Comprehensive) which he defines as ultimate reality, the 'origin' or 'source' of the subject–object relationship.[2] Very broadly speaking, his system divides reality into three such modes which are dealt with by each in turn of the three volumes of his *magnum opus*: '(mundane) existence' in the subject–object dichotomy; '*Existenz*' (or human freedom which is not limited to either pole of the dichotomy)[3] and 'Transcendence' (or God), the Absolute beyond existence, consciousness and *Existenz*.[4] The corresponding philosophical elucidations of these three modes of reality are respectively called '(philosophical) world orientation',[5] 'existential elucidation' and 'metaphysics'.[6] Jaspers is yet another existentialist (though, like most of them, he repudiated the application of the term to himself) who recognizes the logical and psychological need for some measure beyond the human to which human existence answers. He also recognizes the logical requirement that this measure, whether or not imagined in religious or quasi-religious terms, be considered ineffable. He makes a philosophically acceptable version of the claim that Transcendence or God is ineffable and rejects ontotheology by defining the word 'God' as 'the name and sign which lacks all perceivable content' and by repeatedly denying that, as Transcendence, God is an object.[7]

Much of the existing Jaspers scholarship, especially that whose main motive is the aim of recruiting Jaspers's ideas into the service of theology, rightly appreciates the importance of what he calls 'ciphers'. The importance placed on this notion results from the recognition that if theology is to have anything to do with Jaspers's thought, it can either remain as it is, and come to view itself as superstition, or conceive itself as a form of Jaspersian 'philosophical faith', which has ciphers as its contents.[8] However, much of this scholarship is also surprisingly vague on the precise status of ciphers, especially in connection with the subject–object dichotomy. Fritz Buri, for example, fails to appreciate the ambiguity that ciphers have for Jaspers with regard to the subject–object dichotomy. Presenting the Incarnation in superficially Jaspersian terms as 'the cipher that

God objectified himself by becoming man', he simply absorbs an apparent philosophical faith into the objectivity of Christianity's 'saving facts'.[9] Buri describes this operation as the 'use of the Christological dogma as a cipher',[10] a description which sounds convergent with Jaspers's system but, as it turns out, the operation it describes lacks the ambiguity which ciphers are accorded in relation to the subject–object dichotomy in that system. One commentator on the relationship between Jaspers's philosophical thought and its theological appropriation by Buri articulates Buri's understanding of ciphers in terms no different from, and therefore no more satisfactory than, those in which Tillich explained his notion of symbols. For this commentator, the purpose of ciphers, for Buri, is 'to mediate the non-objectifiable in the realm of the subject–object dichotomy'.[11] More recently, David R. Law has briefly acknowledged the ambiguous status of Jaspers's ciphers but has not critically engaged with this ambiguity or drawn out its implications in any detail.[12] To my mind, the ambiguity of ciphers is of crucial importance not only for an understanding of the relation, or potential relation, of Jaspers's ideas to theology and philosophy of religion but also for an understanding of the structure of Jaspers's philosophical system in its own right. I therefore hope that this chapter may go some way towards redressing the state of imbalance between the acknowledged theological importance of Jaspers's theory of ciphers and the level of detail at which theologians and philosophers of religion have typically engaged with that theory.

My main purpose here is to examine in detail and critically to engage with two aspects of Jaspers's thought germane to my argument that open up the possibility of bypassing Tillich's problematic doctrine of symbolic revelation. I look, firstly, at his notion of ciphers, comparing it favourably with Tillich's conception of symbols. Secondly, I consider the (in my view ambiguous) place of the subject–object dichotomy in the tripartite structure of his thought as a whole, with (again) a specific focus on the relation of ciphers to that dichotomy.

Karl Jaspers's Ciphers

Like Tillich's symbols, Jaspers's ciphers are the means whereby the ineffable, 'transcendent' mode of the Encompassing comes to presence to human being in consciousness or *Existenz* since 'Transcendent being in itself is independent of me but inaccessible as such'.[13] It is in the reading of the cipher-script of Being that perceptible reality as a whole is viewed as a presencing, a coming forth, of its Transcendent, ultimately real and ineffable source. Jaspers's aim with his theory of ciphers of Transcendence is to encourage a focus on reality, the world itself, about which human *Existenz* can communicate. According to Jaspers, this relatively concrete kind of experience of Transcendence is very unlike the heights of mysticism, whose experiences are incommunicable to those who do not share them, which, with no worldly practical consequences, lure us to quietism and present us with the illusory possibility of a direct, totally unmediated relationship with Transcendence.[14] In Tillich's language, the theory of ciphers is an attempt to think the concreteness of the (broadly) religious concern in union with its ultimacy: with ciphers, the focus is on the world but with a view to obtaining a sense of what is infinitely beyond that world, that to which human *Existenz* answers. However, the dissimilarity between symbols (like Tillich's) and Jaspers's ciphers is highlighted in a footnote in which Jaspers explicitly distinguishes them. He writes:

> 'Cipher', a word I prefer to the word 'symbol', denotes language, the language of a reality that can be heard and addressed only thus and in no other way – while a symbol stands for something else, even though this may not exist outside the symbol. What we mean by a symbol is the other thing, which thus becomes objective and comes to be present in the symbol, yet symbols may turn into elements of the cipher language.[15]

As David Law insightfully glosses this note:

> What Jaspers seems to mean here is that through the symbol that which is symbolized is made present to us. It is the objectification of that which it symbolizes ... For Jaspers a symbol symbolizes something within and not beyond the sphere of the subject–object dichotomy.[16]

A cipher, Law continues, does not refer to something else in the world but to Transcendence which transcends the subject–object dichotomy. It is therefore not exhaustible by comprehension of the signified object, because what is signified is not an object. Consequently, the cipher's 'content' is in the cipher, and not outside it.[17] Jaspers's note and Law's gloss imply that there is a close connection between the non-objectivity of Transcendence, embodied by ciphers, and the intimacy of ciphers with Transcendence. As we saw with our discussion of Tillich's symbols, it is impossible to give an adequate philosophical account of how what is beyond the subject–object dichotomy and unconditioned by it can be manifest within it. And where Jaspers differs from Tillich is that he excludes objectivity not only from his concept of Transcendence but apparently also from his understanding of the ciphers that embody it and make it perceptible to human *Existenz*. Thus ciphers are not instances of the objectification (even the necessarily inadequate Tillichian objectification) of the ineffable both because they are not purely objective themselves and because they are conceived as intimate with that non-objective reality which they encrypt. It is interesting to note, in this connection, that Tillich identified the origin of the 'half-blasphemous and mythological' notion of the existence of God, and of the 'abortive' attempts to prove his existence, as the paradoxical situation that (1) God is not an object and (2) that everything which is real for us becomes so by entering the subject–object correlation.[18]

Such intimacy is repeatedly stressed by Jaspers and constitutes for him the basic difference between 'mundane' meaning (mediated by the subject–object dichotomy) and the ciphers' 'metaphysical' meaning as regards the relation of the image to what it represents. Whereas, in the former case, the thing represented can be independently grasped as an object, in the case of the latter, metaphysical mode of meaning, 'the image is simply an image for something not accessible in any other way'.[19] If that for which the image stands can be shown directly without it, we are not engaged in metaphysics and the image is not a cipher but a symbol or some other kind of object. With ciphers, what is bodied forth exists for us only insofar as it exists in the cipher, which operates in a metaphysical mode of meaning, that is, it 'must be existentially grasped in the image and cannot be conceived as just an object'.[20] As with Cooper's vision of intimacy, the implication is not that the cipher is accurately *identified* with the Transcendence that it embodies but that Transcendence, being independent of us but inaccessible as such, cannot be acknowledged or experienced without the cipher. Ciphers are our only access to Transcendence and, while they mediate Transcendence to us, they apparently do not do this *via* the subject–object dichotomy. Jaspers expresses this intimacy, or unity without identity,[21] with the help of two illuminating metaphors, one of 'language' and the other of 'physiognomy'.

Deploying the first metaphor, Jaspers writes: 'We call the metaphysical objectivity a cipher because it is the language of transcendence, not transcendence itself'.[22] Jaspers would agree with Cooper's thesis of the human world, believing that the only conceivable world is this, human one. But transcending steers a course between pantheism, which *identifies* this world with the Transcendent, and supernaturalism, which postulates a transcendent world beyond and entirely separate from this world. 'What happens in genuine transcending', Jaspers tells us, 'is the deepest possible affirmation of the world, performed toward mundane existence as a cipher language because that language transfigures the world, and what we secretly hear is the voice of transcendence'.[23] He distinguishes three interrelated 'languages' of Transcendence: (1) the direct language which is the vehicle of our experience of Transcendence, (2) the transmission of this experience between *Existenzen* in communicative symbolism and (3) the philosophical elucidatory penetration to the source of the second language, 'philosophical communication'.[24] Regarding the second, expressive language, Jaspers describes its inseparability from the first, experiential one: 'In communicative expression we also seek to *convey our original perception of symbols*'.[25] One can communicate with oneself in the second language and in this way cause oneself to understand 'what in immediacy is real but murky'.[26] The 'direct symbolism' of the first language 'remains the source, but that symbolism is rarely perceived except insofar as it has become language' of the second, expressive and communicative kind.[27] Although the first language is the source, the second, communicative expression, 'which conveys something else, is language in the proper sense – all other expression can be termed language only metaphorically'.[28] Jaspers's linguistic metaphor has the advantage of illustrating the inseparability of the experience from the expression of the experience of Transcendence and the intimate, immediate relationship between ciphers and Transcendence. It is not that a cipher *is* Transcendence, any more than a language's phonemes *are* what a sentence of that language means, but rather that Transcendence requires the cipher in order to be perceptible and communicable in just the way that linguistic meaning requires the concrete phonemes to be both perceptible and articulable, in other words, to be realized. 'As ineffability precedes all effability in the objective realm', Jaspers writes, 'so does the reality of transcendence precede its language'.[29] The weakness of the linguistic metaphor, however, is its implication that the cipher language is in principle interpretable or translatable into other terms. It implies that what a cipher intends somehow exists outside it and is in principle independently accessible. The physiognomical metaphor, by way of counterbalance, overcomes this weakness.

Jaspers, secondly, describes the way in which, in 'man', an expression of his being is perceptible 'in his physiognomy and in his involuntary gestures';[30] likewise, in ciphers, '*All* things seem to express a being ... we experience this physiognomy of all existence'.[31] Whereas human physiognomy concerns the expression of a kind of being which is accessible in other ways, so that it can be objectively described by empirical psychology, for example, we cannot similarly empirically verify the 'physiognomy' of ultimate reality, for this is inaccessible except in and through that physiognomy. As Jaspers elaborates, again stressing the intimacy that is the point of his metaphorical comparisons:

> This transparent view of existence is like a physiognomic viewing – but not like the bad physiognomy aimed a form of knowledge, with inferences drawn, from signs, on something underneath; it is like the true physiognomy whose 'knowledge' is all in the viewing.[32]

It would strengthen Jaspers's argument if it turned out, contrary to what he seems to assume, that even in the human case, the meaningful 'content' of gesture and physiognomy were inseparable from the gestural expression itself and therefore not a possible object of knowledge derived from inferences from the external and separate signs which it causally produces. It is just such inseparability in the case of gesture for which Merleau-Ponty argues.[33] Asking us to imagine an angry interlocutor who is expressing his anger by gesticulating and shouting, Merleau-Ponty raises the question of where this anger is located. A possible answer is that it is in our interlocutor's mind but Merleau-Ponty objects that '[w]hat this means is not entirely clear. For I could not imagine the malice and cruelty which I discern in my opponent's looks separated from his gestures, speech and body.'[34] He eloquently continues:

> None of this takes place in some other-worldly realm, in some shrine located beyond the body of the angry man. It really is here, in this room and in this part of the room,

that the anger breaks forth. It is in the space between him and me that it unfolds. I would accept that the sense in which the place of my opponent's anger is on his face is not the same as that in which, in a moment, tears may come to his eyes or a grimace may harden on his mouth. Yet anger inhabits him and it blossoms on the surface of his pale or purple cheeks, his bloodshot eyes and wheezing voice ... And if, for one moment, I step out of my own viewpoint as an external observer of this anger and try to remember what it is like for me when I am angry, I am forced to admit that it is no different ... I am forced to acknowledge that this anger does not lie beyond my body, directing it from without, but rather that in some inexplicable sense it is bound up with my body.[35]

Precisely the same point is made rather more perfunctorily by Gadamer when he states that 'what a gesture expresses is "there" in the gesture itself ... [it] reveals no inner meaning behind itself'.[36]

Whether or not we accept that this argument is applicable to both halves of his metaphorical comparison, Jaspers's main point remains that ciphers are not separable from that which they body forth, that what they provide us with access to could not be presented to us in any other way, least of all objectively. Ciphers are significations without there being an object which is signified: 'The significations which cannot be annulled by equating them with the object signified we call ciphers'.[37] Ciphers, Jaspers explains, 'signify, but they do not signify a specific thing. The content is only in the cipher and does not exist outside it.'[38] To put it in even stronger terms: 'Being-a-cipher is a signification which signifies nothing else. Signification is itself only a metaphor for being-a-cipher.'[39] It follows that, though perceptible, ciphers are not interpretable or translatable into any other more literal terms and certainly not into the objective terms of mundane existence, perceptible to what Jaspers terms 'consciousness at large'. Any interpretable symbolism is objective and its sense is soluble in the binary terms of subject and object. But in contrast to symbols, which can be said to be interpretable, ciphers are better thought of as perceptible: 'We no sooner approach the symbol as a cipher of transcendence, however, than it *can be viewed*. A viewable symbolism permits no separation of the sign from its meaning, but embraces both in one.'[40] Although, in practice, we may separate sign from meaning, we do so only to elucidate to ourselves or to others what we have comprehended in the cipher but we do this in a new, communicative system of symbolism (the second 'language') rather than by interpreting one by means of the other. As Jaspers describes this process: 'We only elucidate what we already had. We return and gaze into new depths.'[41] Whereas an interpretable symbolism exists for the consciousness at large whose field is mundane existence, conditioned by the subject–object dichotomy, the viewable symbols 'as sounds of the cipher language are accessible only to such deepening by an *Existenz*'.[42] It is from such depths alone that the cipher-script of Transcendence 'transmits the light of indefinite being'.[43] Thus, for Jaspers, when we apparently interpret ciphers, interpretation never really happens because it is impossible to reach the infinite (which is the ciphers' 'meaning') from the standpoint of the finite without infinite repetition, an endless movement of interpretation.[44] When we read the cipher-script, our starting point is the infinite, since, as a matter of fact, 'it is the infinite presence of transcendence that turns finite things into ciphers'.[45] It is the ineffable, (Being, Transcendence or God) that is present in the cipher and, if it is to be interpreted at all, that which signifies demands, inexhaustibly, an endless movement of interpretation.[46] 'It is nameless. If we speak of it, then we use an infinite number of names and cancel them all again. That which has significance is itself Being.'[47] Ciphers are not translatable into anything but other ciphers and to know a cipher's meaning is not for a subject to be able to translate it, and therefore to know it rationally or objectively, but rather for an *Existenz* to experience, in the cipher's intention, an incomparable reference to the Transcendent and to experience this 'at the boundary where the object disappears'.[48]

Part of the point of Jaspers's linguistic metaphor is to stress that the experience of the incomparably real content of ciphers is not reducible to cognition or translatable into cognitive, subjective and objective, terms. But this is not to say that the content is therefore inaccessible in the cipher. It is to suggest instead that a very different mode of receptivity is required if that which is beyond purely cognitive perception as an object is nonetheless to be concretely perceptible in ciphers. Ciphers must be existentially embraced by an *Existenz*, the kind of being all humans potentially have, not merely comprehended by an existing subject. As Jaspers puts it: 'The cipher is listened to, not cognized'.[49] He expresses his idea of the disappearance or disintegration of the object for *Existenz* (which I shall examine in more detail later) in the following way: though a grasp of Transcendence in phenomena may sometimes look like a materialization, '[i]n the agonies of disappearing empirical reality, the lift to transcendence is the surest manifestation of its not being materialized';[50] 'the truer our grasp of transcendent being, the more decisively will its objective supports be destroyed'.[51] We have heard Jaspers insisting that Transcendence is not detached from the temporal reality in which it appears and, at the same time, that it is wrong to 'materialize' the Transcendent, to see it *as* rather than *in* empirical reality.[52] But he denies that this is the effect of ciphers as they transfigure the human world: 'To transfigure the world does not mean to make it an absolute, and neither does the proposition that whatever has being for man must be present in man mean that man is all'.[53]

By denying both that objectivity is involved on the ultimate side of the cipher-script (on the side of Transcendence) or on the concrete side (by denying that ciphers are soluble in, or reducible to either one of, the terms of the subject–object dichotomy), Jaspers is able to provide a theory of ciphers which improves upon Tillich's symbols by dispensing with the notion of objectivity altogether and thus allowing for a greater degree of intimacy, the 'unity without identity', of Transcendence, embodied in ciphers, with the ciphers themselves.

However, also unlike Tillich's symbols and perhaps owing to their lack of objectivity, Jaspers's ciphers appear to be at some remove from traditional forms of religious experience and expression. Jaspers is clear that, owing to the total absence of objectivity from the process of cipher-reading, the concreteness with which ciphers clothe for us the idea of Transcendence is nowhere near as concrete or specific as the common religious notion of a personal God.

> I quickly shrink from the impulse that would make the deity a thou for me, because I feel I am profaning transcendence. The very idea entangles me in delusions. After all, personality is the mode of self-being that is by nature unable to be alone; relations are its essence; it must have other things, persons and nature, besides itself. The deity would need us, would need mankind, to communicate with. In the idea of God's personality, transcendence would be diminished into an existence.[54]

The failure of objective cognition creates a space that can be fulfilled by the existential reading of the cipher-script of Being. The certainty of Transcendence is elucidated by this process but is given no substance, no concrete content.[55] In Tillich's terms, Jaspers's 'philosophical faith' is similar to Tillich's own 'absolute faith' in that it has been deprived by doubt of all determinate content. However, what such a notion of God lacks in purely rational compulsiveness, Jaspers feels, it makes up for in existential power. 'We find here no personal God of wrath and grace, no relevance of a life of prayer as religious action, no lasting visuality of the deity for our senses in symbols as objects of faith.'[56]

The lack of objectivity in Jaspers's account of what is an essentially philosophical revelation puts it at odds with the specificity of traditionally religious concepts of revelatory experience. Jaspers believes that religion is characterized by the sensuous presence of Transcendence but too often in such a way that the result is not the transparency of the sensuous but rather the concreteness of Transcendence in some specific empirical reality among others, that is, in the objectivity of the religious symbol, which we found that Tillich advocated. In philosophy, by contrast, part of whose goal is to elucidate our existential relations with ciphers in our reading of them, no one single reality is elevated as a definitive cipher of Transcendence. In philosophy, rather, images of the world as a whole are read as hieroglyphics of the cipher-script and that whole world is thereby transfigured.[57] This does not preclude the possibility of specifically religious experience but does acknowledge the need for its philosophical prolegomenon. Again exploiting his linguistic metaphor, Jaspers writes,

> the world is not a direct revelation but a mere language that will not be generally valid, is historically audible to Existenz alone and even for an Existenz is not to be definitively deciphered ... hiding is the way in which transcendence shows.[58]

Like Tillich, Jaspers explains the religious predilection for objective specificity in terms of the power that religious institutions are wont to wield. In his *Dynamics of Faith*, Tillich wrote of the often 'fanatical' religious resistance to the 'breaking' of religious mythologies (the explicit admission of their mythological character), which introduces a measure of doubt or uncertainty into the religious consciousness. Owing to the objective safety and security that an unbroken mythological world provides, 'Such resistance is supported by authoritarian systems, religious or political, in order to give security to the people under their control and unchallenged power to those who exercise the control'.[59] The claim here is not that religion is solely responsible for human unpleasantness or that religion alone, in Christopher Hitchens's phrase, 'poisons everything'. Rather, the claim is that a literal interpretation of religious truth enables the justification of the more generally human desire for power in the name of what is supposedly ultimate and therefore unchallengeable. Law similarly explains Jaspers's critique of theology as a critique of the theological fixing of historical revelation at a specific time or in a specific place which, as a particular kind of objectification, underwrites the power of the religious institutions to whom the specific revelation is supposed to have been granted.[60] Religious claims of the exclusivity of historically and temporally specific revelations can be explained not only in terms of a more generally human desire for hegemony but also in terms of the mistaken objectification of that which is beyond objectivity. This can either take the form of the mistaken idea that ciphers are identical with Being itself and provide us with unmediated, objective access to the ineffable, or of the delusion that Transcendence is an object in another world sealed off from this, human one. When Jaspers speaks of ciphers, he expressly does not mean to refer to

> things, matters, facts, realities, although it seems that the cipher contents have mostly been viewed as realities, like physical realities in space and time. People lived under their pressure as under the pressure of physical threats. It was such that they conquered nations and ages.[61]

But there is an additional problem, famously pointed out by Hume, in that the mutually conflicting nature of the revelations of the world's religious traditions speaks against the absolute or purely objective truth of all of them. And it is a claim to purely objective truth which is necessarily involved in a claim to an exclusive revelation.[62] Jaspers suspects that religious claims to such absolute truth have nonetheless been upheld as the arrogance of some human beings has been disguised as submission to such revelations in order to 'demand of all other men, under the name of humility, submission to their own truth and to themselves as its representative'.[63] The logical results of this objectification, however, take two extreme and opposing forms. One is superstition and magic where the corporeal is regarded as the Transcendent itself and the magical attempt made causally to produce or control this source of the symbolism.[64] The other is the degradation of the world, which happens when the Transcendent is objectified but, rather than being identified with the world, is thought of as sealed off in a realm entirely separate from the human world. In the latter case we may go so far down the mystical and ascetic route as to 'imagine the beyond as if it were another country from whose point of view existence becomes worthless'.[65]

So much for the philosophically uninformed religious consciousness. The 'metaphysical' elucidation of ciphers on the other hand, which philosophy alone can provide and which can provide a firmer basis for religious experience, language and praxis, is able to avoid this idolatrous objectification but has to pay the price of giving up any possibly exclusive or definitive concrete content for the ciphers.

> Never to approach the hidden God directly is the fate which a philosophical Existenz must bear. Only the ciphers speak, if I am ready ... [B]ut only seldom will an eye seem to look at me in the dark. Day in, day out, it is as if there were nothing. In his eerie abandonment man seeks a more direct access, objective guarantees, and firm support; he takes God's hand in prayer, so to speak, turns to authority, and sees the Godhead in personal form – and only in this form is it God at all, while as the Godhead it maintains its indefinable distance.[66]

Far from leaving us in a pure negativity, however, the adoption of this philosophical perspective is also, for Jaspers,

> [t]he great step in which man transforms himself ... when the supposed corporeality of Transcendence is given up as deceptive and the ambiguous cipher language is heard instead – when the contents that have been conceived and visualized are stripped of objective reality. Instead of tangibles there remain ciphers open to infinitely varied interpretation.[67]

Philosophy, Jaspers believes, is required today in a way that it was not in former times when there was no problem with taking ciphers for reality because, in those days, the cipher language was also the public language. 'It was the air you breathed.'[68] With the advent of secularism, where people do not necessarily or always look at the world in a religious light, where theology is no longer *regina scientiarum* (queen of the sciences) and where, for example, miracles are no longer expected to be commonplace, this is no longer the case. An objectively embodied Transcendent reality would be perceived to interfere with the general course of things as they are described by modern science, 'while ciphers give it wings' but only with the help of philosophical reflection, which systematically resists the reduction of the ciphers' content to mere objectivity.[69] This, for Jaspers, is part of what now makes the specific contents of ciphers no longer the final authority. In a secular world, ciphers of any kind, but perhaps especially religious ones, need philosophy to prevent their idolatrous identification with Transcendence itself. Jaspers sets up the contrast between theology and philosophy (both of which he views as species of faith – hence his term 'philosophical faith') as a choice between authority, the authority of a concrete, historical religious tradition, and freedom.[70] However, it is a choice whose very possibility presupposes the primacy of the latter. Philosophy, which, in the absence from a secular society of a specifically religious, exclusive and public cipher language, is the highest court of appeal, must now decide whether there is any truth in ciphers since it is no longer possible for them to be autonomous. The truth or otherwise of ciphers must be judged by 'philosophizing and the living practice of Existenz'.[71]

It may seem at this point that Jaspers leaves us with little doubt about which choice he thinks should be made. Religious symbols, he seems to be suggesting, are failed ciphers which have been mistaken for some other objectified reality, which they were originally meant to body forth and originally succeeded in doing so. In our modern context, however, in which the objective exclusivity of specific ciphers is no longer possible or desirable, the concrete content of religious symbols must be stripped away until we are left with philosophical ciphers, 'world images' in which we may apprehend the whole.[72] The determinate revelations of religious faiths, born of the distorting objectification of the ineffable in fixed, objective forms, should be given up for the sake of an indeterminate philosophical faith with no content but the cipher-script of perceptible reality as a whole. This apparently entails that Tillich's twofold wish to preserve not just a distinctively Christian, but even a distinctively religious, kind of experience could never possibly be fulfilled. However, this is not an altogether accurate picture of Jaspers's position. Jaspers is well aware that ciphers are no less part of a concrete, historical tradition than the religious symbols that he apparently impugns. In temporal existence, Jaspers consistently argues, no cipher is definitive. '*From where I stand*, the cipher remains permanently ambiguous – which means, speaking from the standpoint of transcendence, that transcendence *has other ways yet to convey itself*.'[73] And, as his linguistic metaphor intimates, the cipher-script read by philosophy is no less bound up with a concrete, historical tradition: 'Like languages, the ciphers have their origin in a tradition. We do not invent them, we appropriate them.'[74] Although there can be no such thing as a definitive system of ciphers (for their infinite ambiguity bars this and, if there were, a cipher would be a finite, objective thing rather than a bearer of Transcendence), 'a system can itself be a cipher, but it can never be a draft that meaningfully covers the authentic ciphers'.[75]

This possibility implies that both philosophical and religious symbols,[76] comprehended as part of such a system, can be reread, as it were. They can be interpreted as hieroglyphics of the cipher-script of Transcendence rather than, at least in the religious case (but more likely in both cases), as objectifying potential instruments of social and political power. Jaspers states that the religious ideas of revelation and incarnation as traditionally understood are inconceivable within this frame of reference: 'in this framework of ours it is neither thinkable nor imaginable for Transcendence to find a specific incarnation as a divine reality, distinct from any other, in the world of time and space'.[77] Though we cannot conceive of an incarnation, 'We can do something else, however. Aware of the phenomenality of all that we know, we can visualize the presence of something altogether different, something underlying ourselves and all that we know'.[78] In this context, the Christ-myth can be read as a hieroglyph of a cipher that indicates that 'everything human has the possibility of relatedness to God'.[79] The same possibility exists with regard to the notion of the Trinity. Jaspers claims that whenever a cipher is manifest, a circle is closed: 'out of mere presentness speaks the hidden essence; the hidden essence makes the presentness comprehensible'.[80] In the specific case of the Trinity, God is conceived as triune by way of metaphors drawn from the world of ordinary experience but the Trinity is also thought of as the ground or condition of possibility for these worldly phenomena. But, for Jaspers, 'this circle does not dissolve this whole as a delusion but is itself the cipher of Being which is just as lost in an objectivization into a presumed knowledge of God as in a reduction into empirically experienced triplicities'.[81] Research on the level of the subject–object dichotomy may at first appear to destroy the mythological, potential cipher-script insofar as the mythology's corporeality 'contained a moment of untruth and superstition' but the true purpose of such research is to lead us towards the real cipher-script precisely by discouraging or eliminating (by showing to be unbelievable) objectively transcendent interpretations and by preventing its dissolution in empirical categories.[82] It is in such a way that for Jaspers the concrete, historically conditioned symbols of religious faith are today made possible bearers of the ineffable only by the philosophical faith that recognizes that these symbols are best viewed as the potential hieroglyphs of a cipher-script, which can be read philosophically. To put it another way, the authority on which religion depends is made possibly only by its opposite: the freedom which philosophy, specifically *Existenzphilosophie*,[83] presupposes. The philosophical activity of reading the 'hieroglyphics of Being' must therefore guard against usurpation by a particular kind of religious faith, which makes explicit or implicit claims of the specificity and exclusivity of its revelation of the ineffable. Such a claim not only relies on a necessarily distorting objectification but also can all too easily become a particularly unpleasant instrument of hegemony. Far from attempting to destroy such religious faith, however, philosophy must guard against this potential usurpation 'while recognizing at the same time a cipher truth in the claims of the usurper'.[84]

Ciphers and the Subject–Object Dichotomy

Jaspers's theory of ciphers looks at first like a promising improvement on the Tillichian theory of symbols. Though critical of much in religion, Jaspers allows for the possibility of rehabilitating religious symbols as hieroglyphics of Being on the firmer ground of the philosophical cipher-script. He appears to be extending the possibility of interpreting religious experience and expression as instances of the perception, within a concrete, historical and potentially religious tradition, of ciphers of the ineffable. While their status as such ciphers rules out claims to objectivity and exclusivity, much of what has historically been unsavoury about religion is also ruled out while the ability of religion to attune its adherents to what is ultimately real, philosophically ultimate *and* religiously significant, is attractively preserved. It was also the objectivity of religious symbols, here apparently abandoned, that we found objectionable in Tillich's argument. But it does not, so far, seem very clear just what kind of reality ciphers have, what is the status of ciphers in relation to the various modes of the Encompassing and, specifically, what is their relationship to the subject–object dichotomy. Unlike Heidegger and Cooper, as Cooper himself observes, 'Jaspers does not believe that thinking in terms of subject and object is an eliminable mistake'.[85] This fact is a source of ambiguity in Jaspers's thought and, since it has a direct and important bearing on his theory of ciphers and ultimately on the status of Cooper's own arguments for the notion of ineffability, it is this ambiguity that I now want to address.

Jaspers often speaks of the 'phenomenality' of existence in terms that are consonant with Cooper's thesis of the human world: 'Whatever exists for us does so in the forms in which we become conscious of it'.[86] His distinction here is similar to the Kantian one but, for Jaspers, there is only one, phenomenal world, indistinguishable from another, noumenal one. It is in this way that Jaspers avoids subscribing to what Cooper pejorates as the 'two levels' position which Cooper directly associates with (at least some interpretations of) Kant. While the light of our phenomenal world is 'the only light there is', this is not Being, or what is ultimately real.[87] 'To our cognition, Being in itself is a boundary concept, not an object. The concept indicates nothing beyond our imprisonment in appearance.'[88] Since we cannot cross the boundary to an unworldly kind of being, nor adequately locate Transcendence within the world, the thought of Being lies solely in the process of transcending.[89] Transcendence, therefore, 'leaves the world but does not lead out of the world to something else'; its meaning is derived from the boundary concept, not from an object nor from an alternate world of objects.[90] Jaspers's frequent expression that the cipher transfigures the world and his description of ciphers as 'world images' are meant to express the idea that: 'All existence becomes a phenomenon of transcendence'.[91] He has made clear his view of the status of Transcendence: that it is not to be understood as a further object of which the world becomes a phenomenon and that it is beyond the subject–object dichotomy. However, the question now prompted is: what is the status of the 'phenomenon'? Does a cipher, as a phenomenon of transcendence, appear within the subject–object dichotomy or not? Although useful for other purposes, Jaspers's linguistic and physiognomical metaphors are of little help in settling this question. The linguistic metaphor is open to the interpretation that phenomena, like a language's phonemes, are objectively accessible but Jaspers is also clear that the 'physiognomy' he has in mind is not of the 'bad' kind which yields objectively accessible information but of the more immediately meaningful kind about which Merleau-Ponty writes, the kind of physiognomy whose knowledge is 'all in the viewing'. Jaspers also states that everything known is within the subject–object dichotomy and consists of objects, phenomena, rather than things-in-themselves.[92] As long as we are awake and conscious, Jaspers unequivocally states, we are involved in this 'basic condition of our thinking', the subject–object dichotomy: 'Twist and turn as we will we are always in this dichotomy, always oriented toward an object'.[93] If we are not in this dichotomy, as Jaspers elaborates, we are unconscious:[94]

> Consciousness is the basic phenomenon of the split into subject and object ... What does not enter into this dichotomy is for us like non-being. We can conceive of nothing without this dichotomy. Whatever we speak of has come into the dichotomy as we speak it.[95]

Thus, the subject–object dichotomy is, as it were, the stage on which anything that is and can be for us must appear. 'In realizing the stage', Jaspers states, 'we simultaneously become aware of the phenomenality of whatever appears on it'.[96] It is in this way that the phenomenality of whatever appears in the subject–object dichotomy is distinguished from the Encompassing nature of Being itself which is neither subject nor object but beyond the dichotomy, encompassing both of its poles. Not only that, but in a manner reminiscent of Tillich's quasi-ontological argument for the validity of the idea of God, Jaspers interprets the ultimate meaning of the dichotomy in which phenomena appear as the indication of the Encompassing nature of Being which, as such, is itself neither subject or object but (it seems) necessarily manifest in the dichotomy if it is not to be indistinguishable by us from non-being.[97] (Also like Tillich, Jaspers identifies this meaning as that in which (religious or philosophical) 'faith' is rooted perhaps because he has in mind especially the 'Transcendence' or 'God' mode of the Encompassing of Being itself.[98]) If that which 'authentically is' is not an object then it is beyond cognition. 'But since everything that is an object for us reveals to us its phenomenality in contrast to its being-in-itself, phenomenal being points to authentic being, which speaks and is perceptible through it.'[99]

While the phenomenality of all things is not identifiable with or reducible to Being-in-itself, neither is Being itself a separate, independently accessible object of which reality is a phenomenon: it 'is' for us only in and through the phenomenality of the world. Since the presence of Being is in the transcending movement that 'grasps and permeates simultaneously' subject and object, we take possession of Being, if we can take possession of it at all, in the polarity of subject and object,

> but in such a way that subject and object mutually overlap. While we are directed towards the object, Being in its essence is not already before our eyes as an object but is present only in the Encompassing, through object and subject simultaneously, as that which permeates both.[100]

It follows from these ideas that the ciphers that constitute the mechanism whereby Being is manifest to us, especially in its mode as Transcendence or God, have an ambiguous status with regard to the subject–object dichotomy. Their purpose is to allow us to escape from it to the Transcendent but they can only appear to us within the dichotomy. As a result, therefore, ciphers have an ambiguous status with respect to that dichotomy:

> Ciphers are objective: in them something is heard that comes to meet man. Ciphers are subjective: man creates them by his way of apprehending, his way of thinking, his powers of conception. In the subject–object dichotomy ciphers are subjective and objective at once.[101]

It could only be owing to this ambiguity of ciphers that an experience, necessarily undergone within the subject–object dichotomy, could point us beyond that dichotomy. This experience takes place for mundane consciousness but with a view to the transformation of that consciousness into an *Existenz*, which 'appears in the intertwining of subjectivity and objectivity'.[102] Since 'Existenz is either in relation to transcendence or not at all', and since 'Transcendence ... does not exist as empirical reality',[103] '[t]he consciousness of Being has thus a double foundation in both objectivity and subjectivity', *pace* the history of philosophy, much of which is, Jaspers believes, the history of the mistaken absolutization of one or other of the dichotomy's poles.[104] As he summarizes his view of the ambiguous status of ciphers: 'The cipher is neither object nor subject. It is objectivity which is permeated by subjectivity and in such a way that Being becomes present in the whole.'[105] This ambiguity of ciphers has two main implications with regard to the subject–object dichotomy, which, in tension with each other, bring into focus some difficulties surrounding the place of ciphers in Jaspers's theory of reality, or the Encompassing, as a whole.

Firstly, the ambiguity outlined by Jaspers implies that ciphers are irreducible to specific instances of objectivity, indeed that ciphers are incompatible with pure objectivity. As Jaspers suggests, when Transcendent Being comes into the presence of a human *Existenz*, it becomes immanent Transcendence, since there is no meaningful difference between there being a beyond that is not experienced by humanity and there being no beyond at all. But it does not do so as itself (for if it were immanent as itself, *Existenz* and Transcendence would have to be identical, which they are not) but rather as a cipher

> and even then not as an object that is this object, but *athwart all objectivity*, so to speak. Immanent transcendence is an immanence that has instantly vanished again, and it is a transcendence that has come to exist in the language of a cipher.[106]

The cipher, correspondingly, 'is that which brings transcendence to mind without obliging transcendence to become an objective being, and without obliging Existenz to become a subjective being'.[107] Thinking in these terms, Jaspers defines ciphers' status in relation to the subject–object dichotomy as 'absolute objectivities': just as mundane objects fill consciousness at large in the subject–object dichotomy, so ciphers, as absolute objectivities, fill the consciousness of *Existenz*, which is not soluble in the dichotomy but in which subject and object mutually overlap so that the Encompassing nature of Being itself becomes perceptible. Ciphers, Jaspers claims, elude our grasp in a direct approach but we must attempt to touch their 'existential roots'. Such contact initially validates the objectivity of ciphers since they have an objective content, which 'will have been felt'.[108] But it is in questioning, and eventually negating, this objectivity that the existential roots of ciphers are touched, that they come to be viewed as the 'existentially deciphered handwriting of something else', something else which is, nonetheless, inaccessible without them.[109] Jaspers reminds us that it would be wrong to confuse the objectivity of (or in) the cipher with Transcendence itself but claims that, in the cipher, something absolute is also visible to *Existenz* (in which subject and object are inseparably intertwined), something incomparably real: 'In the disappearance of its objectivity it makes true being manifest to Existenz'.[110] As consciousness transforms itself into *Existenz*, objects are transformed into absolute objectivities whose objectivity disappears as the absolute in them is existentially grasped:

> There is no permanence in which we definitively find the absolute. The objectivities will melt ... Existenz can live a life of its own with an absolute objectivity that will always be specific, will always dissolve, but will shed light even in disappearing.[111]

A cipher, as Jaspers's argument continues, is that in which Transcendence and mundane being are unified to an *Existenz*. This unity is lost if a cipher 'means' or intends something else which is independently accessible but, in the simultaneous transformation of human existence into *Existenz* and of mundane objects into ciphers, '*the symbol is inseparable from that which it symbolizes*' in the cipher-script.[112] In this way, the function of the cipher language is to make

Transcendence intelligible to *Existenz*. The objectivity involved is 'absolute' or 'metaphysical', is prior to all finite concretions and enables an *Existenz* to bring to mind what is unknowable to it as a merely existing consciousness at large, conditioned by the subject–object dichotomy. To the consciousness of mere existence, what is in fact the cipher language of Transcendence looks like another world of objects, perhaps a supernatural realm. But such language is only really audible to 'possible Existenz' and, correspondingly, 'everything objective is a *possible* cipher'.[113] In the freedom of Transcending, *Existenz* becomes transparent to itself and realizes that it *is* only in relation to Transcendence, which is inaccessible to the consciousness of mere existence.[114] At the same time, objective questioning 'fades' before the cipher: 'For the questioned object would promptly cease to be a cipher; as mere existence it would be the cipher's shell'.[115] It is in the simultaneous transition from existing consciousness to *Existenz* and from objectivity to cipher, i.e. the disappearance of the object, that transcending is located. Jaspers describes this dialectic of transcending as

> not just a transcending from a conception to the inconceivable, but in that act the very thinking that voids itself: a not thinking that makes me lucid because I am not thinking something and am not thinking nothing either. This self-annihilating dialectics [*sic*] is a specific thinking that means nothing to me as long as objectivity and visuality are my only conditions of meaning.[116]

At first glance, this argument simply repeats Tillich's difficulty, which was associated with the question of the possibility of the self-negation of the objectivity of symbols. However, the difference is that Tillich's more thoroughgoing and unqualified commitment to the subject–object dichotomy in principle allows for the religious shift from objectivity to non-objectivity to be conceived as a change either in our consciousness of reality or in reality itself, ruling out the idea that the change occurs in both simultaneously. By contrast, Jaspers's notion of the Encompassing and of the distinctively human possibility of the state of *Existenz* in which subject and object are undifferentiated implies that the shift in which objectivity disappears is necessarily conceived as a simultaneous shift in both human consciousness and in reality itself. Although the implication is that Tillich's problem is not simply reproduced in Jaspers's vision of simultaneous change (which follows from his notion of the Encompassing), the latter perspective suffers from similar difficulties. I will discuss these difficulties in the next section after critically engaging with Jaspers's commitment, more qualified and measured than Tillich's, to the subject–object dichotomy.

Secondly, then, as we have already seen, Jaspers places a great deal of importance on the subject–object dichotomy, which occupies an important place in his philosophical system. He repeatedly reminds us that we can never really escape the dichotomy as long as we are conscious, that *Existenz* is always in existence (in the subject–object dichotomy),[117] and that the Encompassing is always manifest precisely in and through that dichotomy. We ascertain the Encompassing, Jaspers thinks, 'by transcending the object within the object thinking that remains for ever inevitable, i.e. to break through the prison of our being that appears to us as split into subject and object, even though we can never really enter into the sphere outside it'.[118] It is only in 'object knowledge' that our consciousness can remain clear, though that knowledge can cognize, but (*pace* Feuerbach) not transgress, its own limits. 'Even in the thinking which transcends object knowledge we remain in it. Even when we see through the phenomenon it holds us fast.'[119] It is as though we plunge through the world to Transcendence but find that 'we remain in the world and find ourselves not in Transcendence but in heightened presentness. Whatever there is for us, becomes more for us than it seemed at first to be.'[120] In this way, the cipher shows us what without it would be totally hidden from us. Continuing his metaphor of incarceration, Jaspers constructs one of his most lucid descriptions of the state of affairs which obtains when the objectivity of ciphers disappears from the consciousness of a being the limit of whose consciousness is constituted by the subject–object dichotomy:

> We remain in the subject–object split, but our realization of it takes us to limits where the sense of our condition in encompassing effects a change in us. It does not free us now, in time, from the reality of our jail, but it does liberate by reflection on an unknown whence and whither felt as our destiny. The phenomena in the dichotomy grow brighter. We sense the encompassing in them. The prison walls are not toppled ... but if we know the prison, if we see it from the outside as well, so to speak, the walls become transparent. The unfoldment of phenomena in time, in the light of encompassing, makes the jail less and less of a jail.[121]

To put it another way, thought becomes acquainted with ciphers despite, or rather precisely through, the disappearance of all of its contents. Although thought requires sensuous support in the form of images, signs and language, this sensuousness can be transcended, or, better, 'consummated'[122] in the collapse of thought (or 'logical collapse'[123] – thought's awareness of its own limits) so that in the 'evaporation' of all contents, Being, which ultimately makes thought possible, becomes palpable for us.[124]

It is a puzzling consequence of these opposing ideas of Jaspers's, initially in apparent tension, that the disappearance of objectivity and its consummation are supposed to amount to the same thing. The passage just quoted may, too, leave us with the uneasy sense that the experience which Jaspers is trying to cultivate is of a delusive kind: ciphers of Transcendence are supposed to provide us with the means of escaping our prison but, if that prison *is* a reality, they can never really do so. With the aid of ciphers, we find ourselves, at most, in the same prison but with transparent walls. And it is difficult to see how our condition, as Jaspers here describes it, is any different from that of the lunatic who manages to convince himself that because the walls of his cell are made of glass, they do not really confine him.

Critical Remarks: The Problem of the Ambiguity of Ciphers

As already intimated, it is my opinion that, given Jaspers's theory of the Encompassing, the ambiguous status which ciphers are required to have in connection with the subject–object dichotomy, described in detail above, causes problems for Jaspers's argument. I now want to highlight some major difficulties concerning the relation of Jaspers's ciphers to the subject–object dichotomy in the context of his general theory of the Encompassing.

First of all, Jaspers is clearly very committed to the validity of the subject–object dichotomy. However, read with Heidegger's and Cooper's arguments in mind, it looks like a dispensable part of his system or, at least, inessential to his account (which is of most interest to me) of the operation of ciphers as the means whereby a human *Existenz* gets a sense of its ineffable source or measure in Transcendence. Human beings, when authentically themselves, are in a state in which their *Existenz* (which is always both subjective and objective)[125] is transparent to itself as being necessarily related to Transcendence or God, which is itself unconditioned by the subject–object dichotomy. Given that it is not required in order to make sense of Jaspers's notions of *Existenz*, Transcendence, ciphers or the relations between them (i.e. his ideas about what is essential to the distinctively human way of being) why does he introduce the dichotomy at all? One obvious way of resolving the tension between the requirement that ciphers be irreducible to objectivity (or subjectivity) and the idea that anything that is perceptible to us must be soluble, or at least somehow manifest, in the dichotomy is, with Heidegger, Dewey and others, to jettison the latter idea. It seems an attractive option to think, with Heidegger and Cooper, of human beings as instances of *Existenz*, for whom there is primordially no subject–object dichotomy but only unmediated instances of meaning (which lend themselves to existential phenomenological description), and as beings who are necessarily related through those meanings to their ineffable measure beyond themselves. On this account, ciphers (or whatever name we give to what, when experienced, attunes us to the ineffable – one of Heidegger's terms is 'things'[126]) need not be at all explained in relation to the subject–object dichotomy. This is because if there is no such dichotomy, meaning is not a thick concept and therefore does not need to be mediated through instances of objectivity. With Heidegger's and Cooper's arguments in mind, which are firmly oriented towards the dissolution of the subject–object dualism, it is hard to understand why Jaspers creates problems and tensions for himself by holding onto it. We may suspect that there are other reasons, reasons unrelated to philosophical argument.

To indulge in a brief biographical excursus, there is an oddly blurred photograph, taken in 1902, in which a young Jaspers, at this time a medical student, and two colleagues are pictured.[127] They are shown engaging in a light-hearted, yet quasi-religious, 'oath to the spirit of science (*Schwur auf den Geist der Wissenschaft*)'.[128] Jaspers's colleagues, Professors Fano and Cornelius, are pictured outdoors in Sils Maria, kneeling on cushions, each with his right hand solemnly placed on an open book which is held by the standing, and slightly smiling, Jaspers. While his biographer describes the photograph as depicting a 'jovial pledge', she also interprets it as indicative of the seriousness with which Jaspers regarded this gesture of respect to the scientist's reputation.[129] Jaspers's contribution to medicine, and to psychiatry in particular, is far from negligible and we may observe that his early respect for scientific enquiry remained throughout his life and, very likely, penetrated to his later philosophical thinking. One commentator even suggests that it is impossible to understand Jaspers's philosophy without reference to the scientific background.[130] This may or may not be the correct biographical explanation for Jaspers's tenacity to the subject–object dichotomy, even after he has formed the opinion that there are forms of experience and enquiry of a more all-embracing, and perhaps even of a more important, kind. But we may observe that his philosophical argument in favour of it is not terribly convincing. He writes:

> When we move through the phenomena of the world, we come to realize that we possess being itself neither in the object, which becomes continuously more restricted, nor in the horizon of our always limited world taken as the sum of phenomena but only in the Comprehensive which transcends all objects and horizons, which transcends the subject–object dichotomy.[131]

Indeed, Cooper harshly describes Jaspers's argument, given expression here, for the conclusion 'that Being-as-a-whole can be neither subject nor object, but some kind of "ground" on which this distinction appears', as 'startlingly feeble'.[132] Cooper continues:

> He seems to think that since not everything is a subject and not everything is an object, then everything is neither. One might as well argue that since not everyone is male and not everyone is female, then everyone is neither male nor female.[133]

Jaspers's argument for the Encompassing, especially in its Transcendent mode, suffers from this weakness, as does Tillich's quasi-ontological argument for the Unconditioned. What differentiates both of these arguments from those of Heidegger and Cooper is their commitment, in differing degrees, to the subject–object dichotomy, to a dualistic understanding of the subject–object distinction.

Secondly, and on a related note, let us grant that Jaspers is right about the inescapability of the subject–object dichotomy. There remains the familiar difficulty of explaining precisely how it is that what is essentially beyond it and unconditioned by it can nonetheless be manifest in it. When discussing the Encompassing *per se*, Jaspers sets out its various modes in the following way: the Encompassing, conceived as being itself 'is called Transcendence and the world, while as that which we ourselves are it is called being-there, consciousness, mind and existence';[134] 'on the subject side lie consciousness at large, existence, the mind, Existenz; on the object side lie the world and Transcendence'.[135] This way of describing things implies that the subject–object dichotomy accounts for and conditions the whole structure of the Encompassing, whereas Jaspers's philosophical position is that it is the other way round: it is the Encompassing that ultimately holds together subject and object. The Encompassing is that of which the poles of the dichotomy are modes, the ground or stage on which the distinction appears. But if 'subject' and 'object' can never be wholly appropriate terms for *Existenz* and Transcendence, as the structure of Jaspers's system implies,[136] then they cannot accurately be thought of as (subjective and objective) modes of the Encompassing. They should not be thought of as soluble in the dichotomy, reducible to either of its poles. Jaspers is well aware of this and concedes that, given the inescapability of the dichotomy, to think or speak of the Encompassing at all (to attempt to escape from it) is, in a self-defeating manner, to put oneself back into it. Not only that but, as we have seen in Jaspers's own discussion of the Encompassing, the dichotomy 'also comes to guide us in organizing the idea of encompassing'.[137] Jaspers takes the result of such inappropriate but unavoidable objectification of the Encompassing to be 'The Paradox of Mutual Encompassing' which he seems to think resists any philosophical elucidation beyond statement of the paradox, if that elucidation itself takes place within the subject–object dichotomy, as he thinks it must. E. B. Ashton's English translation of this statement interestingly exploits the ambiguous grammatical status of the word 'encompassing' as present participle as well as noun: 'The encompassing that we are confronts the encompassing that is Being itself: the one encompassing encompasses the other. The being that we are is encompassed by encompassing Being, and Being is encompassed by the encompassing that we are.'[138] Elsewhere, Jaspers puts it like this: 'The being that I am comprehends, as it were the Comprehensive that Being is and at the same time is comprehended by it'.[139]

The import of this thought, which is a paradox from the point of view of the subject–object dichotomy, is the interdependence of subject and object, mind (and body) and world; it implies the refusal to distinguish subject from object in a dualistic manner, on the grounds that this kind of distinction fails adequately to express the reciprocity of Encompassing which is essential to Jaspers's theory of reality.[140] In short, it indicates that human existence has, at least potentially, the character of what Jaspers calls *Existenz*.

It is my view, however, that with regard to the concept of ultimate reality, either the subject–object dichotomy is generally valid and the objectification of the Encompassing is both inevitable and defensible, or, consonant with my notion of ineffability, it is not valid and the Encompassing should never be objectified. Jaspers's attempt to have it both ways, by claiming that the objectification of the Encompassing is inevitable but inappropriate and results in an inarticulable paradox, is unconvincing. Not least because the statement of that 'paradox' only amounts to a paradoxical statement within the subject–object dichotomy (whose thoroughgoing and exhaustive validity is assumed) and because, from a different perspective, it amounts to the existential phenomenological claim that, in human *Existenz*, subject and object are logically interdependent and not differentiable in anything but a provisional or pragmatic sense.[141] As we shall see in the following chapter, this is not only a claim that can be rationally defended (and which some existential phenomenologists do, in fact, defend) but also one whose rational implications can be drawn out. In other words the existence of the 'paradox' indicates, for some, not only the limitations of the differentiation of 'subjective' from 'objective' in which it originates but the *rational* validity of the alternative, existential phenomenological view, according to which 'subject' and 'object' are thought of as logically inseparable and the dualistic distinction between them is regarded as misleading. Not only does this illustrate the limits of one mode of the subject–object dichotomy but also makes clear that those limits do not constitute the limits of what is articulable since further articulation is always possible in the terms (whose precise status I shall examine in the next chapter) of existential phenomenological description. Jaspers claims that *Existenz* is *always* in existence and that within the dichotomy of subject and object *Existenz*, together with ciphers, is both subjective and objective inseparably. But the notion of mutual encompassing challenges the ambiguous status that Jaspers requires *Existenz* and ciphers to have with regard to the subject–object dichotomy. This is because, as a paradox within that dichotomy (conceived as exhaustively valid), it implies that we cannot claim without contradiction that something is both inescapably in the subject-object dichotomy *and* subject and object simultaneously.

This challenge is supported by Merleau-Ponty's discussion of the most obvious candidate for the ambiguity of subject-and-object status, the human body. In his existential phenomenological analysis of the experiences of vision and touch, Merleau-Ponty shows how the inappropriate objectification of the body leads to the 'confused' notion of it as a 'subject-object', which is inconsistent with actual experience.[142] With regard to vision, he suggests that this confusion results because the parts of our bodies that are far away from the head are more amenable to objectification whereas those nearer to the eyes are experienced as a 'quasi-space' to which we have no direct visual access. This 'gap' in experience at the level of the head is filled by biological knowledge with the eyes, brain and retina conceived as objects and pieces of matter like any other. However, this objectification does not alter the primordial visual experience of the body as the vehicle of subjectivity alone, our point of view upon the world, however hard we may try to repress this experience on account of its incompatibility with the objectification of the body. Similarly in the case of touch: when we consider the experience of feeling (with our left hand) our right hand as it touches some object, we become aware of a conflict between the experience of the right hand as a touched object (a 'system of bones, muscles and flesh' at a particular point in space) and that of the right hand as it touches ('shoots through space like a rocket', 'alive and mobile, which I thrust towards things in order to explore them').[143] This conflict reveals the incommensurability in experience itself of the two notions (body-as-subject and body-as-object) which, in our reflective objectification of the body, we are forced to entertain simultaneously in our attempt 'objectively' to account for certain aspects of that experience. In experience, '[i]n so far as it sees or touches the world, my body can therefore be neither seen nor touched. What prevents its ever being an object ... is that it is that by which there are objects.'[144]

We cannot, Merleau-Ponty argues, *actually experience* simultaneously body-as-subject and body-as-object in the way that, when we objectify it, we *conceive* it.[145] What we actually experience is the passage from the experience of our hand touching to that of our hand being touched: 'in passing from one rôle to the other, I can identify the hand touched as the same one which will in a moment be touching.'[146] This kind of analysis indicates that the subject–object dichotomy is unreal and that what Jaspers calls *Existenz* is not, and cannot be, in existence. Although Jaspers claims at times that *Existenz* is in existence, he also claims, as seems more likely, that mundane existence is incommensurable with the free being of *Existenz* and that we cannot close the gap between the two even in our minds. 'Measured by the being of things', he writes, 'there is no freedom; measured by freedom, the being of things is not true being'.[147] The question concerning which measure is primary, whether life in the phenomenal world is 'like an awakening from sleep, from the darkness of primeval consciousness' or is instead 'a dream life' which obscures authentic, free *Existenz*, is easily settled.[148] The possibility of the question, the freedom to choose either answer, presupposes the primacy of free *Existenz*: 'The answer cannot be given by any wisdom, but, astonishing as it sounds, by making up one's mind'.[149] Therefore, the most compelling way to resolve Jaspers's paradox, which not only arose from an inappropriate objectification but which also has the character of a paradox only within the subject–object dichotomy, is to deny the exhaustive validity of that dichotomy.

There are two further problematic implications of the involvement of the subject–object dichotomy in Jaspers's system that militate against the idea that a dualistic split between subject and object, and the inappropriate objectification which follows from it, is inevitable. The first implication of the presence of both the subject–object dichotomy and the Encompassing in Jaspers's system, and his attempt to derive one from the other, is that the shift from ordinary experience (conditioned by the dichotomy) to what might be called religious experience (that awareness of the Encompassing, especially in its mode as Transcendence or God, in which 'we founder neither on the subject nor on the object but dwell in the Encompassing', that in which 'faith' consists)[150] requires a simultaneous change in us and in reality. This is required because the supposed shift is from a state of affairs in which we and reality are in principle separable (mundane existence, or *possible Existenz*, in which the subject–object dichotomy obtains) to the state of *Existenz* in which they are not. If either the subjective term representing us or the objective term representing reality survived the shift without change, the other term would be absorbed into it. The effect of this would be to reinforce, rather than to overcome, the dualistic distinction between subject and object. This absorption would be another example of the absolutization of one or other of the dichotomy's poles, which Jaspers impugns throughout the history of philosophy. So the transformation of objective being into a cipher[151] takes place at the same time as a change in the posture of consciousness – a change in the human attitude towards everything objective.[152] As Jaspers describes it, Transcendence is on the border of two worlds, which interact like being and non-being. As consciousness at large, empirical objects are real whereas all else is unreal, while as *Existenz*, empirical objects are unreal in comparison to the true reality of Transcendence. If, as Jaspers believes, thought is inevitably bound by the subject–object dichotomy, this relationship must not only be reversed according to the mode of the appercipient self-being, existence or *Existenz* on the subjective side of the Encompassing, but also according to the mode of reality on the objective side: world or Transcendence.[153] The question now prompted is, if the change occurs on both subjective and objective sides and there is no constant term to measure it against, how can the change be assessed? In what terms, in terms relative to what, can it accurately be described? It cannot be measured against existence or world since objectivity disappears as mundane subjective existence becomes *Existenz* and as world, or objectivity, becomes a cipher-script. Nor can it be measured against Transcendence, for this is inaccessible to mundane existence until it becomes *Existenz* and mundane existence can only undergo this change when there is a cipher-script to read. But as Jaspers states, that there is a cipher-script can never be known by mundane existence. The fact could never be apparent to consciousness at large: no experience within consciousness at large can show that there is Transcendence and therefore that *Existenz*, in its necessary relatedness to Transcendence, is a possible or desirable mode in which to be.[154] It seems to follow that if human existence and reality are even possibly interdependent, as Jaspers's definition of human being as 'possible Existenz' and many of his other remarks imply, then it is always distorting rather than illuminating to separate them, perhaps even for the provisional purposes of analysis. Jaspers often claims that *Existenz* only appears to itself in existence but also that, as (or in) existence, *Existenz* slips through the net of cognition:

Whatever I am existentially I cease to be when I make it an object of knowledge. As soon as my existence becomes a research object, as the entirety of existence, I myself slip through the meshes of the cognitive net.[155]

The latter point is more in harmony than the former with Jaspers's view, of most relevance to religious questions, that the point of *Existenz* is its relation to Transcendence. It would make more sense to deny that *Existenz* must always be in existence than to try to overcome the insuperable difficulty of giving an account of the simultaneous transition from existence to *Existenz* and from object to cipher. Jaspers could claim at most that an undeciphered cipher is present to existence (possible *Existenz*) whereas a deciphered one, embodying Transcendence, is present to *Existenz*. But, leaving aside the unanswerable question of what an 'undeciphered cipher' would mean to a being in existence for whom ciphers of any kind are impossible, it is impossible to explain how an 'undeciphered cipher' could get deciphered at the same time as a being in existence (for whom such deciphering is *impossible* because it involves the disappearance of the object) is transformed into an *Existenz* (for whom the deciphering is *necessary* for its self-realization as a being related to Transcendence). In short, Jaspers shares Tillich's difficulty that, given the validity of the subject–object dichotomy, it is impossible to explain how what is beyond that dichotomy can be manifest within it. And the relative complexity of Jaspers's system does nothing to attenuate that difficulty. At best, it merely disguises it.

Secondly, it follows from this difficulty that Jaspers, again like Tillich, is also unable to explain how the disappearance of the object, which supposedly happens when what is an object for existence becomes a cipher for *Existenz*, takes place. Jaspers claims that '[a]s a cipher the object is, as it were, in suspension'.[156] Perhaps, like Tillich, Jaspers thinks it important to keep religious experience separate from everyday experience. Perhaps it is his view that the latter is qualitatively marked off from the former by being unconditioned by the subject–object dichotomy. The world of ciphers is not a new objective demesne, Jaspers states, but is 'hidden in all objectivity'.[157] But as we saw earlier, Jaspers believes that the suspension of objectivity somehow also amounts to its consummation. An object becomes a cipher, he writes,

> through a transformation of the mode of being-an-object in the act of Transcendence. While the formal transcending occurs through a movement of thought in which all objectivity disappears, this substantial transcending is a consummation of cipher-reading in which the concreteness, stability and definiteness of what is objective vanishes at once in the suspended Objectivity [i.e. Transcendence or God] which makes it possible.[158]

Jaspers goes on to state that it is only *via* the polarity of subject and object that an object can attain such suspension, which at the same time 'elevates' it, makes it transparent, and allows it to exist.[159] Transcendence is articulated for *Existenz* 'in the medium of bright consciousness, *with the subject–object dichotomy maintained*'.[160] As well as neglecting to explain precisely how the suspension and consummation of objectivity can be identical, Jaspers also makes clear elsewhere that he has intuited the impossibility of the required simultaneous transition from objective to non-objective and from existence to *Existenz*. In short, Jaspers has intuited the impossibility of a satisfactory philosophical account of how Transcending, or religious experience, is possible:

> In existence, inquiry leads me from thing to thing, from thing to ground, without end. I would have to set an arbitrary ultimate and forbid myself all further questions. I must make a leap, rather, as I transcend from the objective to the nonobjective, from the thinkable to the unthinkable; nothing short of such a leap will without arbitrary fixation take me, if not to cognition of the source, at least to a kind of rumination toward it.[161]

We may conclude that disappearance of the object for Jaspers, aside from being oddly indistinguishable from, or even identical with, the object's *consummation* in the context of his thought, is not really possible because the subject–object dichotomy is so fundamental to his system. Moreover, although it occupies a fundamental structural role, it is philosophically dispensable – inessential to his account of *Existenz*, ciphers and Transcendence (or God) and of the way in which these interrelate. It is his view of the subject–object dichotomy as constitutive of the limits of consciousness, too, which entails that the Paradox of Mutual Encompassing resists any further clear or cogent articulation. For the pure existential phenomenologist, who denies the validity of the subject–object dichotomy, what Jaspers thinks of as statement of the paradox actually amounts to an existential phenomenological description of the logical interdependence of, and the lack of a dualistic distinction between, human being and world, 'subject' and 'object'. For the existential phenomenologist, in addition, this is an interdependence that can be articulated in other terms.[162]

The great benefit of Jaspers's theory of ciphers, over Tillich's symbols, is the greater degree of intimacy allowed between ciphers and Transcendence on the one hand and, on the other, the immediacy of the relationship between ciphers and the *Existenz* that perceives or reads them. Jaspers's theory shows us cursorily how a philosophical account of religious ciphers might work, without involving the subject–object dichotomy, by allowing for the possibility of the ineffable God (or Transcendence) to become present to human *Existenz* in the concrete, immediately meaningful forms or 'phenomena' which constitute that human world. It paves the way for a more detailed account of how this possibility might be realized in the more concrete context of the world's historical and living religious traditions, which is what I want to take away from the detailed critical engagement with Jaspers's thought carried out in this chapter. However, the main problem entailed by Jaspers's theory is that that possibility of the transfiguration of the world into the divine cipher-script for human *Existenz* is compromised by the re-involvement of the subject–object dichotomy in his account. As I have tried to show, the coherence of his account of the possibility of the experience of the ineffable by *Existenz* is compromised by Jaspers's insistence that *Existenz* is always in existence, in the subject–object dichotomy. This observation not only draws attention to the implicit assumption, made by Macquarrie and Tillich, of the validity of a dualistic distinction between subject and object but also makes it even clearer why their shared symbolic account of religious experience was philosophically unsatisfying.

The question remains, however, whether the fact of Jaspers's tenacity to the subject–object dichotomy might not be illuminating; whether there may not be some sense in which the subject–object *distinction*, if not formally valid in an exhaustive, dualistic or dichotomous way, makes possible a kind of philosophical discourse in which it is useful for certain limited, provisional purposes. In my view, it is defensible, indeed necessary, to rehabilitate a pragmatic distinction between subject and object for the restricted dual purpose, firstly, of constructing a philosophical argument against a purely rational method but in favour of the existential phenomenological one and, secondly, of the rational demonstration of the limits of a purely rational enquiry. The assumption made by the existential phenomenologists in using the language of the subject–object dichotomy is not that the dichotomy 'really' or exhaustively conditions human being-in-the-world as Jaspers seems to believe,[163] but rather that the terms of the distinction between subject and object are useful for philosophically defending the very notion of being-in-the-world against rival conceptions, most of which assume the formal validity of the dichotomy. If the subject–object dichotomy is the structure within which most people view reality much of the time, as even many of its most trenchant repudiators seem to believe, the best way of arguing against it would be to argue within the terms of the distinction, taking it to the point where it is unable to answer its own questions, as it were, thereby revealing its limits from within. Indeed, this is the only option open to someone whose eventual aim is to jettison the dichotomy but whose argument itself inevitably draws a pragmatic distinction between subject and object and thus makes initial use of that dichotomy's language. Although Jaspers accords a different, more thoroughgoing, dualistic value to the distinction, he seems to have intuited this idea when, in connection with scientific world-orientation, he writes: 'the meaning of science, the point of the search, is not an object of knowledge, of possible insight, but its limit'.[164] However, it is my impression that Jaspers does not test the subject–object distinction to its limits. Rather, he kicks it away too soon and by merely suppressing it, rather than finding the point where it destroys itself, therefore allows for it to resurface later on in a more thoroughgoing, dualistic way, namely, as a continuous aspect of the human condition, occupying a third of his tripartite system and for ever compromising the possibility of the relationship, conceived by Jaspers as necessary, between the other two parts: *Existenz* and Transcendence.

In Part III of this book, I revisit the problem of ineffability in the light of the insights gleaned from detailed engagement with the work of Macquarrie, Tillich and Jaspers. I attempt to construct a more convincing philosophical solution to the problem of ineffability, with better prospects for theological application. Following up on the main issues raised by the engagement with Jaspers's philosophy, I turn, in the next chapter, to the related questions of the use of the subject–object distinction and the status of existential phenomenology, carrying out a closer examination of Cooper's defence of the notion of ineffability in the hope of shedding light on these questions.

5 THE NATURE OF PHILOSOPHICAL EVOCATION OF THE INEFFABLE

The Use of the Subject–Object Distinction: On the Status of Existential Phenomenology

In the framework that I have been advocating in response to a dissatisfaction with the most valiant theological and philosophical attempts to solve the problem of ineffability, our necessary starting point is existential phenomenology, rather than the subject–object dichotomy. As critical engagement with Jaspers's philosophical system has shown, the validity of the idea of a measure beyond this dichotomy cannot be shown in that dichotomy's binary terms. Nor, even if we accept the validity of the notion of such a measure for argument's sake, can a convincing account be given of how what is unconditioned by that dichotomy can nonetheless be manifest in it. In addition, a dichotomous or dualistic construal of the subject–object distinction entails apparently insoluble philosophical problems, the difficulty of some of which initially prompted the practitioners of existential phenomenology to embark on their project of phenomenological description in the belief that the terms of subject and object would never be wholly adequate. This turn to phenomenology is not made arbitrarily but with rational defence.

To give one example, criticizing what he takes to be the Cartesian insistence on the use of the terms of subject and object, Heidegger claims that it is only when there is such insistence that a difficult epistemological problem arises. That is the problem of how the knowing subject is able to venture into another, external sphere (in order to grasp its object) without being transformed into something else in the process. It is the problem of 'how knowing can have any object at all'.[1] He maintains that the dichotomy requires us to think of the subject's consciousness as a sort of box or cabinet. Only then does the problem arise of how one (as the knowing subject), in the processes of perceiving and knowing, can return 'with one's booty to the "cabinet" of consciousness after one has gone out and grasped it'.[2] What Heidegger labels as the Cartesian presuppositions about knowledge being conditioned by the subject–object dichotomy for him lead to the problem of knowledge since the dualisms created by a dichotomous distinction between logical opposites are apparently impossible to reconcile. How, for example, are we to think of two substances as different as 'mind' (*res cogitans*) and 'body' (*res extensa*) as ever coming into any kind of relationship? If, in our empirical search for causal interaction between mind and body, we were to discover an event which caused a contingent physical event, 'wouldn't we decide *for that very reason* that we had discovered a new sort of *physical* event' rather than a mental one and *vice versa*?[3] This question becomes the problem of interaction in analytic philosophy of mind. How can a knowing subject ever grasp knowledge from an external sphere, one that is, by definition, essentially other, and return with it to the cabinet of consciousness? The problem is then one of how knowing can have any object at all, the problem of knowledge.

Not only that, but so-called objective inquiry can be seen not to be self-sufficient and without firm foundation. As Jaspers pointed out, there is in principle no end to inquiry within the subject–object dichotomy that is not purely arbitrary, that is not a kind of 'leap' of faith from the objective, on which subjective impressions are supposedly based, to the ground of both, beyond the dichotomy: a leap from the thinkable to the unthinkable.[4] If, in the absence of firm ground for the dichotomy, the objective is at best arbitrarily grounded, then the same is true, by implication, of the subjective, which is in turn supposedly based upon it. It follows that, each being as arbitrary as the other, subjective impressions cannot be measured against reality because they constitute our only access to that reality. As is shown by the sceptical notion of equipollence, even the Cartesian sceptical premise, that the senses sometimes deceive us, is suspect for this reason.[5] Equipollence, or *isostheneia*, is illustrated as follows:

(1) x appears F in situation S
(2) x appears F* in situation S*

where F and F* denote incompatible properties and S and S* different situations.[6] An example of the supposed 'disparity between an object and its idea' of which Descartes wrote might be a stick appearing bent when partially immersed in water and then, when taken out of the water, it appears straight.[7] But equipollence entails that we cannot assume, on this basis alone, which of the appearances is veridical. As Sextus Empiricus put it:

> By opposed accounts we do not necessarily have in mind affirmation and negation, but take the phrase simply in the sense of conflicting accounts. By equipollence we mean equality with regard to being convincing or unconvincing: none of the conflicting accounts takes precedence over any other as being more convincing.[8]

Applied to our example, this view entails suspension of judgement since, for all we know, we may only be seeing the stick correctly when it is in the water and our conflicting perceptions of it in other situations are illusory. For the existential phenomenologist (and also for certain pragmatists),[9] by contrast, there can be no such sharp distinction between the way things are and the way things appear to us, precisely because of the impossibility of an account of reality that is not already rooted in experience. Since a dichotomous distinction between subjective and objective dimensions to the notion of experience is dissolved by the existential phenomenologist, his concern is not with how things are in comparison with the way in which they are experienced (for equipollence shows this comparison to be impossible), but rather with the way things are precisely as experienced. He regards the alleged possibility of an account of reality separated from its human experience to be bogus. In the face of scepticism, experience is one phenomenon whose real existence, as Husserl understood, it would be otiose to doubt.[10] As we saw Merleau-Ponty arguing in the case of his analyses of vision and touch, the true ground of philosophical enquiry must be lived experience. Hence the existential phenomenological description of that experience is self-sufficient in a way that objective enquiry cannot be. It is a ground for which rational defence can be provided and which is less disputable in philosophical terms.

The presence of the arguments just outlined in the writings of existential phenomenologists indicates that there is a rational moment to the phenomenological method. Heidegger and Merleau-Ponty have been arguing that their forms of the thesis of the human world better account for reality as we experience it than those opposing accounts that would draw a sharp, dualistic distinction between human experience and reality. Such rational arguments for that thesis involve a distinction between subject and object, even though the eventual aim of those who advance them is the dissolution of any dualistic construal of that distinction. I shall illustrate later on, having defined my terms more clearly, how, crucially for my purposes, the rational dimension to phenomenology can be used by the existential phenomenologist for the primary purpose of demonstrating reason's own limits. But I want first to illustrate that it is also the rational dimension to existential phenomenology that importantly allows the phenomenologist to provide arguments in favour of her method as opposed to others. (It is philosophically important that one rationally defend one's methodology rather than arbitrarily indulging in it. If the argument is going, at least potentially, to win round a philosophical opponent,[11] its premises require the kind of defence that could possibly convince such an opponent.) I make this illustration by showing that Sartre's phenomenology of nothingness, much of which is drawn from the early Heidegger,[12] proceeds on the basis of undefended assumptions. I show that this generally bad philosophical practice results, in this particular case, in bad phenomenology.

Sartre is a well-known example of an existential humanist who speaks of the absurdity or ultimate groundlessness of the human world. His relevant remarks begin with the observation that the experience of nothingness is, as it were, the shadow cast by the experience of meaning in which the human world consists, that the two kinds of experience have a symmetrical structure. Sartre illustrates this in his famous phenomenological vignette of Pierre and the café. In perception, as Merleau-Ponty, too, was well aware,[13] there is always the appearance or construction, determined by one's practical concerns, of a figure against a background.[14] If I walk into a café in the hope of finding Pierre, my absent friend, the figure is absent. In that case, 'the café remains *ground*; it persists in offering itself to an undifferentiated totality to my only marginal attention; it slips into the background; it pursues its nihilation'.[15] The absent figure (Pierre) intervenes between my look and the other objects and people of the café 'precisely as a perpetual disappearance; it is Pierre raising himself as nothingness on the ground of the nihilation of the café'.[16] This vignette shows the way in which the expected perception of an absent figure mirrors the structure of the meaningful perception of a present one: both take place against a background referential totality which organizes itself around the central figure of concern and against which that central figure appears. In the negative experience of an absent figure, however, nothingness is revealed. What is revealed is the lack of basis for the meaningful perception of the human world that is independent of the human concerns that condition that perception. In the absence of the figure of concern, the totality of that meaningful world appears, in Heidegger's phrase, to 'slip away'.[17] And just as our ordinarily meaningful predicament of finding ourselves in the world is mediated by affective states (*Befindlichkeit*) the experience of Heidegger's 'the Nothing (*das Nicht*)' is famously revealed by *Angst*.[18]

The assumption being made by Sartre is that the human world in which the experience of meaning consists is absolute, that it makes no sense to speak of what is beyond the human world. The meaning of Sartre's 'being' is just human being, the *Pour-soi*, just as Heidegger's central concern, in this early period (1929), is the being of *Dasein*, human being-in-the-world. For this reason, it is not believed that there is a 'void' transcendent to the human world that is responsible for the experience of nothingness any more than it is believed that there is any independent 'source' of human meanings. There is therefore no question, either, of there being *two* coeval sources, one of being and one of nothingness, engaged in some sort of unending Manichean battle. Therefore the experience of nothingness is accounted for by absorbing it into the human world: this experience, Sartre tells us, only takes place within the limits of being. It is not that human being is logically subsequent to nothingness, to a void on which it imposes itself. In that case, this void would become the Absolute instead of (human) being. As Sartre puts it, the disappearance of (human) being (*Pour-soi*) would not entail the reign of nothingness but rather 'the concomitant disappearance of nothingness'.[19] The consequence of this absorption of nothingness into the human world, then, is the existential phenomenological description of specific modes of its experience, just as it is in the case of the interpretative experience of the meanings that also constitute that world as a whole. This is because rationality, dependent on the subject–object dichotomy, is not deemed adequate to the character of experience either in the case of meaning (recall Merleau-Ponty's argument invoked above) or in the case of nothingness. It is Heidegger's view, for example, that the logical act of negation depends on Nothing, rather than the other way about, and since negation is an act of reason, reason depends on the Nothing and cannot be used to decide the issue of the experience of the Nothing.[20] Like Sartre's, Heidegger's focus is thus on an 'encounter' with, an experience of, the Nothing on which he thinks the logical act of negation depends.[21] It is in this way that for Heidegger 'The very idea of "logic" disintegrates in the vortex of a more original questioning.'[22] Sartre, too, illustrates the same point by drawing attention to the fact that the absent (but expected) Pierre 'haunts' the café in a way that the also absent (but unlooked-for) Valéry or Wellington do not. In the latter case, I merely abstractly imagine Valéry being present and then negate the thought, whereas in the former case, where a concrete concern is involved (I am anxious to see Pierre), the primordial experience of nothingness, on which a purely abstract and intellectual negation depends, is forced upon me. As Sartre expresses this thought, the fact that Pierre haunts the café in a way that Valéry does not shows that 'non-being does not come to things by a negative judgement; it is the negative judgement, on the contrary, which is conditioned and supported by non-being'.[23] The implication is drawn that the necessary condition for the logical act of negation is 'that non-being be a perpetual presence in us and outside of us', that 'nothingness *haunt* being' in just the way that the absent Pierre haunts the café.[24] Sartre provides a number of similar metaphors: 'Non-being exists only on the surface of being'; 'Nothingness carries being in its heart'; 'Nothingness lies coiled in the heart of being – like a worm'.[25] What is being called for here is not rational argument, which can only inadequately capture the character of any experience (whether of a meaningful world or of nothingness) but phenomenological description of experienced reality considered in opposition to reason.

Having prepared the ground for the more primordial enquiry in the vortex of which logic dissolves, Heidegger proceeds to provide a phenomenological description of the experience of *Angst* revealing the Nothing. In Angst, he says, the Nothing functions as the totality of what is, just while this totality is experienced as slipping away.[26] The essence of the Nothing is 'nihilation' which he describes as a repellent quality. The Nothing, in its nihilation, repels us back into what is just as this is slipping away.[27] Nihilation reveals to us that what is *is*, 'and is not nothing'.[28] This last verbal appendage, Heidegger suggests, is an *a priori* explanation that makes possible any revelation of what is.[29] It is needed because human beings are, for the most part, immersed in their practical dealings with entities and turned away from the Nothing.[30] What Heidegger is trying to describe here is the experience of the human world as one in which we are inextricably engaged but which is without a basis independent of that engagement, a world whose ultimate basis is 'null'.[31] Similarly, what Sartre calls the 'absurdity' with which we have to live, as Cooper suggests, is the tension between the seriousness with which we cannot but be freely engaged with the world and the lack of external measure or ground for that engagement in, for example, an independent system of rationality or a way in which things 'really are' apart from the human contribution.[32] The character of this phenomenological description, which squarely locates the phenomenon of nothingness within the boundaries of the human world, is determined by the undefended assumption I flagged earlier, that the human world is what is absolute and that it makes no sense to speak of an independent measure for or source of that world. The phenomenology would be rather different if it were assumed, for example, that nothingness, as a kind of void, were independent of the human world and would be left over if the human world disappeared. In this case, arguably, it would not even be an existential phenomenology at all but a nihilistic metaphysics. It is at this point, where it becomes clear that it is this assumption that determines the character of the phenomenology, that the demand for its defence becomes all the more urgent. How, for example, are we supposed to choose between a phenomenology, like that of the later Heidegger, which describes human meanings as answerable to an ineffable source beyond the human (functioning also as a rhetoric of attunement to that source) and one in which it makes no sense to speak of such a 'beyond'?

The answer, I shall shortly suggest, can be provided by phenomenology's rational dimension whose purpose is to push rationality to its limits. But, for the benefit of Sartre who does not seem to want explicitly to acknowledge even this relatively confined vision of the rational dimension to his discipline, the choice in favour of the latter can also, I think, be made on his own phenomenological grounds. For the existential humanists like Sartre and the early Heidegger, as we have seen, the experience of meaning, like that of nothingness, is the experience of something's relation of appropriateness to life. Just as the experience of something's meaning occurs against this meaningful background, so the experience of something's absence or absurdity must take place against a background, which, 'nihilating' or slipping away, reveals nothingness. When it comes to considering life as a whole as the ultimate background to these experiences, therefore, it has itself to be experienced as equally meaningful and absurd, depending on the character of the experience that takes place against it. It is only as itself meaningful that it can be the background against which experiences of meanings take place and only as 'nihilation' that it can be the background against which experiences of nothingness occur. In the latter kind of experience, aspects of that background 'detain me for an instant (Could this be Pierre?) and ... as quickly decompose precisely because they "are not" the face of Pierre'.[33]

The rather odd twofold implication is that experiences of absurdity always take place against a background that is at least potentially meaningful and, more worryingly, that experiences of meaning always take place against a background that is at least potentially absurd. Both experiences, Heidegger and Sartre tell us, routinely take place. We may object at this point that the phenomenology here is wrong: that the experience of the even potential absurdity of life as a whole would necessarily undercut the possibility of any experience of meaning, which would ultimately have to take place against that background. As a matter of fact, as Cooper insists, referring to Robert Nozick, 'we want meaning all the way down. Nothing less will do.'[34] The idea that our perspectives and projects are meaningful in virtue of a contribution to a life-world that is itself meaningless, slipping away and answerable to nothing beyond its 'nihilating' self, is unendurable because 'An activity whose point is to contribute to something that itself turns out to be pointless retrospectively inherits this pointlessness'.[35] We could not actually bear to carry on living our lives if experience really were structured in this way. The fact that most of us do bear it suggests that it is not usually so structured. We may, with Cooper, draw the conclusion that, insofar as they engage in meaningful perception and activity, those who, like the 'uncompensated' existential humanists, claim that human meanings are answerable to a life that is itself experienced as appearing as potentially absurd as it appears potentially meaningful 'cannot really believe what they are saying'.[36] The challenge to such existential humanism on its own terms, then, is a phenomenological one. It consists in the objection that experience is just not (and could not be) structured in a way that allows the experience of meaning to be derived from, or answerable to, what is, even potentially, experienced as absurd. To put it in Sartre's terminology, the worm of nothingness coiled at the heart of (human) being compromises that being's role as the inexhaustibly meaningful background against which, with the aid of our human freedom to constitute the world, meanings always appear. The reverse is, of course, also true: we cannot get experiences of *Angst* and absurdity out of a description of them as being ultimately answerable to life as a whole, when that life is even potentially experienced as meaningful. In short, it is just not possible to experience life as a whole in the opposing ways that are required if it is itself to be experienced as the ultimate background against which *both* the opposing experiences of meaningfulness *and* absurdity take place.

Cooper's arguments for the existential phenomenological thesis of the human world, as we have seen, echo those advanced by Heidegger and Merleau-Ponty, which, in contrast to those of Sartre (and whether they were aware of it or not), exemplify phenomenology's rational dimension. Beyond this defence of the presuppositions of existential phenomenology (which is really directed at the philosophical opponent who subscribes to the thoroughgoing validity of the subject–object dichotomy), the rational dimension has a second function, which Cooper also exploits, namely, the rational demonstration of the limits of reason. This demonstration takes the form of his argument for the necessity for a measure beyond the human world, which could not only convince philosophical opponents (the practitioners of a supposedly purely rational philosophical method) but also fellow existential phenomenologists insofar as they have any time for the rational dimension to their discipline, whatever limitations that dimension may turn out to have. This argument from the (now defended) thesis of the human world to the validity of the notion of an ineffable measure for that world has no strict parallel of which I am aware in the works of the existential phenomenologists. This is the case even though these thinkers are eventually concerned, like Cooper, to dissolve the subject–object dualism and some of them, such as Heidegger and Marcel, are also concerned to affirm the meaningfulness of talk of an ultimate 'mystery' to which human life answers.[37] Cooper's argument has its closest parallels in the quasi-ontological argument of Tillich and in Jaspers's attempt to argue that the subject–object dichotomy necessarily manifests the Encompassing. But as we saw in some detail on pp. 67–72 and 95–103 above, these arguments, which at some level assert the appearance of the ineffable within the subject–object dichotomy, fail to convince. Cooper's argument, on the other hand, involves the explicit dissolution of this dualism, initially in its humanist thesis of human being-in-the-world to and *via* which the ineffable manifests. However, that argument still seems to be advanced, at least in part, in rational language, which apparently presupposes the subject–object dichotomy. It exploits the apparently inevitable subject–object structure of thought and language by arguing from premises to conclusions and by avoiding contradiction and circularity. I now want to look at the precise status of the argument in more detail, specifically its relation to 'rationality', after clarifying precisely how I interpret the meaning of this term.

What I am here calling 'rationality', and aim to criticize, is not confined to the *a priori* knowledge of necessary truths but also incorporates scientific enquiry. It may be distinguished from 'reason', which I take to require nothing stronger than a pragmatic distinction between subject and object, deemed to be useful for specific provisional and limited purposes. My eventual target (rationality) is a particular understanding of reason which, in its presupposition of a dualistic distinction between subject and object, leaves open the possibility of reason's in principle *unlimited* operation in isolation from other forms of human engagement with the world. I want to argue that the main point of the phenomenologist's use of reason is the demonstration of reason's own limits, a demonstration that refutes rationality. And although the phenomenologist's use of reason inevitably assumes a pragmatic distinction between subject and object, that distinction is not conceived as a dichotomy, that is, in the unlimited and dualistic way in which rationality conceives it. Rationality is sharply distinguished from ordinary experience of a pre-reflective kind. In a typical account, Langley draws this distinction by expressing such ordinary experience as a process of flux, which involves the relation of a changing subject to a changing world.[38] In pre-reflective states of this kind, we are affected by reality as it makes a more or less emotional impression on us, just as the various dimensions of our relation to reality affect reality itself. Thus, purely rational mental activity, by contrast,

> implies the subject–object relation in which the subject regards himself as a detached spectator, and in which he endeavours to ensure conditions where the objects contemplated are not changed by his voluntary action and the interpretation is not distorted by any emotional prejudice he may possess.[39]

Rationality, Langley continues, proceeds analytically, discriminating the component parts of the wholes presented to direct experience. Although rationality does engage in synthesis as well, it is synthesis of the component parts identified by rational analysis rather than of the directly experienced wholes. On this typical view, reason is opposed to passion and is a kind of purification of lived experience, an in principle exhaustive attempt to get at objective reality by exuviating it of the subjective, evaluative and emotional accretions which it acquires from human subjects as they pre-reflectively experience it. It involves the division of reality into 'subject' and 'object' in a dualistic way so that the subject may either itself be objectified or entirely eliminated from the field of enquiry. If, as Iain McGilchrist has more recently suggested, experience is in a constant state of Heraclitean flux, then reason, according to rationality, is the attempt 'fix' it as it flies, to remove ourselves from the immediacy of experience and to step outside the flow. The result of such an attempt is a 're-presented' version of experienced reality, which contains

> static, separable, bounded, but essentially fragmented entities, grouped into classes on which predictions can be based. This kind of attention isolates, fixes and makes each thing explicit by bringing it under the spotlight of attention. In doing so it renders things inert, mechanical, lifeless.[40]

The viability of rationality, so understood, may be denied by extending the point made earlier (itself founded on rational considerations), in sympathy with the existential phenomenologists' dissolution of one mode of the subject–object dichotomy, that such immediate experience, indistinct from any supposedly independent reality 'behind' it, is the only firm basis for enquiry. If, as Langley suggests, rationality implies a dualistic understanding of the subject–object distinction, anyone who argued for the limits of the validity of that distinction, thereby rejecting such a dichotomous picture, would have also to reject rationality, with its picture of reason as a comprehensive or archetypal model of intellectual enquiry. For such a recusant, the inadequacy of the supposedly comprehensive lifeless, rational 're-presentation' to the character of lived experience, behind which there is nothing purely objective to uncover, is enough to discredit the rationality which not only produces that representation but also takes it to be exhaustive. The dissolution of the broad and overarching dichotomy of subject and object entails the dissolution of narrower, more specific, dependent ones such as fact versus value and, importantly, reason versus passion.[41] The relevant point here is that immediate, lived experience is inescapably constituted by the evaluative and affective human concerns which have, nonetheless, traditionally been relegated to the spheres of value and passion. The idea that there is an independent and objective way in which the world is, onto which subjective evaluations, moods or affective states are subsequently plastered, and which is rationally recoverable from beneath that superficial layer, is a fiction. For the existential phenomenologist, the dimension of mood or affectivity, which, on a view like Langley's, it is the goal of rationality to eliminate, is in fact an essential component of our fundamental relation to the world. As Cooper puts it, 'Beings who only stand and wait, stop and stare, would have no world to understand and reason about'.[42] In Putnam's neo-pragmatist terms: 'A being with no values would have no facts either'.[43] Any attempt to recover a stripped-down, purely factual world initially devoid of any kind of significance would simply miss the phenomena in which any real world necessarily consists. Our being-in-the-world, for the existential phenomenologists, not only constitutes the experiential ground that properly forms the basis for philosophical enquiry but also involves inseparably what are often distinguished as belonging to the separable and opposing spheres of fact and value, reason and passion.

We have seen that Cooper's defence of the humanist thesis proceeds rationally, as does the defence provided by some of the existential phenomenologists, not including Sartre. But does his argument from the thesis of the human world to the validity of the notion of ineffability proceed by way of rationality understood in the above sense? Surely if it does proceed in this way, the possibility of the necessary step of dissolving the subject–object dichotomy is compromised. If it does not, how can there be a rational justification for the insistence that phenomenological description must, at the same time, be a poetry of attunement to the ineffable? Someone who just indulged in such phenomenological poetry (as the later Heidegger arguably does) without rationally defending that indulgence would be in no better a position than that of Sartre who, in a philosophically suspect manner, engaged in phenomenological description without rational defence. I want to suggest that although Cooper's argument does not proceed by way of rationality, understood as an unbridled confidence in the power of reason exhaustively to describe an allegedly independent reality, it does make use of reason. It does so, however, to the sole end of rationally demonstrating reason's limitations and thereby opposing rationality.

In this respect, Cooper's argument can be interpreted as an example of the general philosophical impulse recently described by Iain McGilchrist in the context of his fascinating discussion of the differences between the hemispheres of the human brain and of the way in which these differences can be seen to be reflected in cultural and intellectual history.[44] Supported by a thorough argument based upon a mass of empirical neurological data on hemisphere differences and lateralization, McGilchrist suggests that the default approach of philosophy has reflected the specific kind of attention that the left hemisphere accords to the world. Attention is not just responsive to the world but, in a relationship of reciprocity, the world is responsive to it: 'It is not just that what we find determines the nature of the attention we accord to it, but that the attention we pay to anything determines what we find'.[45] The differences in the kind of attention each of the hemispheres pays to the world amount to different, indeed incompatible, ways of being in the world for which each hemisphere is distinctively responsible. As a result, the approach to philosophy which has predominated in the West for much of the last two millennia can be seen also to reflect the characteristics of the specific kind of world which, as its 'neurological substrate',[46] the left hemisphere brings into being,

> since it is via denotative language and linear, sequential analysis that we pin things down and make them precise, and pinning them down and making them clear and precise equates with seeing the truth, as far as the left hemisphere is concerned.[47]

McGilchrist believes dichotomies, principally that of subject and object, to have dominated philosophy for much of the last two millennia, something which he believes to have been made possible by the 'either/or' world delivered by the left hemisphere. But he discerns in the phenomenological tradition, anticipated by the classical pragmatists (especially John Dewey and William James), progressing through Husserl's transcendental phenomenology to the existential phenomenology of Heidegger and Merleau-Ponty (and, I would add, also present in contemporary pragmatism), a way of philosophizing more reflective of what he takes to be the world according to the right hemisphere. In that world, by contrast, dualisms are out of place since here 'what appears to the left hemisphere to be divided is unified, where concepts are not separate from experience, and where the grounding role of "betweenness" in constituting reality is apparent'.[48] So far as reason is concerned, McGilchrist sees the beginning and end of much of Western philosophy to be in what I have called rationality, a misplaced and excessive confidence in reason's exhaustive scope. But he discerns, in the phenomenological tradition, the implicit admission that reason has limitations and that, while it is important, it is not the only, or even the most effective, way of getting in touch with reality, with that which is other than ourselves, independent of the human contribution. He gives as early examples of the kind of philosophy the limitations of whose methodology he wishes to demonstrate pre-Socratic paradoxes such as that of Zeno of Elea.[49] Openness to a reality that is held to be independent of the human contribution would involve the willingness to countenance the idea that our ordinary ways of thinking are inadequate to the nature of reality.[50] It is for this reason that a constructive paradox would reveal something contrary to expectation and received opinion. The pre-Socratic paradoxes mentioned reveal, by contrast, something counterintuitive for precisely the opposite reason, 'that it is *reality* that is inadequate to our *ordinary ways of thinking*'.[51] We find here the assertions that, despite appearances, 'arrows do not move, Achilles cannot overtake the tortoise, there can never be a heap of sand, Theseus' [sic] ship is not really a ship after all, Epimenides was inevitably talking nonsense'; we find, in other words, the assertion that 'the real world isn't the way we think it is *because logic says so*'.[52]

In phenomenology (and pragmatism), by contrast, McGilchrist finds a healthy scepticism about reason's limitations and a turn towards lived experience as the most philosophically reliable guide, more resistant to scepticism,[53] as to the nature of Reality. For McGilchrist, much Western philosophy, as a product of the world of the left hemisphere (where language is normally lateralized),[54] buys explicitness and certainty at the cost of being further tied to what is already known and, ultimately, at the high price of self-reference and emptiness.[55] Whereas phenomenology, more reflective of the world of the right hemisphere (which alone understands metaphor),[56] yields results which are less explicit, but which are able, for that very reason, to put us in touch with whatever is apart from us and independent of the human contribution. It provides us with the potential to transcend the rational cognitive structures through which we assume Reality necessarily appears to us precisely by revealing them to be of our own making. This process requires a discourse that is implicit rather than explicit, metaphorical rather than literal, since explicit, literal discourse reflects and contributes to those very cognitive structures. It involves such necessarily metaphorical talk as that of the 'semi-transparency' of the 'objects' of our focus, talk of our attention needing 'both to rest on the object and pass *through* the plane of focus' to a Reality that is independent of the meaningful 'objects' of attention but inaccessible without them.[57] An attempt at an explicit, literalistic, analytical description of experience (as something onto which concepts are mapped in a relation of correspondence, for example) would ignore the holistic, meaningful, *Gestalt* forms of experience in which the right hemisphere generally traffics.[58] It would be like 'the joke explained, the metaphor laboriously restated'.[59]

McGilchrist's reading of the phenomenological tradition suggests that it consists not in an arbitrary preference for, and turn towards, experience over logic. Phenomenology begins, after all, with the conventional tools of philosophy: clarity of thought and expression, striving towards precision, consistency and cogent argument. He interprets phenomenology as the unusual philosophical impulse to account for the specifically right hemisphere attention, characterized by a disinterested openness to whatever is other than the mind. Unusual, because as a *philosophical* impulse, its starting point is the contrasting kind of attention characteristic of the left hemisphere's view of the world: rational, literalistic, explicit, analytical. McGilchrist describes this distinctively philosophical impulse to transcend the usual scope of philosophical enquiry, perhaps appropriately, with the aid of a bizarre simile.

> Admittedly, trying to achieve it at all using the conventional tools of philosophy would be a bit like trying to fly using a submarine, all the while making ingenious adaptations to the design to enable one to get a foot or two above the water. The odds against success would be huge, but the attempt alone would be indicative that there was something compelling beyond the normal terms of reference, that forced one to make the attempt.[60]

This reading nicely explains the tendency of some existential phenomenologists to speak of an ultimate 'source' of the experienced human world, or some 'mystery' to which it answers. They are striving towards ultimate Reality, the Absolute, whatever is independent of the human contribution, that on which our being-in-the-world ultimately depends and which, for that very reason, cannot be exhaustively captured in the rational terms with which philosophy quite properly begins. And it is perhaps unsurprising that some such writers find a religious or quasi-religious significance in this idea. Like Cooper, McGilchrist reads the phenomenological tradition as a whole as a reflection of the philosophical impulse to transcend the rational method in which philosophy properly originates. He reads it as the attempt to evoke what is independent of the, specifically rational, human contribution to reality, an attempt that is made initially possible by that contribution. But he does not draw attention to any specific, explicitly rational argument for the limitations of reason in that tradition. Such an argument would be an important contribution to the case that, convergent with my own argument, both writers are trying to make, especially if good philosophy at least begins with explicit, rational argument. Yet, I am not aware of such an argument's existence in the writings of the existential phenomenologists either. To be sure, McGilchrist's reading of the pre-Socratic paradoxes allows him to make the negative point that the prejudice in favour of reason cannot itself be justified by the process of reasoning ('the virtues of reason are something we can do no more than intuit'), that 'every logical system leads to conclusions that cannot be accommodated within it',

> that any enclosed, self-referring system the left hemisphere comes up with if taken strictly on its *own* terms, self-explodes: there is a member of the system that cannot be accommodated by the system. There is always an escape route from the hall of mirrors, if one looks hard enough.[61]

But I suggest that Cooper goes a step further, providing a more positive rational argument for reason's limitations. His argument not only demonstrates that such an escape route must exist, but, as it were, provides us with the map by which we may navigate our way through the secret tunnel.

If the humanist thesis, the (now rationally defended) existential phenomenological perspective from which the argument is made, is genuinely adopted, the most obviously appropriate terms in which to proceed are indeed those of phenomenological description rather than those of rational argument. But it is not a matter of a straightforward choice between them. This would be too early a point at which to jettison the subject–object distinction since, on its own terms, it can go further. Cooper not only exploits this fact in order rationally to defend the humanist thesis, like Heidegger and Merleau-Ponty, but also recognizes that the propositions about meaning that are apparently entailed by that thesis lend themselves to further rational analysis. Someone still convinced of the validity of the subject–object dichotomy will want to carry out this analysis *instead of* simply abandoning that dichotomy and an existential phenomenologist, whose method includes, insofar as this is still possible, a rational dimension, will want to carry out the analysis *before* abandoning the pragmatic distinction between subject and object. So Cooper does proceed in rational terms, observing the logical tension between the two ideas, espoused by the phenomenologists and entailed by their general attitude, that meaning is appropriateness to Life and that Life itself is meaningful only if it is answerable to something beyond itself.[62] Note that, from the perspective of rationality, this initial observation assumes the subject–object dichotomy and involves the objectification or elimination of the subject to the extent that the procedure's form implicitly conceptualizes 'Life', treating it as though it were something objective to which other objects can be in a relation of appropriateness called 'meaning'. From the existential phenomenological perspective, though, this is literally inaccurate. The rational dimension to phenomenology does not extend to the objectification of being-in-the-world; it merely facilitates the rational defence of that humanist thesis. But this move is a provisional stage on the way to fulfilling the second function of the rational dimension to existential phenomenology, that is, to demonstrate the limitations of the subject–object distinction, which grounds reason, especially to the philosophical opponent who subscribes to the more thoroughgoing, perhaps exhaustive, validity of that distinction and dualistically conceives it as a dichotomy. Although it is hoped that we shall reach the point where the objectification of being-in-the-world is seen to be a formally invalid operation, that perspective can be defensibly adopted only once the limits of reason have been rationally demonstrated. It is important to note, too, that there is nothing inherently irrational about simultaneously subscribing to both these ideas about life and meaning. It would be too early to jettison the rational perspective of the subject–object distinction here on the grounds of the logical tension between them.

Cooper points out that 'uncompensated humanism' and 'absolutism', which are respectively reflected in the two ideas about life and meaning, are contraries rather than contradictories: they cannot both be true but each may be false. And they will indeed both turn out to be false if the thought in which he finds the resolution to the tension is correct: 'there is a way the world anyway and independently is, but this way is not discursable'.[63] The (still rational) resolution of the tension, reminiscent of Wittgenstein, is found in the doctrine of ineffability, which holds that life is answerable to a measure beyond itself but, to avoid circularity, this measure is not thought of as one that is invested with the concepts and values with which life itself is invested and is therefore ineffable. At this point reason is still operating, even though the concept of ineffability constitutes a challenge to the subject–object distinction by which reason is conditioned and grounded. The concept of ineffability, though determinately empty and, in this respect, unlike all other concepts, can still be legitimately viewed as a genuine concept. In order to understand its meaning, we have to think of a subject who has a concept to which no determinate object corresponds. But this does not prevent us from submitting that concept, thus interpreted, to further rational analysis. Reason shows that any disjunctive picture of the ineffable (i.e. what the concept of ineffability evokes) would invest it with at least some of the concepts with which life is invested, those of space, time and existence, for example.[64] Since this picture, incompatible with the concept of ineffability, would abrogate the meaning of the term 'ineffable', it must be rejected and (since silence is not an option where that which confers meaning on life is concerned)[65] replaced with a vision of the intimacy of the human world with its ineffable measure, which is not similarly incompatible. But it is here, on such a vision of intimacy, on this vision of unity without identity (and no earlier) that the subject–object distinction is shipwrecked, requiring as it does a feat of 'double exposure'. This simultaneously reveals human life as both that to which meanings ultimately answer and, if it is itself to be experienced as meaningful (answerable or measurable), as a 'gift', as the coming to presence of the ineffable beyond the human.[66] This human world is revealed by such a double exposure as 'not simply a human world unthinkable in isolation from us, but at the same time a realization of, a coming forth of, something to which we can strive to answer and measure up'.[67] The rational terms in which Cooper initially presents his argument only here begin to give way. He ends his 2005 article on 'Life and Meaning' with the following words:

> The delicacy of performing this feat of 'double exposure' should not be in question. So it is not very surprising, perhaps, that I find myself drawn, in my two claims, to speak in ways that are difficult simultaneously to combine.[68]

The import of this difficulty is that the terms of the subject–object distinction should be given up as inadequate to the 'phenomenon' (the reality precisely as experienced) whose character is being submitted to attempted expression. Couched in the language of this distinction itself, Cooper's argument does not leave an open choice between the existential phenomenological perspective and the rational one of the subject–object distinction to which the only response is the Kierkegaardian leap of faith or the making up of one's mind of which Jaspers speaks. Rather, it recognizes that the rational language has further yet to go since the existential phenomenological position can, from the perspective of reason, which it incorporates, be seen to entail certain ideas, those encapsulated in the propositions about meaning, for instance. These propositions, and they way in which they are entailed by the phenomenological standpoint, are susceptible to further analysis in the rational terms that assume the subject–object distinction. And it is *this* analysis that reveals, especially to someone persuaded by the thoroughgoing validity of a subject–object *dualism* or *dichotomy* (i.e. the perspective of 'rationality'), that the terms of that dichotomy fail where those of existential phenomenological description succeed. What rational analysis of the (rationally defensible) existential phenomenological position reveals is the limit of the purely rational. It rationally demonstrates the existence of the point where reason must be kicked away. This is not the point where the psychological need of some existential phenomenologists to postulate a measure for life, beyond the human, is arbitrarily indulged. Rather, it is the point at which we arrive having been led by reason away from 'rationality' towards a phenomenology that incorporates a rational dimension. We are then led, through the implosion of rationality and the limit of the subject–object distinction, to a kind of phenomenology which is, as the same time (as it is for the later Heidegger), a rhetoric or poetry of the ineffable. Such a rhetoric is what underwrites the view (or 'enables the faith') that 'lives led in certain ways do answer to, are consonant with, the way of things' by gesturing towards 'a sense or vision of the mysterious'.[69] Recall Cooper's description of the twofold 'double exposure' which existential phenomenological description can effect: there is, firstly,

> that of 'seeing through' something – a tree, say – to the network of relations, the 'relational totality of significance', on which that depends, whilst also 'seeing' that whole 'gathered', 'con-centrated', in the tree. Then, second ... the experience of seeing things as ordinary particulars, while also 'seeing through' the world as a whole, a sense of which is cultivated in the first experience, to [the ineffable].[70]

Thus Cooper does not merely assert that existential phenomenological description and its corollary poetic evocation of the ineffable are to be preferred to the supposedly purely rational, objective inquiry. Rather, he shows that, if we give any credence to rational implications in general, the rational implication of the incompatibility of these alternatives is that the latter destroys itself at the feet of the former.

It is in this way that the answer to the question 'Is the argument rational?' is inseparable from the meaningfulness (or otherwise) of the question, which in turn depends upon the particular philosophical viewpoint of the inquirer. There is no absolute or objective answer to this question. It is only meaningful to someone who accepts the validity of the subject–object distinction and, to such a person, the answer has to be 'Yes'. It is just the rational nature of the argument, moreover, that will eventually convince this interlocutor of the meaninglessness of the question, that is, of the argument's conclusion, which implicitly involves the relinquishing of the idea of an enquiry or discourse of the purely rational, which I have been calling 'rationality'. Putting it differently, we might say that the argument is rational 'up to a point'. That is, up to the point where the subject–object distinction by which reason is grounded and conditioned, is kicked away like Wittgenstein's ladder.[71] But by the time we have reached this point, our perspective will have changed so that we no longer find the question (or its affirmative answer) properly meaningful. From this new perspective, the word 'reason' no longer signifies anything specific, distinct from what is denoted by the word 'passion', for example. Having reached this perspective, there seems little point in speaking of a purely rational dimension to our being-in-the-world. Here the demand becomes palpable for a philosophical discourse of the existential phenomenological kind: one that, unlike rationality, is not purely rational but which, in line with the phenomena in which experienced reality consists, inextricably includes what are often abstractly separated as 'rational', 'evaluative' and 'affective' dimensions.

Cooper's rational argument from the thesis of the human world to the validity of the notion of ineffability can be interpreted as part of a broader phenomenology which, owing to the inclusion of this argument, is unusually transparent and thus tells us something about the nature of existential phenomenology which is easily missed in reading the standard works of the existential phenomenologists. It highlights the fact that phenomenology has a rational moment which not only defends its own presuppositions but also demonstrates the limits of reason and thus refutes and opposes 'rationality'. This rational moment aptly suits phenomenology's opposition of rationalistic accounts of human beings' engagement with the world, which, as Heidegger suggested in *Being and Time*, take the subject–object distinction too far and conceive it as an exhaustively valid dichotomy. But it is also liable to occlusion by the descriptively poetic form that existential phenomenology is wont to take. I take as an illustration of this often poetic form a passage from Heidegger's phenomenology of art in which he is discussing Van Gogh's painting of a pair of shoes.

> From the dark opening of the worn insides of the shoes the toilsome tread of the worker stares forth. In the stiffly rugged heaviness of the shoes there is the accumulated tenacity of her slow trudge through the far-spreading and ever-uniform furrows of the field swept by a raw wind. On the leather lie the dampness and the richness of the soil. Under the soles stretches the loneliness of the field-path as evening falls ... This equipment is pervaded by an uncomplaining worry as to the certainty of bread,

the wordless joy of having once more withstood want, the trembling before the impending childbed and shivering at the surrounding menace of death.[72]

An extreme example, perhaps, but this poetic form is aptly suited to the articulation of a human sphere in which rational and affective, factual and evaluative are separable only provisionally and artificially. The descriptive and poetic form is suited, too, to the *logical and psychological* need which (with the help of Cooper's argument) we can see existential phenomenology demonstrating, illustrating and fulfilling, for a rhetoric of the intimacy of the human world with its mysterious, independent source in the ultimately Real – what Heidegger, in this essay, called 'earth'. In his description of the way in which this need is met Cooper, true to his word, begins to deploy that rhetoric:

> we need to remember that the point of the rhetoric is not to lend dramatic or poetic expression to what, here at the limits of language, could be articulated in literal terms, but to attune to a way of experiencing the-world-and-us as – to invoke a bit of that rhetoric – a mysterious 'gift'.[73]

While reason is compelled, by its own operation, to recognize the demand for such a vision and its articulation, it cannot by itself fulfil that demand without contradiction, without, as it were, pulling the rug out from under its own feet; from the point of view of 'rationality', the required ways of thinking and speaking are, to put it mildly, 'difficult simultaneously to combine'.[74] The vision of intimacy to which the operation of the rational dimension to phenomenology leads simultaneously shipwrecks rationality and necessitates such rhetoric. It does to by showing itself to constitute the limit of the subject–object distinction and thus showing the error of a dualistic distinction between subject and object. It thus undermines the vision of the thoroughgoing, exhaustive validity of the subject–object dichotomy on which rationality is based. What is nonsense from the perspective of rationality may be (in the same breath) phenomenologically and religiously illuminating. The resultant rhetoric must simultaneously be, on the one hand, an example of existential phenomenology, articulating the phenomena of the human world in a way that does not reduce them to dualisms of reason versus passion or subject versus object but which provisionally includes a rational dimension. And, on the other hand, it must also be a way of attuning us to the mysterious source of that world, which, though infinitely beyond the human world and independent of it, is entirely intimate with it and inaccessible without it.

Admittedly, the rational moment to phenomenology can hamper the poetic moment just as much as, *vice versa*, the poetic dimension can hamper the rational one. In the former case, philosophers committed to rationality will complain that the descriptive and poetic discourse in which phenomenology consists is just not philosophy. But the phenomenologist may answer that the phenomenological and poetic discourse is what philosophy, even as such philosophical opponents understand it, necessarily becomes. It is the consummation of philosophy even when philosophy is modelled on 'rationality' but certainly when (as in good phenomenology and all good philosophy) it takes reason as its guiding light in the absence any other, when it follows through the implications of its own logical operations. Itself still philosophy, it is no longer mere rationality but rather the consummation of reason. In the latter case, on the other hand, it would be easy to draw the conclusion that, because existential phenomenology is poetic, and because it criticizes rationality, it does not itself involve reason. The phenomenologist can reply that existential phenomenology does involve reason to the limited end that, firstly, within the terms of the subject–object *distinction*, it might defend its own methodology in opposition to rationality's *dichotomy* between subject and object. And, secondly, that it might show that its own consummation in a poetry of attunement to the ineffable takes place not as an arbitrary substitute to reason but only with reason's shipwreck. Although, unlike Cooper, Jaspers (with whom we began this line of thought) does not appear to provide us with a clear and convincing articulation of this view, as a more or less implicit intuition, it is an abiding theme in his writing on the place of reason in philosophy:

> That the whole of my rationality rests upon the basis of non-reason – such a phrase does not assert that reason can be denied out of some general right drawn from existential philosophy. Nothing which lacks reason or which is contrary to reason can raise up argumentative claims out of itself, for precisely this process enters into the medium of rationality. Neither the positivity of mere empirical existence, nor that of the existential basis has a right without reason. Every premise of justification enters into the medium of the rational. The truth of the non-rational is impossible unless reason is pushed to its limit.[75]

The Identity of Meaning and Absurdity: The Phenomenological Dialectic

I explained earlier the inability of Sartre's phenomenology properly to account for experiences of *Angst* and absurdity as well as those of meaning. The kind of phenomenology that I have been arguing attunes us, in its poetic mode, to the ineffable ultimate Reality, not only has the advantage of being able rationally to defend its presuppositions. It also, unlike Sartre's description, can cope with the coexistence of experiences of meaningfulness and absurdity without the existence of the latter experience undermining and compromising the possibility of the former. In other words, its role as rhetoric of attunement to the ineffable allows it to be a more adequate phenomenology, i.e. a truer description of the human experience of reality. For, even given the rational demonstration of the validity of the concept of ineffability, no one would seriously want to deny that experiences of *Angst* and absurdity actually take place. It would be unrealistic to expect these deeply affective psychological phenomena to be submerged in the wake of a rational argument. But the character of the notion of ineffability allows such phenomenology, without contradiction, simultaneously to account for the opposed experiences both of meaning in the human world and of that world's absurdity, or a sense of nothingness. On the one hand, the experience of meanings is possible because those meaning are experienced against a background of life. Life is itself meaningful in virtue of being experienced as being in a relation of appropriateness to what is beyond itself. And it is only as determinately meaningless that what is beyond the human can, in a non-circular manner, function as the measure for all human meanings, including the meaning of life as a whole. It is only to the determinately meaningless that the meaning(s) of the human world can be experienced as answering. Only the notion of ineffability, to repeat Nozick's phrase, can give us meaning all the way down. On the other hand, it is the determinate meaninglessness of the ineffable, the peculiarly contentless and empty nature of the concept of ineffability, which can give the impression, especially to one still impossibly committed to rationality (or to the uncompensated humanism discussed in Chapter 2, above), that it is no measure at all. The results of such an impression are experiences of Heideggerian *Angst* and Sartrean absurdity: there is no measure for life, therefore life, the meanings that we impose on it and the projects which contribute to it are absurd. I cannot but be engaged with the world but that engagement is *ultimately* groundless. Jaspers describes the proximity of the ineffable, which, as the ground of meaning, cannot itself have a determinate meaning, to absurdity in this way: 'Where transcendence is concerned, no kind of meaning could fail to be delimiting and constrictive ... All that I can do is to search for the unthinkable transcendent being in the *identity of meaning and absurdity*.'[76]

This proximity is exploited by what Jaspers refers to as the cipher of 'foundering', which he describes as the 'passing away' of the objective, and even determinately meaningful, specificity of the experience of the world. What is revealed in foundering – 'the nonbeing of all being accessible to us – is the being of transcendence'.[77] But this formula, Jaspers continues, says nothing for it is like breaking a silence that cannot be broken; it says merely *Being*. Foundering, as 'uninterpretability', is the ultimate cipher 'but it is no longer a definable cipher. It remains open, hence its silence. It may well become the absolute void as the definitive fulfilment.'[78] The True Ground of meaning and being, the ultimately Real, the Absolute, has to be bought at the high price of indeterminacy of being and meaning. It is the human 'fear' and 'sheer dread' (the early Heidegger's *Angst*) in the face of such indeterminacy that 'blurs my perception of foundering; holding on to supposedly known realities makes me faithless'.[79] This apparent proximity of phenomenological nihilism[80] with the kind of philosophical faith Jaspers advocates seems unavoidable for as long as its subject matter is the truly ultimately Real, the ineffable. In order to serve as the true ground of all determinate meanings, the ineffable has itself to 'be' determinately meaning*less*.

Jaspers's opinion seems to imply that, with regard to the poetic evocation that is the suggested human response, a poetry of attunement to the ineffable should consist in a phenomenological dialectic of affirmation and negation. Just as, for Jaspers, the whole world becomes transparent in the experience of faith directed towards Transcendence, so no determinate meaning should in principle be debarred as a valid imagining or evocation of the ineffable.[81] Not if that meaning is understood in Jaspers's sense of a cipher, on the basis that the ineffable is the ground of all such meanings: such faith is what turns what appeared to Jaspers to be objects into ciphers. It is what turns existential phenomenological description into a simultaneous poetry of the ineffable and allows us to experience the meaningful fabric of life itself as a mode of ineffability, intimate with the ineffable. But, at the same time, the ineffable must be literally denied any determinate meaning because only on account of this denial can it serve as the ground of all such meanings. As Jaspers put it, 'we use an infinite number of names and cancel them all again'.[82] Indeed, as I hinted in the previous chapter, Jaspers himself seems to have discerned the value of a dialectical methodology: a methodology which prompts a kind of thinking which is not thinking of something but not thinking of nothing either.[83] As a methodology, he claims, the dialectic brings to mind 'what I live by but cannot refer to'.[84] He approvingly finds in Anaximander's notion of *apeiron* and in Parmenides both a radical setting off of Being from Nothingness and an identification of Being *as* Nothingness. *Contra* Sartre, such dialectical thinking aims at what is beyond or above being, what, like Jaspers's notion of Encompassing and Macquarrie's dialectical theism, encompasses both Being and Nothingness.[85] The dialectical methodology, however, is open to abuse. On the one hand, 'The eternal, perfect, self-sufficient universal source and goal that we call Being or Nothingness is nothing only as an intellectual conception; as encompassing experience it is the true reality'.[86] But, on the other hand, the misuse of such dialectical thinking occurs when, in the opposite direction, 'an objective reality, an objective claim, is fixed, allowed to call for blind obedience, and then supposed to be justified by dialectics' – hence the deeply felt need for the mutual correction of the dialectic's poles.[87]

Each pole of this dialectical response loosely corresponds to each of the moments to existential phenomenology: the rational and the poetic. If, in our haste to find a firm ground for human meanings in the ineffable measure, we mistakenly and idolatrously invest it with determinate meanings (or, worse, concepts), the rational reminder of the necessarily determinately meaningless or contentless nature of the concept of ineffability, together with phenomenological description of the concomitant experiences of *Angst* and absurdity, will stop us short. And if *Angst* overwhelms us as we become inappropriately mindful of the determinately empty character which the notion of ineffability must have if it is to measure our concepts and meanings, a poetry of ineffable inexhaustibility and the concomitant phenomenological description of the experienced meanings of the human world, will reassure us that it is only as indeterminate (determinately meaning*less*) that the notion could evoke the ultimate measure for all the determinate meanings that it is possible for us to experience as we engage with the world with creative receptivity. Given my eventual aims, it is perhaps not surprising that the dialectic I have just outlined sounds consonant with the suggestion of Denys Turner, for which he finds a long theological pedigree, that, in religion and theology, apophatic and cataphatic 'ways' (the *via negativa* and the *via eminentiae*) must be held in tension and continual dialogue.[88] Arising out of reason, the dialectic is phenomenological and poetic and, as such, makes itself transparent as an imaginative and mutually correcting process rather than a literal, but paradoxical, description of the way things independently are. Through the dialectic, as through the pre-Socratic paradoxes as constructively viewed by Jaspers and McGilchrist, we become aware of the 'limit to literal conceivability for us'.[89] As for what lies beyond this limit, we may attune ourselves to the ineffable through the phenomenological dialectic. On the one hand, that dialectic's rational roots keep it always transparent, always self-aware as a piece of phenomenology. With regard to the ineffable, '[r]eason cannot think it; it can only keep it undefiled'.[90] The dialectic's poetic dimension, on the other hand, consists in the articulation of the paradox with which reason was left. It consists in attunement to what lies beyond the limit of literal conceivability. Both dimensions together show that such articulation is not mere nonsense but a valuable, indeed rationally required, description of a certain religious dimension of human experience which eludes a purely rational articulation, a kind of description which may also help to cultivate and bring about that experience.

As to whether such a dialectical oscillation is for ever the inevitable and imperfect way in which we must attune ourselves to what lies beyond it and in which opposites are reconciled, the answer has to be 'Yes' for as long as we are engaged in philosophy, conventionally understood, i.e. as in some (albeit limited or pragmatic) way involving the most fundamental of our human distinctions by which reason is necessarily conditioned – that of subject and object. The phenomenological dialectic is an articulation of reality that arises out of reason and continues to involve reason at one of its poles. Its dialectical and phenomenological form owes to the fact that what it articulates is a paradox according to pure rationality. But, as philosophy, phenomenology always has to have a rational dimension. As Jaspers rightly stated, 'Once Reason is lost, philosophy itself is lost'.[91] It may be that there is a point where the phenomenological dialectic can be transcended, where it is possible to undergo the rationally paradoxical experience of the *simultaneous* identity of meaning and absurdity, where the oscillation between the poles of the dialectic ceases as the rationally incommensurable poles of the dialectic have a simultaneous effect on our experience and where, therefore, reason is entirely abandoned. But, although such an experience must arise out of philosophy, its articulation and attunement will not themselves (at least not without vigorous controversy) be agreed to constitute philosophical operations. These might consist in a kind of poeticizing similar to that of the later Heidegger, but the relation of this to philosophy, as traditionally conceived, is notoriously contentious. In any case, as a work of philosophy, this book would not be an appropriate place to indulge in such poeticizing. The philosopher can raise the question of the possibility of such a rationally paradoxical experience, its articulation and cultivation. And for as long as the philosopher maintains her grip on the rational dimension to her discipline (which she must never loosen if she is to continue to philosophize) her articulation of the answer to such questions, which transcend pure reason, will be necessarily dialectical. However, beyond such dialectical articulation, the philosopher may also indicate places other than philosophy where the rational dimension is not so important, where this dimension may be deliberately lost and where the articulation and cultivation of such experience can therefore be non-dialectical. Indeed, this will be my task in my final chapter's discussion of art and ritual. If such philosophical indication itself turns out to contribute to the cultivation of the kind of experience in question, so much the better, but it cannot be counted upon to do so *a priori*. As Jaspers realized, to follow a philosophical path on the search after Truth 'means an incessant searching, trying and risking, all in a state of ignorance'.[92] But I hope it will be clear that the dialectical, rational appraisal of these non-rational spheres of human experience and activity that philosophy provides (in aesthetics or philosophy of art and in a focus on ritual and religious practice) remains indispensable if the conceptual, and consequent practical, dangers inherent in these spheres (especially that of religious practice) are to be avoided.

Our engagement with Jaspers, then, opened up the possibility of overcoming Tillich's difficulty in accounting for the possibility of religious experience (or revelation) caused by Tillich's thinking the concept of ineffability only in terms of transcendence of the subject–object dichotomy. The advantage of Jaspers's line of argument was found to be the rethinking of ineffability in terms of meaning which, although it apparently involved placing less emphasis on the notion of objectivity (for example the notion of ciphers as world images rather than objects), did not involve sacrificing the ciphers' concrete character. Jaspers showed that, without being thought of as mere objects, ciphers, as determinate meanings, can be experienced as transparent to their indeterminate ground. However, Jaspers's suppression of the subject–object dichotomy ultimately meant that he could never properly overcome that dichotomy, as the notion of ineffability requires. In this chapter, I have tried to correct this and to show, with the help of Cooper's argument, that existential phenomenology makes use of the subject–object distinction, in its rational dimension, only to the degree that this is required to defend its presuppositions, demonstrate its own limits and thus to overcome it. This use of the subject–object distinction, I maintained, opposes the dualistic understanding of the distinction as a dichotomy, an understanding that unhelpfully underwrites and bolsters an implausible rationality. I showed that the poetic dimension to phenomenology is there to take over when the subject–object distinction implodes, enabling a dialectical attunement to the ineffable and to the vision of the intimacy of the ineffable with the human world. *Pace* Tillich, we can move from the rational to the ineffable only *via* the rational phenomenology and the phenomenological poetry of existential phenomenological description. The phenomenological dialectic consists in this: that, as well as being understood as the articulation of human meanings, phenomenological description is seen equally as effecting the following. On the one hand, the *rational* defence of its specific way of articulating life's meanings and of the validity of the notion of life's ineffable measure. And, on the other hand, and inseparably, an articulation of life's meanings which is, at the same time, a *poetic* attunement to the ineffable to which those meanings (viewed as ciphers) ultimately owe and with which they are entirely intimate.

Unlike a Procrustean (if rather popular) direct theological application of Heidegger's rather vague suggestion (outlined in Chapter 2) that philosophical discourse properly consists in 'thinking' and 'poeticizing', this clearer and more transparent view of the various modes of philosophical discourse, informed by engagement with Jaspers and Cooper, can more appropriately be applied to address religious concerns and to account philosophically for religious experience (or revelation), language and practice by locating them within a philosophical framework. While this view is clearly not disconsonant with that of the later Heidegger, it has the advantage of being able to retain the concreteness and historicity of such experience and practice, crucial to any religious tradition, in the form of religious ciphers.[93] Within this framework, such ciphers (though, *pace* Jaspers, without any direct relationship to the subject–object dichotomy) can be seen to constitute the concrete religious meanings which belong to a historical tradition and which are, in the respects which Jaspers outlined, like the 'language' and 'physiognomy' of the ineffable God, intimate with both God and human being-in-the-world and directly perceivable by us. They are the 'contents' of historical religious experience. In other words, they are the concrete points of focus, the 'world images' of an ineffable God's immediate revelation in the human world, even though such a God, as the Absolute, is independent of that world but inaccessible as such. Owing to their lack of relationship with the subject–object dichotomy, and therefore unlike Tillich's symbols, they can still be consistently understood as such after the rejection of ontotheology. The religious language or expression, corresponding to what Jaspers called the 'second language', is the communicative attunement to those religious ciphers by means of the, strictly inseparable, phenomenological description and poetic attunement. Such attunement, like Heidegger's 'thinking/poeticizing', involves a comportment which incorporates linguistic and non-linguistic dimensions. These dimensions are respectively captured in Jaspers's metaphors of language and physiognomy or gesture. And as we also saw with Jaspers, this communicative expression is inseparable from the original perception of the religious ciphers and, also like Heidegger's 'poeticizing' (and a little like John Cottingham's 'praxis', as we shall see in the next chapter), is able actually to *establish* the human experience of the ineffable God in its appropriation of religious ciphers.

In other words, engagement with religious ciphers as such enables them to function as the concrete, historically and culturally mediated, foci of immediate religious experience – or of divine revelation to an entirely intimate human world. The philosophical framework within which religious experience, language and practice are located and understood in this way enables the resolution of the tension, noted at the outset, between ineffability and answerability and the potential appropriation of that resolution by religious thought. As we have seen in this chapter, it has the added advantage of being able, on this basis, to show philosophically the inevitability of such religious experience. It is able to show the necessity for and appropriateness of such linguistic and non-linguistic religious practice to anyone who is, at least initially, committed to the validity of the operations of reason. It does this by identifying religious experience as the experience of God where 'God' is understood to refer to the concept of ineffability and thereby to evoke what is truly ultimately Real, the Absolute, in terms of which the meaning of life must be explained. It shows that such experience is implied by our lived experience of the world, and identifies specifically religious expression and practice as a species of the poetic attunement which is, correspondingly, the rationally inevitable consummation of the existential phenomenological description of that lived experience. Such phenomenological description, as we have also seen, is itself the inevitable result of the operations of reason. Finally, it is in the phenomenological dialectic of (poetic) affirmation and (rational) negation of meaning that, given the notion of ineffability, a philosophical account of religious experience and expression properly consists.

So there is, too, an important corrective tendency here to the kind of theology that believes itself to have any determinate content to its concept of God. The identity of meaning and absurdity, which the notion of ineffability implies, entails that every statement about God is as false as it is true and points beyond the dichotomy of 'truth' and 'falsity', conceived as correspondence to the facts.[94] It points towards 'Truth' with a capital 'T' – the condition for any truth at all to be apprehended, which, as Heidegger was well aware, involves as much concealment as it does revelation and which therefore entails the phenomenological dialectic. What is revealed in any given case is dependent on the attendant concrete human concerns (McGilchrist's 'attention'), the horizon within which it is viewed. Jaspers addressed the question whether the reality that religious revelatory experience has for the faithful could possibly become, in his sense, a cipher of Transcendence. His answer was as follows:

> The paradox seems inescapable: the contents of revelations would become more pure, more true, if their reality were discarded. The reality as such would turn into a cipher of the presence of God, lending an extraordinary weight to the contents.[95]

This rational and negative pole of the phenomenological dialectic implies that, viewed as a cipher, the revelation of a specific religion could no longer be regarded as any more valid than any other cipher from another religious, or non-religious, tradition. Such a cipher would be one

> that allows man's boundless yearning for the real presence of God to be satisfied for an instant, so to speak – but only so as to thrust him back at once into the hard, great, free state he was created in, and in which God remains inexorably hidden.[96]

In Jaspers's view, the 'poison' of exclusive claims must be removed in order for religious revelatory experience to become, by being interpreted as, the reading of a cipher.

> Removing the poison consciously takes a simple and momentous insight: that exact, generally valid truth is relative, dependent on premises and methods of cognition but compelling for every intellect, while existential truth is historic, absolute in each man's life but not to be stated as valid for and [sic] all others.[97]

This corrective impulse has thoroughgoing implications for religion at the dialectic's positive, imaginative and poetic pole, which Jaspers briefly sketches. If, say, the Christian revelation were understood as a cipher, faith in it would 'metamorphose'.

> Dogmas, sacraments, rituals would be melted down, so to speak – not destroyed, but given other forms of conscious realization ... Not the substance, but the appearance in consciousness would change. Philosophy and theology would be on the road to reunification.[98]

It is the nature of just such 'appearance in consciousness' that I want to address in the final chapter. The bulk of this book has consisted in the development of the philosophical framework. Ideally we shall now be in a position to locate religious experience and practice within that framework and to appreciate that, by being located within it in this way, these can be accounted for in the light of the notion of ineffability. And while the foregoing remarks reiterate that the historical concreteness of the spiritual and religious practices of the Christian tradition can in principle be accommodated by this philosophical framework (to which the notion of ineffability is central) I have not yet shown in any detail how this accommodation might happen. In the following chapter, therefore, I want to look more closely at a specific instance of religious practice in order to show in more detail how it may be philosophically interpreted as the place, within Christianity's historical and concrete religious tradition, of the experience or revelation of the ineffable. I want to show how religious practices (in this case, the language and rites of the Christian tradition) can be seen to be the hieroglyphics of the religious cipher of the truly ultimate, and therefore ineffable, God. For, as we have seen, it is only by appeal to such a God that the meaning of human life can be explained. I proceed by drawing analogies between religious experience and expression and those of art with a view, finally, to making philosophical sense of what is, in many traditions, the central Christian rite, namely, the Eucharist.

6 THE AESTHETIC AND RITUAL EMBODIMENT OF THE INEFFABLE

In this chapter, I want to develop further my neo-Jaspersian account of religious ciphers. This account differs from Jaspers's own account, as we have just seen, in that such ciphers cannot have a direct relationship to the subject–object dichotomy if they are to succeed in bodying forth the ineffable. As Jaspers described ciphers, his rather narrow focus was on the possibility of an *experience* connected with Transcendence or God. *Mutatis mutandis*, I want to broaden the focus in keeping with the philosophical demand, left hanging at the end of Chapter 2, for an account of modes of comportment that consist in a constellation of experience, language and practice and, comparable to what Heidegger called 'dwelling', cultivate an awareness of, and therefore body forth, the ineffable. In a religious connection, I want to provide an account of religious practices, specifically religious ritual (and, even more specifically, the Eucharist) in the light of my foregoing argument according to which the notion of ineffability must be central to a convincing philosophical account of religion. I hope that, in this way, I may at least begin the appropriation by religious thought of the philosophical resolution of the tension between ineffability and answerability that I have been advocating in this book. Such an appropriation will show how religious ritual can be philosophically interpreted as one means of bodying forth the ineffable. Jaspers said that, although a religious system could itself be a cipher of Transcendence, it could never be a 'draft' that covers the authentic ciphers. Thus, when I speak of 'religious ciphers', I mean, in Jaspers's terms, something more akin to the hieroglyphs of one cipher-script among others. I mean elements of Christianity's historically concrete cipher-script which, properly understood, does not make an exclusive, objective claim on the ineffable. As we have seen, claims to exclusivity and objectivity are inconsistent with the concept of ineffability. As John Macquarrie puts it, 'the operation of the divine Spirit is not confined to the recognized sacraments any more than it is confined to the Christian religion'.[1] Religious ciphers, then, are the concrete points of focus, within a religious tradition, where the ineffable may be understood to be manifest to human beings. These are the terms in which Macquarrie understood the notion of 'sacrament' ('the places where Being makes itself present-and-manifest in and through particular beings')[2] and he realized that the Christian conviction that the human world as a whole is a sacramental one implies that the range of possible sacraments is very great and that there is no reason to suppose that divine action is 'confined to the ecclesiastically recognized channels'.[3] Brown has more recently reiterated such a synoptic view.[4]

I want, here, however, to remain relatively uncontroversial and to focus on those places where God's presence is self-consciously evoked and invoked, namely, religious, and specifically sacramental, rites. Such rituals, I suggest, make use of such ciphers: pieces of language, artefacts, gestures, works of religious art including music and architecture, and so on. There is an important sense in which rituals, as such ciphers themselves, are just made up of such potentially 'hieroglyphic' phenomena. If my attempt, in this chapter, to locate the phenomenon of religious ritual within the foregoing philosophical framework has any success, the nature of religious ciphers, and rituals as (perhaps pre-eminent) examples of such ciphers, should become clear. It is my aim, in this chapter, to show how we may understand art and ritual as instances of the 'phenomenological poetry' in which, I suggested in the previous chapter, authentic ciphers must consist. Art and ritual are spheres of practice and discourse where the phenomenological dialectic can be transcended since the rational dimension is here somewhat muted in comparison to philosophical discourse. Once reason is lost, as Jaspers aphorized, philosophy itself is lost but the same is not true of art and ritual. In these spheres, I suggest, it is possible to experience the identity of meaning and absurdity, which, in philosophy, can be evoked only dialectically. Here, the world can experienced as answerable to the ineffable, simultaneously *beyond* the human world and entirely intimate with it. The concept of ineffability refers to no objective or determinately meaningful measure but evokes, for that very reason, the most enduring measure possible. And, although these forms of practice may be in some respects similar to phenomenology, they are not so strongly motivated by the impulse to make rational, as to make emotional, sense of the world. If these pieces of phenomenological poetry are to be self-aware, conscious of their nature, scope and limitations, they themselves invite philosophical reflection, with its rational dimension, such as I hope to carry out in this chapter.

There are further reasons for my focus, in this final chapter, on ritual. It is not just that this practical dimension to religion seems most compatible with the demands for a mode of comportment laid down earlier. Ritual quite obviously incorporates both experience and expression and the linguistic and non-linguistic dimensions of these, as is respectively reflected in Jaspers's metaphors of 'language' and 'physiognomy'. Rituals are, too, (it intuitively seems) peculiarly closely related to the meaningful fabric of people's lives in structure and content and, in this connection, ritual's creative dimension comes to light. It is not just that ritual reflects a meaning that certain human lives already had, rather, it seems, these lives would not have had the meanings they do for those who live them were it not for the ritual. Ritual not only expresses life's meaning but seems, in an important sense, to create and cultivate such meaning and its lived experience. Finally, the topic of ritual has received surprisingly scant philosophical attention. Before looking at these issues in more detail, and providing these preliminary intuitions with some solid philosophical support, one obvious objection to my proposed focus on religion's practical dimension seems worth parrying.

This objection could take the form of the question 'Isn't religious practice dependent on theory?' Surely, it will be argued, religious practices are most often underpinned by doctrines; it is therefore impossible to treat such practices except as products of those metaphysical beliefs which apparently justify them and in terms of which their meaning is typically explained. Ronald Hepburn has advanced an argument of this kind. Citing the idea of Heidegger and Bachelard that the sacred (a sense of which, in my view, might be cultivated by the arts and by religious language and practice) is 'older than the Gods',[5] he argues that sense can be made of the concept of the sacred, only once the concept of deity has already been grasped. Hepburn says that the assertion 'God is holy' is not an analytic truth for, if it were, 'believers would be unable to rejoice in his holiness, singing "*Sanctus, sanctus, sanctus*" with thankfulness and wonder'.[6] He sees the logic here as parallel to that revealed by the familiar analysis of 'God is good'. The ability to praise God for his goodness, or to see the assertion that he is good as news-giving, cannot be simply a linguistic matter. Therefore, the concept of the sacred is logically independent of the concept of deity. So far, I agree with Hepburn. But he does not think it follows from this that the sacred is older than the gods or that we can therefore employ the concept of the sacred, in an aesthetic, ritual or any other context, irrespective of whether we hold the belief that there is a God in what turns out to be the traditional, ontotheological sense. His suggestion is that to hold the 'religious–metaphysical meanings consistently in abeyance inevitably draws off what attracts us to the term ["sacred"] in the first place'.[7] He continues:

> Perhaps centuries of Christian theism have so impregnated 'sacred' with its religious relational qualities – belonging to God, emanating from God – that those strands are by now unsuppressible, cannot admit of bracketing, but reassert themselves whether we like it or not, and no matter whether the sacred was or was not older than God or the gods.[8]

Perhaps. But, then again, perhaps not. It is odd that Hepburn, someone for whom Christianity's metaphysical beliefs constituted the major obstacle to religious commitment, should claim to be attracted to the concept of the sacred by precisely those religious–metaphysical meanings which he finds intellectually unacceptable. Whether his argument holds depends upon what, precisely, attracts us to the concept of the sacred. Theologians who seek to reject ontotheology (the successful ones at least) *must* disagree that the concept of the sacred is irreparably steeped in, and attractive on account of, an intellectually offensive metaphysics. Not only that, but many of Hepburn's fellow atheists would surely not agree that the concept is unrecoverable from beneath the metaphysical layers accumulated over the centuries, any more than they would submit that a sense of awe and wonder is still today contaminated by an ignorance of the causes of natural phenomena which, no doubt, in less enlightened times long produced that sense in human beings. For these reasons, I am not convinced by Hepburn's argument either against the logical independence of (practical) ritual or aesthetic uses of the term 'sacred' from (theoretical) religious–metaphysical understandings or for the logical priority of the latter.

An argument for the non-dependence of practice on theory in this context may be found in the later work of the most prominent twentieth-century philosopher to have written on the topic of ritual, Ludwig Wittgenstein. One of the main purposes of his *Remarks on Frazer's* Golden Bough is precisely to resist the suggestion that ritual practices must rest on (in this case mistaken) beliefs. Here Wittgenstein argues that showing someone an error in their beliefs will not be sufficient to make them change or cease engaging in the ritual practice which is supposedly founded upon those beliefs.[9] For Wittgenstein, rituals should be compared to acts, like that of kissing a picture of a loved one, which are clearly not based on the belief that the action will causally effect the object represented.[10] In addition, rituals do not typically *replace* actions directed at practical ends as one might expect on the misinterpretation Wittgenstein is attacking. The 'savage' who breaks an effigy of his enemy into pieces, apparently in order to kill him, really does build his hut of wood and hunts for food; he does not do these things, essential for his survival, in effigy.[11] Wittgenstein pursues this line of thought, providing a further example: 'towards morning, when the sun is about to rise, people celebrate rites of the coming of day, but not at night, for then they simply burn lamps'.[12] What this indicates is either that such people do not believe that the rite causally produces the rising of the sun or that this belief is irrelevant to the real point of their performance of the rite. In either case, the rite's significance cannot depend upon its performer's holding the belief. One commentator suggests that rituals, for Wittgenstein, are based not on beliefs but on forms of life and that their performance is in this way more like an art than a science.[13] Suzanne Langer takes up the Wittgensteinian line of argument, and the comparison of ritual with art, suggesting that ritual consists in the 'slow deposit' of people's imaginative insight into life.[14] She suggests that a supposedly 'magic' effect, such as rites are often assumed to aim at, is not the desired causal result of a ritual but its completion.[15] Giving a better example than Wittgenstein's dawn rites, she argues that a rain dance is not a practical mistake but a ritual in which the appearance of rain has a part. This explains why, in her words,

> [n]o savage tries to induce a snowstorm in midsummer, nor prays for the ripening of fruits entirely out of season, as he certainly would if he considered his dance and prayer the physical causes of such events. He dances *with* the rain, he invites the elements to do their part.[16]

Thus, the failure of rain to come does not discourage the 'savage' from performing the rite. Perhaps, indeed, it further encourages him. The rite is not ineffective in this case but unconsummated. The ritual's real import is its power to articulate the relationship between man and nature. Its supposed physical power to produce rain is one metaphorical way of recognizing and expressing this import.[17] Langer sees the origin of sacrament in such rituals and believes this type of action to run the gamut 'from blind compulsive behaviour, through magical conjuring, to the heights of conscious expression'.[18] It is for these reasons that she reverses the usual formulation that religion has its origin in magic and claims instead that magic begins in religion. In her view, magic's 'typical form – the confident, practical *use* of a formula, a brew, and a rite to achieve a physical effect – is the empty shell of a religious act'.[19]

To understand one of Wittgenstein's examples in these terms, we might say that rites begin as acts comparable to the kissing of a picture of a loved one and that magic would be the result if the metaphorical understanding of the meaning of this act came to dominate, collapsing into the literal belief that the loved one is causally affected by this action. Elsewhere, Wittgenstein writes:

> Everything ritualistic (everything that, as it were, smacks of the high priest) must be strictly avoided, because it immediately turns rotten.
> Of course a kiss is a ritual too and it isn't rotten, but ritual is permissible only to the extent that it is as genuine as a kiss.[20]

The act of kissing the picture, mentioned in the *Remarks*, would come to smack of the high priest if it were contaminated by the magical belief that it could produce some pleasant effect in the absent beloved. As Wittgenstein succinctly expresses the conclusion of his argument: 'What makes the character of ritual action is not any view or opinion.'[21]

More recently, too, John Cottingham has sought to downplay the metaphysical dimension to religious belief in favour of the practical dimension in his recent advocacy of the 'primacy of praxis' in philosophy of religion.[22] The kind of spiritual and ritual praxis he has in mind does not consist in mere trappings since he sees its nature as the vehicle for the kind of depth of existential and emotional response to the human world that, in his view, characterizes the religious perspective. If we were to do away with the rituals, he suggests, we would run the risk of losing our only means of access to the deeper meaning of life as a whole, provided by daily ritual rhythms, or of significant points in life, provided by rites of passage.[23] Whereas the only rational position to take on traditional, metaphysical theism is, in Cottingham's view, agnosticism, religious practices reveal what is not fully graspable by human reason, what, like Descartes's mountain, is a 'mystery to rationality': an emotionally charged view of the world that is irreducible to propositions and is perhaps only available by way of those practices which are, for Cottingham, the precondition for this religious outlook.[24] He advocates an adaptation of Pascal's exhortation to act as (Pascal claims) those who are already committed once did 'by acting as if they believed. In the natural course of events this in itself will make you believe, this will train you.'[25] We must behave and live *as if* the world had a divine source, though the question whether it does is unanswerable by appeal to human rationality or to the evidence available to empirical investigation. Pascal's word (*'abêtir'*) is not, Cottingham insists, to be understood in the malign sense of some Orwellian crushing of rationality.[26] It is used, rather, in the sense of the cultivation of a particular world view which, although it cannot be epistemically validated, can only operate against a background of other, rationally validated, beliefs and, insofar as it is tenable, in harmony with them.[27] The rationally unanswerable metaphysical questions can be bypassed, Cottingham thinks, by engaging in religious praxis. Aping the early Wittgenstein, he suggests that 'the domain that "cannot be spoken of" must be *handled through praxis* – the practice of spirituality'.[28] As well as challenging the view that practice depends on theory, Cottingham's work also brings out the creative dimension to religious practice, the idea that the religious view of the world is perhaps only available once we have engaged in the practices that not only express but also help to cultivate that outlook. One sociologically inclined writer speaks, in a similar register, of ritual as that which 'opens up a space within quotidian paramount reality so that new or renewed formulations of reality (or orientations to lived experience) can be constructed'.[29] In Langer's more philosophical vocabulary, it is ritual's central aim to 'to aid in the formulation of a religious universe'.[30] Although Cottingham's suggestions nicely bring out this often neglected creative dimension to ritual, I cannot help but feel that his central notion of the primacy of praxis reinforces, rather than overcomes, the division between theory and practice which we have consistently found to be rather unhelpful in this demesne and which, in my view, eventually does violence to Cottingham's argument. I suggest that, in this area, Wittgenstein's approach, which gestures towards the dissolution of this sharp division, is more constructive. Just as he does not want to reduce rituals to primitive actions based on (mistaken) beliefs, he also speaks of beliefs themselves as being potentially ritualistic.[31]

I want, finally, to counter the suggestion that, in religion, practice is necessarily dependent upon theory by way of a counterexample. Macquarrie reminds us of the historical course of the, relatively late, development of Mariological dogmas and expresses doubt as to whether they would ever have been formulated at all had it not been for the existence of the ritual practices that had been centred around Mary (intercessions directed towards her, hymns composed and sung in her honour) since the very earliest Christian times.[32] In the fourth century, according to Macquarrie, Bishop Epiphanius anticipated the later doctrinal distinction between being worthy of 'worship' and 'veneration' as a result of having to restrain the excesses of Marian devotion in his diocese. While he recognized that devotion to Mary could meet sincere spiritual needs, Epiphanius saw that excessive exuberance could very easily lapse into the idolatrous worship of a human person. Here we see, in addition to the arguments rehearsed above against the *logical* priority of theory over practice in religion, the suggestion that, in some cases, practice enjoyed *historical* priority over theory. In any case, we can see from Macquarrie's example that the relationship between religious practice and religious beliefs is more complex than one of the simple dependence of ritual on dogma. If anything, the arguments we have been considering have gestured towards the dissolution of a sharp division between theory and practice. And this idea turns out to be remarkably consonant with the constellation I referred to at the beginning of this chapter of experience and practice of both linguistic and non-linguistic kinds.

My focus on ritual is justified, I think, by the suggestion already encountered that it is not simply an expression of beliefs nor can it be said, in a straightforward sense, to create beliefs. Religious ritual is, inseparably, the expression and cultivation of a mode of comportment towards the world as both essentially shaped by human consciousness and answerable to the ineffable. Quite obviously amongst religious phenomena, it is also a sphere in which the linguistic and non-linguistic dimensions enjoy equal importance. Having justified this chapter's topic, I now want to show, in service of my account of religious ciphers, how ritual meaning operates and to consider how it is to be understood within the philosophical framework I have developed. I want to suggest that, in four important ways, ritual meaning operates in an identical manner to artistic meaning as the latter is revealed by the phenomenology of art. Ritual bodies forth the ineffable in just the way that art does for the phenomenologists. This suggestion prompts what I call an aesthetic account of ritual meaning.[33] This account is bolstered by the fact that ritual not only resembles art but also incorporates works of art into itself. First, though, I set out in some detail the four features of artistic meaning I have in mind.

The Phenomenology of Art[34]

The first point to be made about works of art, which immediately connects them with the concept of ineffability, is that their meaning is inexhaustible. If there is in principle no end to the interpretation of the meaning of artworks, that meaning will be in principle unconceptualizable and literally inexpressible – ineffable. Gadamer holds that the concept of inexhaustibility, which he sometimes expresses as 'excess of meaning', is essential to an accurate account of the experience of aesthetic meaning.[35] A commentator describes this conclusion, drawn from Gadamer's phenomenological analysis of the experience of aesthetic meaning, as amounting to Gadamer's 'thoroughgoing rejection of the idea that understanding is ever finished or complete'.[36] Gadamer's premise is that, ontologically speaking, art really consists in the experience of artistic meaning and, therefore, that 'artistic presentation, by its nature, exists for someone, even if there is no one there who merely listens or watches'.[37] Although the truth of this claim is most obvious in the case of the performing arts, Gadamer believes it to be true of art in general. We quite obviously do not experience music or drama, in the fullest sense, by reading a score or a script but by hearing or seeing it, or both, in performance. As Gadamer puts it, 'a drama really exists only when it is being played, and ultimately music must resound'.[38] This claim can be seen as the natural consequence of the application of the phenomenological method to the field of aesthetics since it reflects the phenomenological approach to reality in general. Mikel Dufrenne asks: 'Certainly the aesthetic object realizes itself only in aesthetic perception; is this not true, however, of all perceived things?'[39]

The implication of the idea is that the experience of a work of art is mediated by layers of interpretation provided by both the performers and spectators and, since art really consists in the experience of its meaning, the work is itself inseparable from these interpretative layers. There may well be disagreement over the interpretation of an artwork among and between artist, performers and spectators, such that the criterion of what counts as a correct interpretation becomes 'a highly flexible and relative one'.[40] However, it does not follow that it is not the same thing, the artwork, that comes into being as a result of the creative and interpretative activity of all of them. A new production of *King Lear* is not a new play but a new interpretation of the *same* play and is itself open to as many new interpretations, differently nuanced and with different emphases and resonances, as there are members of the audience. Hence Gadamer can write that such an interpretative performance, and, by extension, the spectators' experience of the work, 'merely completes what works of art already are' since interpretation of this kind is a necessary condition of the experience of the meaning, and therefore of the being, of the artwork – since it is in the experience of its meaning that the artwork essentially consists.[41] The concept of aesthetic inexhaustibility, for Gadamer, draws together these two thoughts: the idea that the interpretation of aesthetic meaning is a flexible and relative business and the thought that this relativity does not abolish or attenuate the bond between the meaningful experience and the artwork itself. Indeed Gadamer's position, as I understand it, is that the ontology of art has to be understood in terms of this bond. It does not follow from the fact that an artwork's meaning is in principle inexhaustible that it does not have meaning at all and therefore, in Gadamer's sense, does not exist or that to speak of 'art' at all makes no sense. This would only be the case if our only conditions for meaning and measure were determinately objective ones. That this is not the case for Gadamer is obvious from his premise that art always exists for someone. The ontology of the work of art is inseparable from, indeed at least partly constituted by, its human interpretation and 'Art demands interpretation because of its inexhaustible ambiguity'.[42]

The second point, briefly met earlier (at the end of Chapter 1) and anticipated above, concerns the intimacy and inseparability of the meaning of an artwork from the work itself. It concerns the inseparability of what is presented from the way in which it is presented. Adapting Malcolm Budd, we might refer to this point, which is well made by several philosophers, as the assertion of the autonomy of aesthetic meaning.[43] In his *Lectures and Conversations* and in various other scattered remarks on aesthetics, Wittgenstein repeatedly returns to his keynote observation of the inseparability of meaning or sense from artwork and the way in which that inseparability is reflected in our sense of the work's irreplaceability. Wittgenstein notes the tendency to speak of the 'effect' of a work of art as though the reason we seek to experience artworks is to get a certain effect (an experience of meaning, say) and therefore as though the work itself is of inferior importance to the effect it produces or does not matter at all. The fact that we can play a minuet once and 'get a lot out of it', and play the same piece another time and get nothing out of it, does not entail that what we get out of it is independent of the minuet: 'A man may sing a song with expression and without expression. Then why not leave out the song – could you have the expression then?'[44] Wittgenstein's suggestion is that we could not have the expression without the song, the meaning without the work of art. It is the intimacy of the 'effect' that the work of art has on us with the artwork itself that explains the oddity of the idea that two works which have the same effect as one another would be interchangeable. Although someone might say that the associations evoked by the work are what matter, Wittgenstein says: 'You can't say: "That's just as good as the other: it gives me the same associations"'.[45] He continues:

> You *could* select either of the two poems to remind you of death, say. But supposing you had read a poem and admired it, could you say: 'Oh, read the other, it will do the same'?
> How do we use poetry? Does it play this role that we say such a thing as: 'Here is something just as good'.[46]

His suggestion is that this is not the way we use poetry, or art in general, and this fact points up the inadequacy of the view that sense and work are logically separable: 'I should like to say "What the picture tells me is itself." That is, its telling me something consists in its own structure, in *its* own lines and colours';[47] 'I should like to say: "These notes say something glorious, but I do not know what." These notes are a powerful gesture, but I cannot put anything side by side with it that will serve as an explanation'.[48] We find a summary of Wittgenstein's position in a 1947 remark in response to Tolstoy's 'bad theorizing' about the way in which a work of art conveys a feeling experienced by the artist and, if successful, infects another person with the same feeling.[49] Wittgenstein writes:

> You might say: the work of art does not aim to convey *something else*, just itself. Just as, when I pay someone a visit, I don't just want to make him have feelings of such and such a sort; what I mainly want is to visit him, though of course I should like to be well received too.[50]

Budd notes a similarity between the account of art Wittgenstein opposes, here represented by Tolstoy, and a view of linguistic meaning which is the principal target of the *Philosophical Investigations*: 'that the sense of a sentence is a process that accompanies the utterance or perception of it'.[51] Indeed Wittgenstein notes this similarity himself when he compares the account of art he is opposing to the 'mistake of thinking that the meaning or thought is just an accompaniment of the word, and the word doesn't matter'.[52]

This similarity begins to bring out the dissolution of a sharp divide between linguistic and non-linguistic forms, which is another tendency of the kind of approach to art with which I am concerned. Dufrenne identifies the term 'expression' as a key word in the phenomenology of art and it will be immediately recognized that the term embraces linguistic and non-linguistic forms.[53] (Merleau-Ponty, it has been noted, conceives aesthetics as part of a general theory of expression.[54]) Dufrenne draws an analogy between both linguistic and non-linguistic forms of meaningful bodily expression and the meaning expressed by works of art. Writing of what he calls the 'physiognomy' of speech, following his conception of language as specifically *bodily* expression, Merleau-Ponty denies that speech is a sign of thought heralding another phenomenon in the way that smoke betrays fire. Rather, he says, speech is 'the presence of thought in the phenomenal world'.[55] Just as a gesture for him, as we saw earlier, does not represent a person's anger but embodies it, allowing the anger to unfold through their body, so language should be understood as a kind of 'phonetic gesticulation'.[56] In just the way that we have one means of representing a word, by uttering it, so 'the artist has only one means of representing the work on which he is engaged: by doing it'.[57] This comparison is the basis for Merleau-Ponty's likening of the body to a work of art since, in the same way that a threatening gesture does not make me *think* of anger but 'is anger itself',[58] so in 'a picture or a piece of music the idea is incommunicable by means other than the display of colours and sounds'.[59] The sense in which the body is comparable to a work of art, Merleau-Ponty explains, is that in which they are both 'beings in which the expression is indistinguishable from the thing expressed, their meaning accessible only through direct contact'.[60]

Merleau-Ponty develops this idea in a lucid and muscular lecture in which he provides the following definition: 'a work of art is something we perceive'.[61] In the lived world of perception, as with the work of art, it is impossible to separate the appearance of something from the *way* in which it appears. He asks us to consider the distinction between the definition and perception of a table. In the case of definition, we withdraw our interest from accidental, specific features such as the shape of the feet, the style of the moulding and so on, so that we end up with a description thought to capture the table's 'essence', something like: 'a horizontal, flat surface used for writing, eating, etc'. Perception, by contrast, does not withdraw its interest from the *way* in which the table performs its function. No detail (the grain of the wood, graffiti) is insignificant when the table is *perceived*.[62] Art's connection with perception, Merleau-Ponty tells us, consists in the inseparability of perception from meaning: 'the work of art resembles the object of perception: its nature is to be seen or heard and no attempt to define or analyse it ... can ever stand in place of the direct perceptual experience'.[63] This explains why I can get a relatively good general impression of a tool I have never seen from a description of its function but no analysis, however detailed, can give me 'even the vaguest idea of a painting I have never seen in any form'.[64] On this basis, Merleau-Ponty denies that art is to do with representation, in which case the meaning would lie beyond the canvas in the objects signified by the artwork (the work's 'subject'), which could be examined quite independently, without the work itself. His suggestion, on the contrary, is that, in art, everything that is to become perceptible must enter the 'world' of the artwork, must become paint, music or poetic language. A work of art does not represent but rather presents. It does not just imitate the world, 'it is a world of its own'; the 'subject' of the work consists entirely in the manner in which the perceptual object is, for example, 'constituted' by the painter with her brushes on the canvas.[65]

These thoughts are closely related to those of Wittgenstein on what might be called, thirdly, the *performative* character of the explanation of artistic meaning. This is the idea that the way in which someone conveys that they have understood the meaning of an artwork is not by making statements which definitively capture the meaning (for, if the sense is (a) inseparable from the work itself and (b) inexhaustible, this is impossible) but in the way in which they perform the work itself, the way they read out the lines of the poetry or play, hum or whistle the musical phrase. This performative character also embraces both linguistic and non-linguistic forms of expression. Invoking an idea akin to Merleau-Ponty's 'verbal gesticulations'[66] Wittgenstein says: 'If you are reading something aloud and want to read *well* ... sometimes ... what matters is the punctuation, i.e. your precise intonation and the duration of your pauses'.[67]

And elsewhere in a non-linguistic connection:

> Appreciation of music is expressed in a certain way, both in the course of hearing & playing and at other times too. This expression sometimes includes movements, but sometimes only the way the one who understands plays, or hums, occasionally too parallels he draws & images which, as it were, illustrate the music. Someone who understands

music will listen ... with a different facial expression ... play differently, hum differently, talk differently about the piece than someone who does not understand.[68]

If the meaning of an artwork is there in the work itself, it should not be surprising that when asked to explain our understanding of the work, we should engage in *performance* in the broad sense outlined above by Wittgenstein. It is said that Schumann's response, on being asked the meaning of one of his compositions, was to play it again.[69]

Wittgenstein had a tendency, noted by Lüdeking,[70] to compare art with the gestures of the human body, a tendency which brought him close to Merleau-Ponty's understanding of art as one sphere of linguistic and non-linguistic bodily expression. For both thinkers, this tendency is indicative of a desire to dissolve the sharp distinction in art (and perhaps, for Merleau-Ponty, in all bodily expression) between linguistic and non-linguistic forms. (Recall, also, the similarity highlighted by Budd between Wittgenstein's view of art and his later view of language.) Therefore the kind of argument that these thinkers advance should be no less applicable to art which takes a linguistic form. Although it is clear, in the case of music, how the work can be understood to refer to nothing other than itself, this is perhaps less clear when the form of the work is linguistic. Nonsense poetry (and nonsense) aside, the main point of any language, after all, seems to be to point to things beyond itself. But the argument is no less applicable in this sphere. Merleau-Ponty takes up a distinction made by Mallarmé, inherited by Valéry, between 'poetic' and 'everyday' language.[71] Whereas the latter is used to refer quickly to some well-known object, in 'the poem, as in the perceived object, form cannot be separated from content; what is being presented cannot be separated from the way in which it presents itself to the gaze'.[72] 'To speak of the world poetically is almost to remain silent, if speech is understood in everyday terms.'[73] For Gadamer, too (in his later essays), there is a sliding scale of language, ranging from its most everyday uses to the prosodic heights of lyric poetry.[74] In all language there is a relationship between 'image' and 'concept' – form and content. Whereas concept predominates and occludes image in language at its most everyday, language in its more poetic mode allows image to shine. Gadamer says: 'Ordinary language resembles a coin that we pass among ourselves in place of something else, whereas poetic language is like gold itself'.[75]

The point of this contrast is to illustrate that, whereas, at its most everyday, language serves to indicate things and disappears behind those things which are intended by its meaning, in its poetic capacity, it 'shows itself even as it points' and perhaps, at its most poetic, shows itself far more than it points.[76] Gadamer follows remarks made by Heidegger, in 'The Origin of the Work of Art', about the importance of the material out of which artworks are made. Heidegger claimed that in everyday objects, tools for instance, the material from which they are made is 'used up'; the material form disappears behind the objects' meaningful function and utility (the grain of the wood in a hammer is not essential to its function). In the artwork, by contrast, pigment and colour are not 'used up' in this way but 'colour ... rather only now comes to shine forth'.[77] It is pre-eminently in the artwork that our attention is drawn to the form of things as well as to their meaning. For Gadamer, the same is true of language as the material out of which the art of poetry is constructed.[78] Since, in its poetic capacity, focus is drawn to what Gadamer calls the 'corporeality' of the language itself (in contrast to everyday language which disappears behind what it points towards), poetry is language in a 'pre-eminent' sense.[79] In poetry, Gadamer claims: '[t]he structuring of sound, rhyme, rhythm, intonation, assonance, and so on, furnishes the stabilizing factors that haul back and bring to a standstill the fleeting word that points beyond itself'.[80]

To be sure, poetic language intends meaning but what is distinctive about it, Gadamer claims, is that, to a greater or lesser degree, this function recedes into the background in favour of the formal characteristics just listed.[81] As he summarizes: '[t]here is not a single word in a poem that does not intend what it means. Yet at the same time it sets itself back upon itself to prevent it slipping into prose.'[82] For Gadamer image is equal to concept, form to content, sound to sense. For him, 'poetry does not consist in intending something else. It consists simply in the fact that what is intended and what is said is there in the poem.'[83] Returning to Mallarmé's simile, he says, 'the language of poetry is not a mere pointer that refers to something else, but like a gold coin, it is what it represents'.[84]

The point may be elaborated in a way that brings out Gadamer's proximity to Wittgenstein and Merleau-Ponty. The presentation of something in poetic form is not a representation, a substitute for a more direct, 'less flowery' representation. Poetic language constitutes its own meaning, realizes itself. As determinate meaning is occluded in poetry, a mysterious realm of inexhaustible excess of meaning is opened up, as the individual words stand only for themselves and gaining in 'presence' and 'illuminating power'.[85] In a piece of poetic language, Gadamer claims, 'what is represented is itself present in the only way available to it'.[86]

Before turning, in the next section, to apply these aesthetic insights to the topic of religious ritual, it is important to guard against a possible misinterpretation of the arguments I have been presenting. Do they not just amount to formalism?[87] Is not the claim that an artwork refers to nothing other than itself an invitation to concern ourselves solely with its formal characteristics and, at an extreme, to deny that it has a meaning at all? Merleau-Ponty quickly disposes of this objection by clarifying that he is not suggesting that content should be ignored at the expense of form but that, instead, 'I mean that form and content – what is said and the way in which it is said – cannot exist separately from one another'.[88] The charge of formalism may be further rebutted by appeal to another remark of Wittgenstein's, which highlights my second feature of artistic meaning: inseparability of sense from work. In answer to the question whether a work of art refers to something outside of itself, Wittgenstein says that it certainly does but that what it points to is nothing determinate but is, rather, the 'background' against which anything is able to show up as meaningful for us; the work of art 'makes an impression on me which is connected with things in its surroundings – e.g. with our language and its intonations; and hence with the whole field of our language-games'.[89] Lüdeking explains that it would be impossible to work out the meaning of an artwork solely by an analysis of its inner structure, the formal characteristics which make it up.[90] The explanation of an artwork's meaning must be given in terms of its role in a form of life. Even if the best way to show that one has understood the meaning of a work, or to explain it, is performative, in the sense sketched above, such performance always takes place within a context, a language-game, a form of life, of which at least aspects are in principle articulable. The artwork points outside of itself, not to theoretical beliefs about the world but to other things in its surroundings in the 'weave of life' and thence to the 'whole scene of our language-games'. This helps us to understand Wittgenstein's remark that in order fully to explain a work of art, one would have to describe an entire culture.[91] It also explains Cooper's claim about the continuity of art with phenomenology;[92] there is a sense in which art is phenomenology by other means: the sense in which it irreplaceably articulates the meanings of the human world.

Let me end this section by reassuring the reader that this last point does not weaken my opening link between artistic meaning and the notion of ineffability. It might be objected that since what artworks refer to, embody or make present, is the culture of a period, they cannot be said to body forth the ineffable since the culture of a period is in principle, if not in practice, graspable in concepts and articulable in literal language. This objection can be countered by highlighting again the fourth feature of aesthetic meaning: its creative dimension. It is not just that a work of art reflects the culture of the period in which it exists but also, as Heidegger said of 'great' art like the Greek temple (which 'first gives to things their look and to men their outlook on themselves'),[93] that it contributes to the character of that culture. As Cooper puts this thought,

> We should not think of the Life to which practices, including art, are appropriate as something fixed independently of those practices. A genre of religious painting, say, may be palpably suited to the consciousness of an age while, at the same time, modifying and honing that consciousness.[94]

The reciprocity of this relationship between artwork and culture entails the inexhaustibility of which Gadamer spoke. There is, firstly, the complex, interpretative and reciprocal 'conversation' between the artwork and the performers and spectators and, secondly and equally reciprocally, between the artwork and the wider culture in which it is set. The work of art is therefore able to open up new ways of seeing, ways, which, without it, would never have existed. Perhaps it can even contribute to the development of new forms of life. As Merleau-Ponty says, the meaning of 'expression' in general does not just refer to and derive from an 'alphabet' of meanings already held in common by members of a cultural and perceptual world.[95] Language and gestures create new sense and even the pre-existing significances which constitute this alphabet must themselves at one time have been new; it is language and gesture that endow an object for the first time with a human meaning and therefore as much constitute the basis of that meaning as they are founded upon it.[96] But, in Heidegger's terms, the artwork does not just 'open up' or 'set up' a 'world' but also 'sets forth the earth'. The materiality of the work as it shines forth in the work itself seems to Heidegger, and to the other phenomenologists of art, to be semi-transparent to the mysterious and ineffable ground on which any world is necessarily founded. In Wittgenstein's terms, the ineffable is inexhaustibly spread over the whole surface of our language.[97] In my view, it is not just spread over the surface of our language but all our meaningful practices, of which some are linguistic in nature. This is just what the phenomenological account of aesthetic meaning helps us to understand. McGilchrist describes the Reformation iconoclasts' error as the failure to understand that 'divinity could find its place *between* one "thing" (the statue) and another (the beholder), rather than having to reside, fixed, in the "thing" itself'.[98] To appreciate such ambiguous, and therefore inexhaustible, 'betweenness' or semi-transparency, to reject the binary options 'either it is God, or it is a mere thing', I suggest, is a precondition to regarding such a 'thing' as a religious cipher of the ineffable.[99]

In this section, we have reviewed four features of artistic meaning which some phenomenologists of art drew out: (1) its inexhaustibility and connection with ineffability; (2) the logical inseparability of meaning from work; (3) the performative character of its expression and explanation and (4) its creative dimension. An abiding theme through all of this was the dissolution of the division between linguistic and non-linguistic forms of aesthetic experience and expression. Towards the end, we saw that artistic meaning, inseparable from the work itself, is also directed towards the meaningful fabric of life, the human world. This justifies the claim that art, as phenomenology by other means, 'opens up a world' and, in its creative dimension 'sets it up'. But, given the ineffability of the 'background' against which the world has meaning for us, the other side of this claim, as we also saw, is that art evokes the ineffable, 'sets forth the earth' on which any human world is necessarily grounded. Since what is present in the work is present in the only way available to it, this inexhaustible evocation of the ineffable is inseparable from the materiality, linguistic or non-linguistic, of the work itself. The intimacy between, indeed the identity of, the two sides of this Heideggerian claim implies that art renders 'world' transparent to 'earth'. In the work of art, as Heidegger says, 'earth juts through the world'.[100] Merleau-Ponty says that I do not just see an artwork, as if it were opaque but, in its transparency, 'I see according to it'.[101]

In a recent essay, Richard Kearney notes that, in Merleau-Ponty, this process gets described in sacramental language.[102] Merleau-Ponty makes it clear that his understanding of sacramental meaning is identical to his understanding of artistic meaning:

> Sacramental words and gestures are not simply the embodiment of some thought. Like tangible things, they are themselves the carriers of their meaning, which is inseparable from its material form. They do not evoke the idea of God: they are the vehicles of His presence and action.[103]

In the same way, just as we could say that an artist 'plucks the signs themselves – the person of the actor, or the colours and canvas of the painter – from their empirical existence and bears them off into another world',[104] so, conversely, we can say that he brings a meaning into being in *this world* in and through his work. In changing everything he wants to present into paint, or another artistic medium, the artist effects 'transubstantiations'.[105] The *Lebenswelt* to which art refers, but which it also embodies in new and creative ways, opening up novel ways of seeing which are in principle inexhaustible, is 'consecrated' by the artist. As Merleau-Ponty puts it,

> the body, the life, the landscapes, the schools, the mistresses, the creditors, the police and the revolutions which might suffocate painting are also the bread his work consecrates. To live in painting is still to breathe the air of this world.[106]

As Kearney summarizes Merleau-Ponty's 'sacramental aesthetic', 'the bread of the world is the very stuff consecrated in the body of the work: the work of art or the work of fiction'.[107]

While, like Macquarrie, Kearney draws out from this the implication that the Eucharistic imagination is not confined to the liturgies of the church but is extended to the whole of quotidian experience, it would be surprising if this idea did not have implications for a philosophical understanding of the Christian liturgies themselves. In my stated desire to remain relatively uncontroversial, it is to the latter that I now turn.

Religious Ritual

P. J. FitzPatrick has criticized both the classical and some revised, twentieth-century, accounts of the doctrine of transubstantiation on philosophical grounds. Both accounts, he argues, are touched by the 'Fallacy of Replacement', which links the meanings of words to 'loftier' criteria than usual. These criteria are made to compete with, and eventually to negate, the 'humbler' criteria, even though the conditions are present for the latter's use, as the decision is made in favour of what is more exalted.[108] In the Eucharistic case, it is said that the host *only looks* like bread. This, according to FitzPatrick, is tantamount to saying that not all the criteria for its being bread are satisfied, an assertion which, whether true or not, at least makes sense. But it does not make sense, he maintains, to say that something *only looks* like bread and, at the same time, to claim that *none* of the criteria for its being bread are absent. FitzPatrick thinks that this claim at once makes an assertion and removes the context which gives the assertion meaning. It rejects the context of investigation which is the only thing that gives sense to the distinction between the way things are and the way they appear. He describes this distinction between appearance and reality as 'theological phenomenalism' and interprets it as a theological variation on the kind of phenomenalism espoused by Bertrand Russell. Russell famously claimed that the real table at which he writes, if it exists at all, is not immediately known. What is seen and felt is the *appearance* of the table, which is taken to be a sign of some *reality* (assumed to be the real table) 'behind' it.[109] As we know, Russell's position led him to doubt whether there was a real table behind the phenomena at all.[110] FitzPatrick concludes that, if there is indeed a *philosophia perennis* underlying the Eucharistic theories (as their proponents claim), it is not the kind of philosophy which those authors had in mind but rather turns out to be a form of philosophical scepticism.[111] In a Eucharistic context, we then find ourselves unable to venture beyond the phenomena since 'all else is hazard. The gap is unbridgeable; the theology that claims to open us to transubstantiation opens us in fact to anything we fancy.'[112] FitzPatrick's suggestion is that, if theology does not want to follow Russell into scepticism, it will have to resist the distinction between appearance and reality, supposedly drawn in service of Eucharistic belief. Since it is impossible to challenge the sceptic on her own terms, it is her formulation of the problem that must be called into question. What must be challenged, in FitzPatrick's view, is the 'time-honoured Eucharistic formula' that the host looks and tastes like bread but it is not.[113] The fact that no investigation could disclose that it is *not* bread simply distracts attention from the real problem which, for FitzPatrick, is to do with the meanings of words.[114]

The Fallacy of Replacement is more pernicious than a simple mistake since it is an abuse of what FitzPatrick takes to be the supremely important insight 'into the divinely bestowed and inexhaustible character of reality, into the quasi-sacramental significance it already possesses, into the limits of all our own contrivings and describings, and into the transcendence of what the Eucharist bestows'.[115] He wants to suggest, in contrast to the existing accounts, that the exalted reality that becomes present in the Eucharist (the divine presence) does not replace the humbler present reality (the bread and wine) but that the former is discerned *in and through* the latter.[116] The 'humbler creation', to be sure, is only part of the story. 'But there would be no story at all without it.'[117] Whereas the distinction between appearance and reality causes no problems when one is talking of fools' gold (which looks like gold but is not), when speaking of the Eucharist, it cannot help us to make sense of the incoherent idea that 'every conceivable perceptual datum for something's being bread must be allowed without bread being there'.[118] FitzPatrick's attempt at the dissolution of this distinction, and his positive proposal for the understanding of the divine presence in the Eucharist, bring us onto the same territory as that of the previous section on the phenomenology of artistic meaning. He advocates what he calls the 'Way of Ritual' which is meant to be a non-reductive account of the Eucharist as a ritual, one which does not reduce a ritual to anything else and starts from the observation that '[w]hatever else the Eucharist is, it is a *rite* of some kind'.[119] FitzPatrick thinks that consideration of the Eucharist according to the Way of Ritual will avoid the Fallacy of Replacement because a proper understanding of ritual requires precisely what the Fallacy of Replacement would deny it.[120]

It is specifically as a ritual meal that the Eucharist embodies what Cooper, writing on gardens, calls the intimate 'co-dependence' of human beings and their world.[121] As FitzPatrick puts it:

> It displays the dependence of our lives upon the Earth and upon what the Earth provides, while at the same time bearing witness to the skills and force we bring to bear upon the Earth and upon what it supports, in order to prepare the food we need.[122]

This dimension of Eucharistic meaning echoes the 'setting up of world' which, according to the phenomenologists of the previous section, was effected by artworks. Not only does the Eucharist, as a kind of meal, reflect these worldly meanings of which FitzPatrick writes, but it also, as a ritual (and echoing the creative dimension of artistic meaning), hones and contributes to those meanings. However, it can do this only when, *contra* the Fallacy of Replacement and the scepticism to which this inevitably leads, the meanings are understood as being embodied in the material phenomena (the bread, words and gestures) in which the rite consists. It can do this only when those meanings are discerned, not in spite of these phenomena, but *in and through* them. Like art, the worldly dimension of the rite goes hand in hand with the more mysterious one which Heidegger called the 'earthly' or 'thingly'. To recall Cooper's favoured terminology, borrowed from D. T. Suzuki,[123] it effects a double exposure. The humble materials of the Eucharist, *qua* humble materials, concentrate in themselves the referential totality of meaning on which their own meaning depends. At the same time, the ineffable, to which that referential totality in turn is answerable, is concentrated in that web of meaning. In Heideggerian language, this ritual makes earth jut through world. It renders the meaningful world transparent to its ineffable ground and measure. In the ritual community that eats the food, FitzPatrick says,

> the meal is a communal acknowledgment of our needs, our abilities, our dependence upon each other, our mutual trust. Given all that, it is natural that a ritual meal should have been linked with the quest for God and with the awareness of God ... where our sharing is with what lacks our weaknesses, surpasses the reach of any skills we can possess.[124]

I would say: not just 'linked with' but, with Cottingham on ritual's creative dimension, a condition for. As FitzPatrick summarizes this second half of the double exposure:

> Just as the sharing of a meal is at the heart of a shared human life, so we make this special sharing into a means of uniting those who eat ... with what is greater than any life with which they are acquainted.[125]

It is in this way that the ritual of the Eucharist can evoke, for Christians, the ineffable God on which the meaning of the human world ultimately depends and with which such a God is wholly intimate. This can only happen, FitzPatrick has made clear, if 'what is exalted does not replace what is humble'.[126] He does not think that his Way of Ritual is able to *explain* the divine presence in the Eucharist since, as a non-reductive way (and like Wittgenstein's interpretation of aesthetic understanding), it ultimately refers us back to the *performance* of the ritual itself.[127] It does not eliminate the mystery of the divine presence but acknowledges the mystery by refusing to reduce it to the result of a '"technique" by which substance and accidents are manipulated' or to puzzles of our own making whose terms are not the solutions they purport to be but yet further labels for philosophical problems.[128] FitzPatrick suggests that the divine presence in the Eucharist should be seen not as concealed by the outward forms, linked with them only extrinsically, but rather as 'a ritually achieved sign [in my terms, a cipher] of [God's] presence', a presence otherwise inaccessible.[129] The ritual, like the work of art, can point to what eludes adequate expression in literal language but not by denying or downplaying the words, gestures and material realities which constitute it. This is because, although they can never be the whole story, they are the embodiments without which there would be no story at all. Ritual 'is touched by what we make of the world, while going beyond the world'.[130] In the Eucharistic ritual, as in art, the reality that we see and touch is what embodies the Ultimate Reality towards which we can *only* gesture.[131] Unlike philosophy's dialectical evocation of the ineffable, described in the previous chapter, the ineffable's ritual (and aesthetic) embodiments are, like Jaspers's ciphers, without a direct relationship to the subject–object distinction. Insofar as they embody the ineffable, aesthetic and ritual phenomena are experienced as semi-transparent, transcending the either/or dichotomy described by

McGilchrist. This thought captures the distinctive ability of art and ritual to embody the ineffable, the identity of meaning and absurdity, in a non-dialectical way. Such non-dialectical embodiment conveys at once the immediate presence of ineffable source of the human world in and through the aesthetic and ritual phenomena (which, given our Jaspersian insights on ciphers, are not here being treated as objects) and the simultaneous sense that, as ineffable, this source is nothing objective, or even determinately meaningful, but is itself determinately meaningless and, to that extent, absurd.

These reflections on the specific example of the Eucharist, which draw on FitzPatrick's critique of the Fallacy of Replacement, illustrate how the foregoing aesthetic account of ritual meaning can be appropriated by religious thought and applied in concrete and constructive ways. But given the identical operation of artistic and ritual meaning in their evocation of the ineffable, in the four respects outlined above (their autonomy, the necessarily performative character of their explanation, their double evocation of worldly meanings and that on which such meanings ultimately depend, their creative dimension), are there any reasons to prefer ritual to art as a way of evoking the ineffable? I should like to end by indicating two possible affirmative answers to this question, neither of which attenuates my aesthetic interpretation of ritual meaning.

Firstly, on a rather pragmatic note, an essential feature of a ritual is that it can be repeated.[132] This feature is what secures the closer relationship between rituals and the fabric of life. If what both art and ritual evokes is what explains the meaning of life, and if ritual turns out to have a potentially closer relationship than art to the life whose meaning both help to explain, ritual should end up being a more effective way of attuning oneself to that which explains the meaning of one's life. Cottingham takes the repeating, rhythmic nature of ritual practices, like saying morning and evening prayer and grace before meals, to be a major way in which rituals provide us with the access to the emotional depth which, rightly viewed, the religious perspective on life provides. They allow the otherwise mundane, repetitive rhythm of eating and sleeping to take on a religious significance. On a broader level, too, the shape of a life as a whole may be religiously structured, in some traditions, by the ritual structure of the liturgical year and, perhaps universally, by the marking off of significant, unique, life events by rites of passage:[133] birth by baptism, copulation by marriage and death by burial. This repetitive, rhythmic dimension which typically characterizes the experience of ritual, and which seems to constitute much of what makes it valuable to those who engage in it, does not seem to characterize the experience of art to the same degree. By contrast, much art (at any rate much Western art) seems intended to be the recipient of a 'special' kind of experience, hermetically sealed off from the quotidian realities of the rest of life: bounded by frames, locked and carefully guarded in museums and galleries.[134] Although one could make the case that the practice of experiencing art in the West has ritualistic characteristics, it does not typically invite the degree of quotidian engagement that is invited by most rituals.

Secondly, and finally, rituals do not just resemble works of art (most explicitly drama), nor do their gestures and words, like all 'expression' for Merleau-Ponty, just *mean* in an aesthetic way, they also clearly *incorporate* works of art into their structure, content and context of their performance. Altarpieces and icons just *are* religious paintings; crosses and crucifixes are religious sculptures; churches and cathedrals are pieces of religious architecture; settings of chorales and the Mass are pieces of religious music; prayers are pieces of (religious) poetic language;[135] and so on. Religious rituals are pieces of religious drama.[136] Given all of that, the claim of one of Gadamer's later essays, that the oldest of the arts had its origin in religious ritual,[137] even if it does not convince, should not surprise us. And neither should his claim, notably and controversially inherited by George Steiner,[138] that all art has to be understood in the theological terms of 'real presence'.[139] If the view that I have put forward in this chapter is right, then the inexhaustible and therefore ineffable import of such real presences ultimately depends upon ritual and aesthetic performance for its experience and expression.

Conclusion and Remarks on Further Research

My focus on one of the central Christian rites in this final chapter has been intentionally theologically uncontroversial. With respect to my broad view of religious experience, however, there is obvious affinity between my own position and the theological ones of Macquarrie and Brown. More controversially than Macquarrie's, Brown's work has sought theologically to explore spheres outside the Christian church, which can be seen to be 'sacramental' in the broad sense he advocates. But he has suggested that such a view has important implications for my own discipline, philosophy of religion, as much as for theology. As he puts it, 'The so-called argument from religious experience has been in my view altogether too narrowly conceived'.[140] I agree that the potential range of philosophy of religion's 'source material' is as great as the scope of human experience. Even all 'revealed' theology, as Macquarrie saw, is to that extent 'natural'. Not only the arts and cultural phenomena but also the whole of the natural world can become the concrete foci of religious experience, i.e. religious ciphers. In this connection, one advantage of the existential phenomenological approach I have been adopting is that a separation between the cultural and the natural is resisted:[141] traditions of interpretation condition the experience of the natural, as much as they do that of the cultural, world. As Brown suggests in a religious connection, a stone stood on its end by man has as much capacity to reveal the divine as one found pointing skywards naturally, which is doubtless why both have been found in contexts of worship.[142]

Therefore, like Brown's theological work, further research might more controversially examine, from a philosophical perspective, the potential religious significance of other aspects of the whole breadth of human experience than its more self-consciously Christian, and religious, modes. And maintaining the existential phenomenological approach I have taken here, it might examine in detail the structure of aspects of that experience. It might, for example, examine the structure of the religious experience of the body, time, space or place. Extending the focus on the philosophically neglected topic of ritual, it might also examine the potential efficacy of non-religious rituals, for example, medical ones,[143] to confer meaning on aspects of life or even life as a whole. While I have sought, in this book, to accommodate self-consciously religious practices within a doctrine of ineffability, further work might broaden the scope to include a range of non-religious practices.

However, the conceptual work carried out in this book, which was the result of a systematic attempt to work out the logical implications of the concept of ineffability, places some significant restrictions on the theological use to which such future philosophical research could be put. Tillich's remarks on the political implications of fanatical resistance to the 'breaking' of religious mythologies and Jaspers's warnings about the 'poison' of exclusive theological claims, remain at least as relevant today as when they were written. If the concept of ineffability entails anything about religious experience, it is that no one has access to the whole truth in this demesne. It would therefore be inadmissible for any theology, connected with any religion, to attempt to absorb the whole range of religious experience, thus broadly construed, into the unavoidably confined radius of its theological circle. I have been arguing that the problem of ineffability can be solved and that religious experience, language and practice can defensibly be viewed as appropriate to the concept of ineffability by being located within the philosophical framework of (what might be called) ineffabilism that I have developed. If this is so, then that appropriateness comes at the cost of giving up any theological claim to exclusivity or certainty. Acceptance of a philosophical doctrine of ineffability implies the acceptance of the integrity of doubt and uncertainty to all our epistemic practices and of the relativity and incompleteness of all human knowledge.[144] Theological knowledge is no exception. Some theologians will probably see this as too high a price to pay. But from the philosophical perspective that I have adopted and tried to develop, the future of theology as a philosophically credible epistemic practice will depend upon its ability and willingness to accept, in dialectical fashion, not only the imaginative freedom but also the doubt and uncertainty that are inescapable and intrinsic to the human condition.

NOTES

Introduction: Philosophy of Religion in the New Style

1. J. Macquarrie, *Principles of Christian Theology* (London: SCM, 1966), p. 41.
2. Tertullian, *De Praescriptione Haereticorum*, VII.15: 'Quid ergo Athenis et Hierosolymis? quid academiae et ecclesiae?'.
3. D. A. Pailin, *Groundwork of Philosophy of Religion* (Peterborough: Epworth, 1986), p. 9.
4. Macquarrie, *Principles of Christian Theology*, p. 42.
5. D. Hume, *Dialogues Concerning Natural Religion* (Edinburgh: William Blackwood and Sons, 1907). I. Kant, *Critique of Pure Reason*, trans. F. Haywood (London: William Pickering, 1848), p. 406 ff.
6. For a more thorough and detailed criticism, see J. Macquarrie, *In Search of Deity: An Essay in Dialectical Theism (The Gifford Lectures Delivered at the University of St Andrews in Session 1983–4)* (London: SCM, 1984), ch. 3: 'A Critique of Classical Theism'. For my own part, I critically engage with the recent modal reformulation of the ontological argument at greater length in Chapter 3, below.
7. Macquarrie, *Principles of Christian Theology*, p. 43.
8. Ibid., pp. 45, 42. See also Chapter 3, below.
9. J. G. Cottingham, 'What Difference Does it Make?: The Nature and Significance of Theistic Belief', *Ratio*, 19 (2006), pp. 401–20.
10. Macquarrie, *Principles of Christian Theology*, p. 45.
11. Ibid., p. 48.
12. S. Freud, *The Future of an Illusion*, trans. J. A. Underwood (London: Penguin, 2004), pp. 31–2.
13. Macquarrie, *Principles of Christian Theology*, pp. 50–1.
14. Macquarrie, *In Search of Deity*, pp. 12–13.
15. G. A. Bennett-Hunter, 'Natural Theology and Literature', in R. Re Manning (ed.), *The Oxford Handbook of Natural Theology* (Oxford: Oxford University Press, 2013), pp. 551–65.
16. Macquarrie, *In Search of Deity*, p. 12.
17. Freud, *The Future of an Illusion*, p. 33. The question of reason's limitations is discussed in more detail in Chapter 5, below.
18. J. G. Cottingham, *The Spiritual Dimension: Religion, Philosophy and Human Value* (Cambridge: Cambridge University Press, 2005), p. ix; J. G. Cottingham, 'What is Humane Philosophy and Why is it At Risk?', in A. O'Hear (ed.), *Conceptions of Philosophy*, Royal Institute of Philosophy Supplement, 65 (2009), pp. 233–55; I. J. Kidd, 'Humane Philosophy and the Question of Progress', *Ratio*, 25 (2012), pp. 277–90.

1 Ineffability and Religion

1. A. Plé, 'Mysticism and Mystery', in A. Plé (ed.), *Mystery and Mysticism: A Symposium* (London: Blackfriars Publications, 1956), pp. 1–17, on p. 5.
2. He writes: 'As has been seen in these mystery texts, while there is something secret or hidden (Col. 1:26; Eph. 3:9); that it was unknown in other generations (Eph. 3:5), but that it was now revealed (Eph. 3:5), manifested (Col. 1:26), declared (1 Cor. 2:7; 15:51; Col. 4:3), explained (Apoc. 17:7), it is brought to light (Eph. 3:9), it is seen (1 Cor. 13:2), and known (Eph. 1:9; 3:3; 6:19; Col. 1:27; 2:2; Matt. 13:11; compare Rom. 11:26)'. Plé, 'Mysticism and Mystery', pp. 7–8.
3. Compare Colossians 1:15.
4. Acts 2:33.
5. Plé, 'Mysticism and Mystery', pp. 3, 1.
6. L. Bouyer, 'Mysterion', in Plé (ed.), *Mystery and Mysticism*, pp. 18–32, on pp. 19–20.
7. Ibid., pp. 20–2.
8. Ibid., p. 24.
9. For a vast amount of detail on this, and the complex historical relationship between '*mysterion*', '*mysterium*' and '*sacramentum*', see B. N. Gordon-Taylor, 'Mystery: A Neglected Aspect of First-Millennium Western Liturgy' (PhD dissertation, Durham University, 2007), esp. ch. 5.
10. L. Bouyer, 'Mysticism: An Essay on the History of a Word', in Plé (ed.), *Mystery and Mysticism: A Symposium*, pp. 119–37, on pp. 129–31.
11. Ibid., pp. 130, 128. By way of support, Bouyer cites Gregory of Nyssa's *Contra Eunomium*.
12. His influence on Vatican II and on Roman Catholic liturgy, and that of other churches, since then is recorded by G. Guiver, *Pursuing the Mystery: Worship and Daily Life as Presences of God* (London: SPCK, 1996), p. 73.
13. To take an example of criticism, Gordon-Taylor, 'Mystery', p. 152, draws attention to Casel's (and his translator's) misquotation of Ambrose. They quote him as saying 'I find you in your mysteries' (O. Casel, *The Mystery of Christian Worship and Other Writings*, ed. B. Neunheuser (London: Darton, Longman and Todd, 1962), p. 7 and n. 2.) whereas the Latin original is 'te tuis invenio sacramentis'. For Gordon-Taylor, this failure on the part of Casel, and his translator, to distinguish between 'mysterium' and 'sacramentum' is enough to call into question their use of the word 'mystery' and to justify Gordon-Taylor's own attempt 'to go beyond and behind Casel'.
14. Casel, *The Mystery of Christian Worship*, p. 97.
15. Ibid., p. 98.
16. Ibid., p. 100.
17. Ibid., p. 40.
18. Guiver, *Pursuing the Mystery*, p. 61.
19. See n. 13, above.
20. Gordon-Taylor, 'Mystery', p. 29.
21. Ibid.
22. J. Toland, *Christianity Not Mysterious: Or, a Treatise Shewing, That There is Nothing in the Gospel Contrary to Reason Nor Above it: And That no Christian Doctrine can be Properly Call'd a Mystery* (New York: Garland Publishing, 1978).
23. Ibid., p. 104. Plé and Toland also share references to Eph. 3:1–6, 9 and 1 Cor. 2:7–8.
24. Toland, *Christianity Not Mysterious*, pp. 96–7. Compare Plé, 'Mysticism and Mystery', p. 5.

25. Toland, *Christianity Not Mysterious*, p. 98.
26. Tillich, too, wishes to avoid 'wrong or confusing' uses of 'mystery'. A mystery is not, he says, 'something which ceases to be a mystery after it has been revealed', nor something which could be 'discovered by a methodical cognitive approach'. Neither is it what is 'not known today, but which might possibly be known tomorrow'. P. Tillich, *Systematic Theology*, 3 vols (Welwyn: James Nisbet & Co., 1968), vol. 1, p. 122.
27. S. D. Boyer, 'The Logic of Mystery', *Religious Studies*, 43 (2007) pp. 89–102, on p. 89.
28. Ibid., pp. 90–1.
29. Ibid., p. 91.
30. Ibid. This kind of claim can also be found in the writings of theologians such as Rahner (see n. 48, below) and J. Macquarrie, *Mystery and Truth: The 1970 Pere Marquette Theology Lecture* (Milwaukee, WI: Marquette University Theology Department, 1973), pp. 55–98. The present paper by Boyer is the fullest attempt I know of philosophically to articulate and defend such a position. His recent book co-authored with Christopher A. Hall deals with related issues from a theological, rather than a philosophical, perspective and is less relevant to the argument of the present book. C. A. Hall and S. D. Boyer, *The Mystery of God: Theology for Knowing the Unknowable* (Grand Rapids, MI: Baker Academic, 2012).
31. E. A. Abbott, *Flatland: A Romance of Many Dimensions* (Oxford: Oxford University Press, 2006).
32. Boyer, 'The Logic of Mystery', p. 102, n. 23. See Bennett-Hunter, 'Natural Theology and Literature', where I draw out this connection in more detail.
33. Boyer, 'The Logic of Mystery', p. 96.
34. Ibid., p. 97.
35. Ibid.
36. Ibid., p. 99.
37. Abbott, *Flatland*, p. 104.
38. Compare Macquarrie, *Mystery and Truth*, p. 87.
39. It is also able to circumvent, without resorting to idealism, Santayana's critique of Herbert Spencer that nothing can be intrinsically unknowable because 'unknowable' only describes something in its accidental relation to the human perspective (a potential, but unsuccessful, knower). This is because existential phenomenology defines everything in terms of its relation to the human contribution. The ineffable then becomes the one and only exception to this general principle. G. Santayana, *The Unknowable: The Herbert Spencer Lecture Delivered at Oxford, 24 October, 1923* (Oxford: Clarendon Press, 1923).
40. C. Yannaras, *On the Absence and Unknowability of God: Heidegger and the Areopagite*, ed. A. Louth, trans. H. Ventis (London: T&T Clark International, 2005), pp. 55, 66.
41. D. Turner, *The Darkness of God: Negativity in Christian Mysticism* (Cambridge: Cambridge University Press, 1995), p. 19.
42. A. Kenny, 'Worshipping an Unknown God', *Ratio*, 19 (2006), pp. 441–53, on p. 443.
43. Compare L. Kołakowski, *Metaphysical Horror* (Oxford: Blackwell, 1988), p. 29 ff.
44. Pseudo-Dionysius the Areopagite, *The Divine Names*, 824B.
45. J. Hick, 'Ineffability', *Religious Studies*, 36 (2000), pp. 35–46, on p. 38.
46. D. W. Brown, *God and Mystery in Words: Experience through Metaphor and Drama* (Oxford: Oxford University Press, 2008), e.g. p. 18. Brown's conception of mystery is stronger and more consonant with our notion of 'ineffability' than Casel's.
47. Ibid., p. 22.
48. This tension is often acknowledged, more or less explicitly, but rarely given any substantial philosophical treatment. For example, K. Rahner, 'The Hiddenness of God',

in *Theological Investigations*, trans. D. Morland, 23 vols (London: Darton, Longman & Todd, 1979), vol. 16, pp. 227–43, acknowledges the tension (p. 229) but, perhaps owing to his overconfident suggestion that 'we should not be worried about whether we are concerned with philosophy or theology' (p. 235), fails to explain just how divine revelation can be understood not as the 'unveiling' of God but as the 'presence' of God precisely as unknowable (p. 237). In this essay, he does no more than to restate the same philosophical problem in different, theological terms.

49. G. Marcel, 'On the Ontological Mystery', in *The Philosophy of Existence*, trans. M. Harari (London: Harvill Press, 1948), pp. 1–31, on p. 15.
50. I have just been arguing that the concepts are not the same but I shall attempt to find a place for the notion of inexhaustibility in the final chapter.
51. W. James, *The Varieties of Religious Experience* (New York: Mentor Books, 1958), pp. 292–3.
52. A. Kukla, *Ineffability and Philosophy* (London: Routledge, 2005), p. 74.
53. Ibid., p. 3.
54. W. P. Alston, 'Ineffability', *Philosophical Review*, 65 (1956), pp. 506–22, on p. 506.
55. W. T. Stace, quoted ibid., p. 507.
56. Ibid., pp. 519, 522. This is also described by Kołakowski as a version of the 'self-reference antinomy'. Kołakowski, *Metaphysical Horror*, p. 44 and, by Cooper, as a 'paradox of ineffability'. D. E. Cooper, 'Ineffability and Religious Experience', in A. de Nicholás and E. Moutsopoulos (eds), *God: Experience or Origin?* (New York: Paragon House, 1985), pp. 189–99, on p. 193. For the same reason, Yandell describes the claim that God is literally ineffable as 'necessarily false'. K. E. Yandell, *The Epistemology of Religious Experience* (Cambridge: Cambridge University Press, 1993), pp. 61–2.
57. W. P. Alston, *Perceiving God: The Epistemology of Religious Experience* (Ithaca, NY: Cornell University Press, 1991), pp. 31–2.
58. J. Kellenburger, 'The Ineffabilities of Mysticism', *American Philosophical Quarterly*, 16 (1979), pp. 307–15, on p. 307. This fourth option seems to be the one preferred by Alston in his early work.
59. Kukla, *Ineffability and Philosophy*, p. 3.
60. He writes, 'the charge of self-refutation applies to any claim to the effect that some being or process or feature or event or thing is indescribable' (Ibid., p. 5) and 'there is no entity that cannot be described'(Ibid., p. 9).
61. Ibid., p. 4.
62. Ibid., p. 53.
63. Cooper, 'Ineffability and Religious Experience', pp. 193–4.
64. Ibid., p. 194.
65. Ibid. It will become clearer that Cooper does not subscribe to this last idea but is here setting out equally unattractive alternatives.
66. Ibid., pp. 194–5.
67. Ibid., p. 195.
68. W. P. Alston, 'Lecture I: The Divine Mystery Thesis', *Divine Mystery and Our Knowledge of God*, Nathaniel William Taylor Lectures, Yale Divinity School, 11 October 2005, at http://www.goodnewsline.com/pastoral_resource/lecture_in.htm [accessed October 2008].
69. Ibid.
70. Ibid.
71. Ibid.

72. Ibid.
73. R. Mason, *Understanding Understanding* (Albany: State University of New York Press, 2003), p. 102.
74. Cooper, 'Ineffability and Religious Experience, p. 193.
75. Alston, 'Ineffability', p. 519; Alston, *Perceiving God*, pp. 31–2. Although Yandell adopts a very similar position to Alston's, he does not discuss this possibility in his critique of various versions of the claim of divine ineffability. Yandell, *The Epistemology of Religious Experience*, Part 2: 'The Challenge from Ineffability'.
76. A. W. Moore, 'Ineffability and Religion', *European Journal of Philosophy*, 11 (2003), pp. 161–76.
77. This is perhaps a little too close for comfort to the unsatisfactory argument, outlined above (the reaction to the supposed self-stultification of statements of the form 'x is ineffable'), that it is not a certain x which is ineffable but a certain experience or state of knowledge.
78. Moore, 'Ineffability and Religion', p. 169.
79. Ibid.
80. Ibid., p. 168.
81. Ibid., p. 172.
82. D. E. Cooper, *The Measure of Things: Humanism, Humility and Mystery* (Oxford: Clarendon Press, 2002), p. 291 n. 26.
83. Ibid., p. 291.
84. Kukla, *Ineffability and Philosophy*, p. 52.
85. D. E. Cooper, 'The Inaugural Address: Ineffability', *Proceedings of the Aristotelian Society, Supplementary Volume*, 65 (1991), pp. 1–15, on p. 14.
86. Kukla, *Ineffability and Philosophy*, p. 53.
87. This focus, as we shall see, owes to Cooper's sympathy with the existential phenomenological viewpoint. It is important to observe in this connection that Cooper's argument does not turn, as Kukla's argument from epistemic boundedness seems to, on there being any limitations to scientific enquiry.
88. Cooper, 'Ineffability and Religious Experience', p. 198.
89. Ibid., p. 196. The import of Wittgenstein's relevant comments is that the sense of a piece of music or a poem is conveyed precisely in and through its performance or reading and could not be exhaustively stated independently of such a performance. We shall return to this argument in the final chapter.
90. Ibid.
91. This issue is addressed in Chapter 3, below.
92. Cooper, 'Ineffability and Religious Experience', p. 197.
93. Ibid., p. 198.
94. D. E. Cooper, 'Mystery, World and Religion', in J. Cornwell and M. McGhee (eds), *Philosophers and God: At the Frontiers of Faith and Reason* (London: Continuum, 2009), pp. 51–62, on p. 54. Compare Alston's suggestion, above, that if I can experience something I must also be able to apply at least some concepts to it.
95. Ibid.
96. D. M. MacKinnon, 'Some Epistemological Reflections on Mystical Experience', in S. T. Katz (ed.), *Mysticism and Philosophical Analysis* (London: Sheldon Press, 1978), pp. 132–40, on p. 135.
97. Ibid., p. 136.

2 Philosophical Defence of the Concept of Ineffability

1. Cooper, *The Measure of Things*; Cooper, 'Life and Meaning', *Ratio* 18 (2005), pp. 125–37.
2. Cooper, *The Measure of Things*, p. 280.
3. Cooper, 'Life and Meaning', pp. 126–7.
4. The capitalized term, which I adopt in this chapter, is meant to convey Dilthey's sense of *das Leben*, life as the 'permanent subject' of meaning. It is also intended to rule out any purely biological senses of the word. Ibid., p. 126.
5. M. Heidegger, *Being and Time*, trans. J. Macquarrie and E. Robinson (New York: Harper & Row, 1962), p. 116.
6. Cooper, 'Life and Meaning', p. 126. He defends this definition at length in D. E. Cooper, *Meaning* (Chesham: Acumen, 2003).
7. Cooper, *The Measure of Things*, p. 239.
8. Ibid., p. 18.
9. Ibid.
10. Ibid., p. 249. See Heidegger, *Being and Time*, p. 228 ff.
11. Cooper, *The Measure of Things*, p. 251.
12. Heidegger, *Being and Time*, pp. 232, 435.
13. Cooper, *The Measure of Things*, p. 251.
14. J.-P. Sartre, *Nausea*, trans. R. Baldick (Harmondsworth: Penguin, 1965), p. 182.
15. Cooper, 'Life and Meaning', p. 128.
16. J. Calder, *The Philosophy of Samuel Beckett* (London: Calder Publications, 2001), p. 3.
17. S. Beckett, *Acte Sans Parole II*, translated in *The Complete Dramatic Works* (London: Faber & Faber, 1986), pp. 207–11.
18. Cooper, *The Measure of Things*, p. 270–1.
19. Calder, *The Philosophy of Samuel Beckett*, p. 61. Italics mine.
20. Cooper, 'Life and Meaning', p. 128.
21. I argue this point in more detail in G. A. Bennett-Hunter, 'Absurd Creation: An Existentialist View of Art?, *Philosophical Frontiers*, 4 (2009), pp. 49–58.
22. Cooper, 'Life and Meaning', p. 136.
23. Ibid., p. 132.
24. Ibid.
25. Ibid., pp. 132–3.
26. Ibid., p. 134.
27. Ibid.
28. Ibid., p. 279 ff.; Cooper, 'Mystery, World and Religion', p. 54.
29. Cooper, *The Measure of Things*, p. 280.
30. Ibid., p. 296 ff., 292 ff. For the relevant distinction, contra the charge of self-stultification, between talking 'about' and talking '"about"' the ineffable, see ibid., p. 286.
31. Although, for the person of a theological turn of mind, the reason for this neglect may be difficult to fathom, it can be explained in terms of Cooper's personal interest in and sympathy for Eastern and Asian traditions and in terms of his failure to see how the Christian significance of, say, Christ could be fitted into his framework (personal communication). In some recent work, with which I deal in a later chapter, Cooper has explored the extent to which a life responsive to a sense of ineffability might invite the label 'religious'. However, in another recent article (Cooper, 'Mystery, World and Religion', p. 61), he has written explicitly on the relation of his notion of mystery to that of the more recondite God of negative theology in the Christian tradition. Here, he writes

that he does not understand the need to introduce the word 'God' to name the mystery. If it is used in order to identify the mystery as the appropriate 'object' of attitudes and practices like fear, love and worship (ones 'that belong to, or intelligibly derive from, a traditional stance towards God as a person'), then Cooper thinks this use indefensible. For we would need to know more about mystery than is, by definition, possible in order for these attitudes, and thus this use of the word 'God', to be appropriate. It is a major aim of this book to show how religious experience, language and practices may be thought of as appropriate to, consonant with, this concept of ineffability.

32. Cooper, *The Measure of Things*, p. 279.
33. I return, more explicitly, to religious concerns in the following chapter after clarifying the notion of ineffability and illustrating how a doctrine of ineffability is at work in Heidegger's later thought.
34. Ibid., pp. 317–8. The other danger for the 'transcendent conception', if it did not do this, would be for it to invoke the concept of mystery and leave matters there since what it refers to is undiscursable. But in this case Cooper's objection to the Kantian 'two-levels' position would still have to be answered. There are problems even given the alternative existential phenomenological doctrine of engagement: either something is part of the human world or it is not. If it is, then it is conceptualizable and if it is not, then it is ineffable. There is no way to bridge the logical gap between the 'two levels' and thus legitimately to describe one level as being answerable to, or measure-providing for, the other.
35. Cooper, 'Life and Meaning', p. 135.
36. Ibid.
37. Ibid.
38. Ibid., p. 137.
39. Cooper, *The Measure of Things*, p. 327. We can here see the full significance of Cooper's wish, recorded at the end of the previous chapter, to dissolve the subjective and objective dimensions to the notion of experience.
40. J. Young, *Heidegger's Later Philosophy* (Cambridge: Cambridge University Press, 2002), pp. 10–12.
41. M. Heidegger, 'The Origin of the Work of Art', in *Basic Writings*, ed. D. F. Krell, 2nd edn (London: Routledge, 1993), pp. 139–212.
42. Ibid., pp. 194, 172, 172, 174, 168.
43. Young, *Heidegger's Later Philosophy*, p. 13.
44. Cooper, *The Measure of Things*, p. 292.
45. One piece of primary evidence to support this claim can be found at M. Heidegger, 'Letter on Humanism', in *Basic Writings*, ed. Krell, 2nd edn, pp. 213–65, on p. 236.
46. Young, *Heidegger's Later Philosophy*, p. 12 ff. With some qualifications, Young even identifies Being with God. Young, *Heidegger's Later Philosophy*, p. 22.
47. Cooper, *The Measure of Things*, pp. 292–3.
48. M. Heidegger, 'On the Essence of Truth', in *Basic Writings*, ed. Krell, 2nd edn, pp. 115–138, on pp. 125, 129.
49. Ibid., pp. 129–30.
50. This can be seen, for example, ibid., p. 236 and M. Heidegger, 'The Thing', in *Poetry, Language, Thought*, trans. A. Hofstadter (New York: Harper & Row, 2001), pp. 161–84, on p. 176.
51. Heidegger, 'On the Essence of Truth', pp. 137–8.
52. S. L. Bartky, 'Originative Thinking in the Later Philosophy of Heidegger', *Philosophy and Phenomenological Research*, 30 (1970), pp. 368–81, on pp. 372–3.

53. Heidegger, *Being and Time*, p. 255 and n. 1.
54. Heidegger, 'Letter on Humanism', p. 238.
55. Ibid., p. 239.
56. Heidegger, 'The Thing', p. 174; M. Heidegger, *What is Called Thinking?*, trans. J. G. Gray (New York: Harper & Row, 1968), pp. 8–9.
57. Ibid., p. 9.
58. Ibid.
59. Heidegger, *Being and Time*, p. 62; Heidegger, 'Letter on Humanism', pp. 240, 234. The gender exclusive language is Heidegger's. I follow this purely for the sake of clarity.
60. Heidegger, 'Letter on Humanism', p. 231.
61. This partly rhetorical point should perhaps be put less strongly and more explicitly from the perspective of the human world. We could say that Being comes to presence in a way of which we humans cannot but conceive in the terms of 'need' or necessity.
62. Heidegger, 'Letter on Humanism', pp. 234, 240.
63. Ibid., pp. 240, 234. In the language of 'The Origin of the Work of Art', the relevant experience is of the transparency of 'world' to 'earth'. See J. Young, *Heidegger's Philosophy of Art* (Cambridge: Cambridge University Press, 2001), pp. 44–45.
64. It is worth flagging up, at this point, the fact that Heidegger's relationship with the language of 'experience', in this connection, is an ambiguous one. It is perhaps motivated by a dissatisfaction, like Cooper's, with the division of subjective from objective dimensions to the concept.
65. Heidegger's relationship with the term 'philosophy' is also ambiguous. It is my view, which I do not defend here (but see G. A. Bennett-Hunter, 'Heidegger on Philosophy and Language', *Philosophical Writings* 35 (2007), pp. 5–16 where I do defend it), that the later Heidegger's project, as the main text is about to describe it, is essentially the same whether he calls it 'philosophy' or 'thinking'. Thus, for the sake of clarity, I here use only the latter term.
66. M. Heidegger, *What is Philosophy?*, trans. W. Kluback and J. T. Wild (London: Vision, 1958), pp. 69, 77, 23.
67. G. Steiner, *Heidegger*, 2nd edn (London: Fontana, 1992), p. 29.
68. Ibid., p. 32; Heidegger, *What is Philosophy?*, p. 77.
69. Steiner, *Heidegger*, p. 29.
70. Heidegger. *What is Philosophy?*, pp. 54–5. We shall return to the connection, in thinking, between 'Being (*Sein*)' and 'being (*das Seiende*)'.
71. Bartky, 'Originative Thinking in the Later Philosophy of Heidegger', p. 369.
72. M. Heidegger, *Discourse on Thinking*, trans. J. M. Anderson and E. H. Freund (New York: Harper & Row, 1966), p. 55.
73. Heidegger, 'The Origin of the Work of Art', p. 172.
74. Heidegger, 'Letter on Humanism', p. 251; Heidegger, *Discourse on Thinking*, p. 46.
75. This is the case at least in the writings that he intended for publication. Consider, by contrast, the bizarre linguistic formulations found in the *Contributions to Philosophy*, which could be interpreted as attempts to eschew the language of 'experience'.
76. Heidegger, 'Letter on Humanism', p. 248.
77. Heidegger, *What is Called Thinking?*, p. 55. Compare Heidegger, *What is Philosophy?*, p. 71.
78. Heidegger, *Discourse on Thinking*, pp. 58–90.
79. Ibid., p. 22.
80. Ibid., p. 69.

81. T. Clark, *Martin Heidegger* (London: Routledge, 2002), p. 88. See also Bennett-Hunter, 'Heidegger on Philosophy and Language', pp. 13–15.
82. Heidegger, *Discourse on Thinking*, p. 54 and n. 4. This editorial note points out the origin of the term '*Gelassenheit*' in the German mystical tradition, notably in Eckhart.
83. Ibid., p. 64.
84. See Cooper, *The Measure of Things*, p. 292. Alternatively, the 'region' could be compared to the '*Sein*' of '*es gibt Sein*' and 'that-which-regions' to '*es*'.
85. Heidegger, *Discourse on Thinking*, p. 68.
86. Ibid., pp. 72–3.
87. Ibid., p. 55.
88. Heidegger, 'On the Essence of Truth', p. 127.
89. Heidegger, *What is Called Thinking?*, p. 79.
90. Heidegger, 'Letter on Humanism', p. 240.
91. Bartky, 'Originative Thinking in the Later Philosophy of Heidegger', p. 374.
92. Cooper, *The Measure of Things*, p. 328.
93. See Heidegger, 'On the Essence of Truth', p. 137. My interpretation of the archaism *Seyn* on the basis of this passage goes against that of Young who identifies it with the use of *Sein* which includes the 'earth' dimension. (See Young, *Heidegger's Later Philosophy*, p. 13.) It is interesting to note that our epistemological activity is forced to work in strict opposition to this ontological flow i.e. from beings to Being. A comparison could be made with Aquinas who argues that whereas, ontologically speaking, attributes apply 'pre-eminently' to God and to creatures only by analogy, epistemologically, the finite human mind is forced to operate in a contrary manner as if the attributes applied pre-eminently to creatures and then apply them to God by analogy. Perhaps Heidegger had read Aquinas during his theological training.
94. J. Young, 'The Fourfold', in C. B. Guignon (ed.), *The Cambridge Companion to Heidegger*, 2nd edn (Cambridge: Cambridge University Press, 2006), pp. 373–92, on p. 373. Compare M. Heidegger, *Poetry, Language, Thought*, trans. Hofstadter, p. 197. Young's reference to Heidegger is incorrect.
95. Young, *Heidegger's Later Philosophy*, p. 16; Heidegger, 'The Thing', p. 171 (see also this passage for evidence against Young's interpretation of the fourfold as 'world' in the ontical sense. There, Heidegger speaks of the fourfold as '[p]receding everything that is present').
96. Ibid., p. 172.
97. Ibid., p. 179.
98. Cooper, *The Measure of Things*, p. 322.
99. Ibid., p. 330; Heidegger, *Discourse on Thinking*, p. 61.
100. Heidegger, *What is Called Thinking?*, p. 16; for a more detailed discussion of the topic of language in the later Heidegger, relevant to the issues raised in this paragraph, see Bennett-Hunter, 'Heidegger on Philosophy and Language'.
101. Heidegger, *What is Philosophy?*, p. 93. See Bennett-Hunter, 'Heidegger on Philosophy and Language', pp. 11–12 for a discussion of this etymological mode of argument.
102. Heidegger, *What is Philosophy?*, p. 92 ('this corresponding is a speaking' (p. 93)).
103. M. Heidegger, 'The Nature of Language', in *On The Way to Language*, trans. P. D. Hertz (San Francisco, CA: Harper & Row, 1971) pp. 55–108, on p. 57.
104. M. Heidegger, 'The Way to Language', in *Basic Writings*, ed. Krell, 2nd edn, pp. 393–426, on p. 411.
105. Heidegger, 'Letter on Humanism', p. 265.

164   Notes to pages 36–41

106. D. E. Cooper, *Heidegger* (London: Claridge, 1996), p. 84.
107. Heidegger, 'The Way to Language', p. 423.
108. Heidegger, 'Letter on Humanism', p. 237.
109. Cooper, *Heidegger*, p. 86.
110. Heidegger, 'Letter on Humanism', p. 234.
111. Steiner, *Heidegger*, p. 7.
112. M. Heidegger, 'Hölderlin and the Essence of Poetry', trans. D. Scott, in *Existence and Being* (London: Vision, 1949), pp. 293–315, on p. 300.
113. Ibid., p. 307.
114. Ibid., p. 304. Italics mine.
115. Ibid.
116. See L. Wittgenstein, *Culture and Value*, trans. P. Winch (Oxford: Blackwell, 1980), p. 84; G. Steiner, 'A Reading against Shakespeare', in *No Passion Spent: Essays 1978–1996* (London: Faber & Faber, 1996), pp. 108–28, on p. 121.
117. Ibid.
118. Ibid., p. 122.
119. See Scaliger, quoted in M. H. Abrams, *The Mirror and the Lamp: Romantic Theory and the Critical Tradition* (New York: Oxford University Press, 1953), p. 273. See ch. 10, section iii for an interesting survey of the idea of heterocosm in Romantic criticism.
120. Cooper, *The Measure of Things*, p. 292.
121. M. Heidegger, '" ... Poetically Man Dwells ... "', in *Poetry, Language, Thought*, trans. Hofstadter, pp. 209–27.
122. M. Heidegger, 'Building, Dwelling, Thinking', in *Poetry, Language, Thought*, trans. Hofstadter, pp. 141–59, on p. 145.
123. Heidegger, *What is Called Thinking?*, pp. 191, 193; Heidegger, *Discourse on Thinking*, p. 55. Compare Cooper's notion of 'measure'.
124. Cooper, *The Measure of Things*, p. 295.

3 Two Attempts at Theological Appropriation

1. Compare the weaker kind of ineffability ascribed to colours and certain bodily sensations in Cooper, 'Ineffability and Religious Experience', pp. 190–1.
2. Alston, 'Lecture I: The Divine Mystery Thesis'.
3. I shall return to the alternative possibility of 'God' referring to a necessarily existent entity later in the chapter.
4. S. Pihlström, *Structuring the World: The Issue of Realism and the Nature of Ontological Problems in Classical and Contemporary Pragmatism*, Acta Philosophica Fennica, vol. 59 (Helsinki: The Philosophical Society of Finland, 1996), p. 123. See also n. 51, below.
5. See http://dictionary.oed.com/, s.v. [accessed October 2008]. The word is not hyphenated.
6. The term was apparently coined by Kant (and his translators), with a meaning very different from Heidegger's (see I. D. Thomson, *Heidegger on Ontotheology: Technology and the Politics of Education* (Cambridge: Cambridge University Press, 2005), p. 7 and n. 1). Kant, *Critique of Pure Reason*, p. 439.
7. J. W. Robins, 'The Problem of Ontotheology: Complicating the Divide between Philosophy and Theology', *Heythrop Journal*, 43 (2002), pp. 139–51, on p. 139.
8. Thomson, *Heidegger on Ontotheology*, p. 2.

9. M. Heidegger, *Identity and Difference*, trans. J. Stambaugh (New York: Harper & Row, 1969), p. 72. For more detail on Heidegger's original conception of ontotheology, see Thomson, *Heidegger on Ontotheology*, ch. 1: 'Ontotheology? Understanding Heidegger's Deconstruction of Metaphysics'.
10. D. Turner, *Faith, Reason and the Existence of God* (Cambridge: Cambridge University Press, 2004), p. 27. Turner stresses that, although ontotheological error may exist in the history of theology, there are important figures who avoid it. In particular, he wants to salvage Bonaventure and, like Macquarrie, Eckhart and Thomas Aquinas.
11. See, for example, M. Westphal, 'Overcoming Onto-theology [*sic*]', in M. Westphal, *Overcoming Onto-theology [sic]: Toward a Postmodern Christian Faith* (New York: Fordham University Press, 2001), pp. 1–28, on p. 2; A. J. Godzieba, 'Ontotheology to Excess: Imagining God without Being', *Theological Studies*, 56 (1995), pp. 3–20, on p. 7.
12. Heidegger, *Identity and Difference*, p. 72.
13. Turner, *Faith, Reason and the Existence of God*, p. 28.
14. Heidegger, *Identity and Difference*, p. 72. In his characteristic etymologizing manner, Heidegger includes *two* hyphens in 'onto-theo-logic'.
15. Steiner, *Heidegger*, pp. xvi–ii. Here, Steiner charts Heidegger's progression from his pre-seminarial origins, through his claim of 1921: 'I am a Christian theologian', to his later flat refusal to form opinions on theological issues. A well-known example of the latter can be found in Heidegger, *Identity and Difference*, pp. 54–5, where Heidegger writes: 'Someone who has experienced theology in his own roots, both the theology of the Christian faith and that of philosophy, would today rather remain silent about God when he is speaking in the realm of thinking ... [etc.]'.
16. Heidegger, 'Letter on Humanism', p. 253.
17. See, for instance, ibid., p. 251, where he shows uncharacteristic optimism about the potential mileage in the concept of God. There, he writes, 'When one proclaims "God" the altogether "highest value," this is a degradation of God's essence'.
18. C. O. Schrag, *God as Otherwise Than Being: Toward a Semantics of the Gift* (Evanston, IL: Northwestern University Press, 2002), p. 68.
19. Tillich, *Systematic Theology*, vol. 1, p. 24.
20. Ibid.
21. Ibid., p. 120.
22. Ibid., p. 122.
23. Ibid., p. 121.
24. Ibid., p. 187.
25. Ibid., p. 227.
26. Ibid., p. 191.
27. See Marcel, 'On the Ontological Mystery'.
28. I shall return to some of the detail of Tillich's use of Heidegger when discussing some objections to it.
29. Tillich, *Systematic Theology*, vol. 1, p. 191. Italics mine.
30. Ibid., p. 227.
31. Ibid., pp. 262–3.
32. Ibid., p. 301.
33. Ibid., p. 227.
34. Ibid.
35. A. Thatcher, *The Ontology of Paul Tillich* (Oxford: Oxford University Press, 1978), p. 85, n. 39.

36. P. Tillich, *The Courage to Be* (London: Nisbet, 1952), p. 175.
37. Tillich, *Systematic Theology*, vol. 1, p. 191.
38. See, for example, S. Hook, 'The Atheism of Paul Tillich', in S. Hook (ed.), *Religious Experience and Truth: A Symposium* (London: Oliver & Boyd, 1962), pp. 59–64.
39. Compare Tillich, *Systematic Theology*, vol. 1, pp. 227–33.
40. Macquarrie, *Principles of Christian Theology*, p. 41.
41. For the detail of his criticism of Classical Theism, see Macquarrie, *In Search of Deity*, ch. 3: 'A Critique of Classical Theism'.
42. Ibid., p. 31.
43. Macquarrie, *Principles of Christian Theology*, p. 45.
44. Ibid.
45. Macquarrie, *In Search of Deity*, p. 27. This an interesting consequence of the notion of ineffability to which we shall return.
46. Ibid., p. 172.
47. Ibid., p. 186. I shall return to the other pole of Macquarrie's dialectic, implied by the final phrase of this quotation, in the next section.
48. Ibid., p. 167.
49. Macquarrie, *Principles of Christian Theology*, pp. 105–6. Herman Philipse has thoroughly described what he takes to be the major 'paralellisms and analogies' between the 'postmonotheist' leitmotif in Heidegger's writing after 1935 and traditional Christian theology (see H. Philipse, *Heidegger's Philosophy of Being* (Princeton, NJ: Princeton University Press, 1998), pp. 189–201). Philipse is of the opinion that the intelligibility of the language of Being, with which he sees Heidegger attempting to replace traditional religious discourse, depends upon such 'structural paralellisms' (ibid., p. 187).
50. This dualism is a problematic aspect of Tillich's thought to which I shall return.
51. The precise connection between the concepts of meaning and existence that I have in mind is the one made by Kołakowski as he reads Husserl: '"Existence" itself is a certain "sense" of an object. Consequently it would be absurd ... to say that an object "exists" independently of the meaning of the word "to exist" – independently of the act of constitution performed by the consciousness'. L. Kołakowski, *Husserl and the Search for Certitude* (London: Yale University Press, 1975), p. 65. Certain classical and contemporary pragmatist philosophers have a strikingly similar view of the most basic ontological categories (Pihlström, *Structuring the World*, p. 123).
52. See the 'Conclusion' to W. J. Richardson, *Heidegger: Through Phenomenology to Thought* (The Hague: Nijhoff, 1963).
53. C. O. Schrag, 'The Three Heideggers', in C. O. Schrag, *Philosophical Papers: Betwixt and Between* (Albany, NY: State University of New York Press, 1994), pp. 159–73, on pp. 169–70.
54. In his article, he uses the relationship between or 'entwinement of' Being and language as the 'illuminative idea' against which he can compare each of the three supposed 'Heideggers' (Schrag, 'The Three Heideggers', p. 162).
55. Heidegger, 'Letter on Humanism', p. 217; Steiner, *Heidegger*, p. 128; Bennett-Hunter, 'Heidegger on Philosophy and Language'.
56. Heidegger, 'The Way to Language', p. 411.
57. Heidegger, *What is Philosophy?*, p. 89.
58. Heidegger, 'Letter on Humanism', p. 265.
59. Cooper, *Heidegger*, pp. 84, 86.
60. Schrag, 'The Three Heideggers', p. 172.

61. Schrag, *God as Otherwise Than Being*, p. 69.
62. Ibid., pp. 14–15.
63. M. Heidegger, *Contributions to Philosophy (From Enowning)*, trans. P. Emad and K. Maly (Bloomington, IN: Indiana University Press, 1999). This work was composed between 1936 and 1938, though not published until 1989.
64. Heidegger, *What is Philosophy?*, p. 71. See also Bennett-Hunter, 'Heidegger on Philosophy and Language', pp. 9–10.
65. Heidegger, 'Letter on Humanism', p. 248.
66. Heidegger, *What is Philosophy?*.
67. J.-L. Marion, *God without Being* (Chicago, IL: University of Chicago Press, 1991), p. 46.
68. Suffice it to say that his desire to posit a God outside the ontological difference on the grounds that even this is too limiting (because, in it, the world 'worlds') is inconsistent with the vision of intimacy in terms of which I have tried, with Cooper, to read Heidegger's notion of Being as ineffable. That the world 'worlds' within the ontological difference is the whole point: only thus can the ineffable be viewed as intimate with the human world and absolutist or two-levels positions be avoided. I am also unconvinced by the guess, on which Marion's whole approach to theology is predicated, as to the reason for Heidegger's statement that, if he were to write a theology, the word 'Being' would not appear. Who knows why Heidegger said that? Marion's reading is, at the very least, controversial and I think it more likely that it was Heidegger's worry that, applied theologically, the language of Being would be contaminated by metaphysics and itself reduced to an instance of the ontotheology it was designed to eschew. (Heidegger made the statement in his reply to the third question at a seminar in Zurich in 1951. The German text can be found at GA15, 436–7. It has been reprinted and translated into English in L. P. Hemming, *Heidegger's Atheism: The Refusal of a Theological Voice* (Notre Dame, IN: University of Notre Dame Press, 2002), pp. 291–2).
69. Young, *Heidegger's Later Philosophy*, p. 16.
70. Heidegger cited ibid., p. 16. The reference is to M. Heidegger, 'On the Question of Being', in *Pathmarks*, ed. W. McNeill (Cambridge: Cambridge University Press, 1998), pp. 291–322, on pp. 310–11.
71. I shall consider the specifically religious significance of this vision of intimacy, at the other pole of Macquarrie's dialectical theism, in the next section.
72. R. Le Poidevin, *Arguing for Atheism: An Introduction to Philosophy of Religion* (London: Routledge, 1996), p. 20.
73. Ibid., p. 25. This way of presenting the argument has been popular since Plantinga. The late Jonathan Lowe is a recent and eminent proponent of the presentation of the argument, which he apparently believes to be sound, to a modern audience using the language of possible worlds and modern modal logic. See E. J. Lowe, 'The Ontological Argument', in C. Meister and P. Copan (eds), *The Routledge Companion to Philosophy of Religion* (Oxford: Routledge, 2007), pp. 331–40, on p. 338.
74. For what follows, see Le Poidevin, *Arguing for Atheism*, p. 25 ff.
75. Ibid., p. 27. The atheistic version of the argument runs as follows: '1 If it is possible for God to exist, then, necessarily, God exists. 2a It is possible that God does not exist. Therefore (from 2a): It is not the case that necessarily, God exists. Therefore: It is not possible for God to exist.' (Ibid., p. 26.)
76. Ibid., pp. 26–7.
77. Ibid., p. 32.
78. Ibid., pp. 27–8.

79. He points out that if God's necessity just belonged to descriptions rather than to what is described, talk of possible worlds would not be relevant to the discussion.
80. Le Poidevin, *Arguing for Atheism*, p. 30.
81. Ibid.
82. Ibid., p. 41.
83. S. Mulhall, 'The Ontological Argument: Wittgensteinian Variations', paper read to the D Society, University of Cambridge, 17 October 2008. References, in what follows, are to the unpaginated typescript of this paper.
84. Ibid.
85. Ibid.
86. Ibid.
87. Ibid.
88. Ibid.
89. Ibid.
90. Ibid.
91. Ibid. Compare Wittgenstein's 1931 remark to this effect (Wittgenstein, *Culture and Value*, p. 16e), cited in Cooper, 'The Inaugural Address: Ineffability', p. 1.
92. Mulhall, 'The Ontological Argument'.
93. Ibid.
94. Ibid.
95. Wittgenstein, *Culture and Value*, p. 82e. Compare S. Mulhall, '"The Presentation of the Infinite in the Finite": The Place of God in Post-Kantian Philosophy', in B. Leiter and M. Rosen (eds), *The Oxford Companion to Continental Philosophy* (Oxford: Oxford University Press, 2007), pp. 494–522, on p. 500.
96. Macquarrie, *In Search of Deity*, p. 33.
97. Macquarrie, *Principles of Christian Theology*, p. 107.
98. R. Williams, 'Simone Weil and the Necessary Non-Existence of God', in *Wrestling with Angels: Conversations in Modern Theology* (London: SCM, 2007), pp. 203–27, on p. 203.
99. Simone Weil cited ibid., p. 203.
100. Ibid., p. 208.
101. T. A. Carlson, 'Postmetaphysical Theology', in K. J. Vanhoozer (ed.), *The Cambridge Companion to Postmodern Theology* (Cambridge: Cambridge University Press, 2003), pp. 58–78, on p. 58.
102. Marion, *God without Being*, p. xx.
103. If a 'name', in Marion's sense, is not a philosophical term at all, then the possibility of applying it to God hardly constitutes a challenge to my argument.
104. Carlson, 'Postmetaphysical Theology', p. 63.
105. For the existential phenomenologists the only possible concept of love is a human one because human thought and discourse capture only a human world.
106. K. Jaspers, *Philosophy*, trans. E. B. Ashton, 3 vols (Chicago, IL: University of Chicago Press, 1969), vol. 3, p. 146.
107. Ibid.
108. For the most part, Macquarrie leaves his affinity with Tillich unvoiced but does mention it obliquely at times, e.g. in Macquarrie, *In Search of Deity*, p. 163. Macquarrie, however, is more explicit than Tillich in acknowledging his debt to Heidegger.
109. Macquarrie, *In Search of Deity*, pp. 158–9. Macquarrie claims that it is inaccurate and misleading to say that God exists since he exists no more than (Heidegger's) Being does (Macquarrie, *Principles of Christian Theology*, p. 108).

110. Ibid., p. 103.
111. Macquarrie, *In Search of Deity*, p. 174.
112. Macquarrie, *Principles of Christian Theology*, p. 186.
113. Ibid., p. 85.
114. Macquarrie, *In Search of Deity*, p. 13.
115. Macquarrie, *Principles of Christian Theology*, p. 51.
116. Ibid., p. 80.
117. Ibid., p. 103.
118. Ibid., p. 105.
119. Ibid., p. 108.
120. Ibid., p. 108 n. 12. Compare Psalm 94:9 (Macquarrie's reference is incorrect). Tillich, referring to the correct Psalm, also quotes these lines in Tillich, *Systematic Theology*, vol. 1, p. 268. Here, the import of the quotation is that the statement, for example, that 'God lives' is symbolically applicable to God insofar as he is the ground of life.
121. Recall that, for Macquarrie, the word 'God' is synonymous with 'holy Being'. Conversely, he interprets atheism not as the denial that God exists as 'a being', since this much is denied by Christian theology, but as the denial of the holiness of Being (Macquarrie, *Principles of Christian Theology*, p. 109).
122. Ibid.
123. Ibid., p. 108.
124. Ibid., p. 107.
125. J. Macquarrie, *Two Worlds are Ours: An Introduction to Christian Mysticism* (London: SCM, 2004), p. 142.
126. Macquarrie, *Principles of Christian Theology*, p. 110. We may again question the tactical strength of Macquarrie's choice of language. He is using 'letting-be' in a very different sense to Heidegger's own (see Chapter 2, above) and surely 'event' would be better than 'act' since it does not imply an objective agent. It is at this point in the book, significantly, that Macquarrie begins to capitalize 'Being'.
127. Macquarrie, *In Search of Deity*, p. 233.
128. W. P. Alston, 'Lecture III: The Need For True Statements about God and How to Reconcile This with Divine Mystery', *Divine Mystery and Our Knowledge of God*, Nathaniel William Taylor Lectures, Yale Divinity School, 13 October 2005, at http://www.yale.edu/divinity/video/convo2005/alston_lecture_03.shtml [accessed October 2008].
129. Macquarrie, *In Search of Deity*, p. 177.
130. Tillich, *Systematic Theology*, vol. 1, p. 265.
131. Ibid., p. 263.
132. Ibid., p. 266.
133. Ibid., p. 121.
134. Ibid., p. 122.
135. Ibid., p. 123.
136. Ibid., pp. 123–4.
137. Ibid., p. 130.
138. Ibid., pp. 130–1.
139. Ibid., p. 131.
140. Ibid., pp. 133–4.
141. Ibid., p. 149.
142. Ibid., pp. 149, 155.
143. Ibid., p. 148.

144. P. Tillich, *Dynamics of Faith* (London: George Allen & Unwin, 1957), p. 97.
145. Tillich, *Systematic Theology*, vol. 1, p. 156.
146. Ibid., p. 210.
147. Ibid., p. 164; R. Re Manning, *Theology at the End of Culture: Paul Tillich's Theology of Culture and Art* (Leuven: Peeters, 2005), pp. 115–6.
148. Tillich, *Systematic Theology*, vol. 1, pp. 93–4.
149. Ibid., p. 94.
150. Ibid.
151. Ibid., p. 166.
152. Ibid., p. 167.
153. Ibid., p. 234.
154. Ibid., p. 238. The existential phenomenologists argue that we humans can speak of anything only on the basis of our relation to it.
155. Ibid., p. 173.
156. Ibid., p. 227.
157. Ibid., p. 173.
158. Ibid., pp. 265–6.
159. Ibid., p. 301.
160. Macquarrie, *Principles of Christian Theology*, p. 84.
161. My criticism of Tillich below considers in more detail this separation between being and meaning.
162. D. Olson, 'Paul Tillich and the Ontological Argument', *Quodlibet Journal*, 6 (2004), at http://www.quodlibet.net/olson-tillich.shtml [accessed 21 January 2009].
163. Ibid. Tillich thinks that the intimacy is also apparent in acts of faith as ultimate concern: 'The ultimate of the act of faith and the ultimate that is meant in the act of faith are one and the same ... In the act of faith that which is the source of this act is present beyond the cleavage of subject and object. It is present as both and beyond both.' (Tillich, *Dynamics of Faith*, p. 11.)
164. Olson, 'Paul Tillich and the Ontological Argument'. The reference is to Tillich, *Systematic Theology*, vol. 1, p. 230.
165. J. M. Russell, 'Tillich's Implicit Ontological Argument', *Sophia*, 32 (1993), pp. 1–16, on pp. 7–8.
166. Ibid., p. 6.
167. Tillich, *Systematic Theology*, vol. 1, p. 227.
168. Olson, 'Paul Tillich and the Ontological Argument'.
169. I discuss the possibility and nature of such a demonstration in more detail in Chapter 5, below.
170. See D. E. Cooper, *Existentialism: A Reconstruction*, 2nd edn (Oxford: Blackwell, 1999), ch. 2: 'Philosophy and Alienation' and pp. 80–2.
171. M. Merleau-Ponty, *Phenomenology of Perception*, trans. C. Smith (London: Routledge, 2002), p. xii.
172. J. Dewey and A. F. Bentley, *Knowing and the Known*, at https://www.aier.org/sites/default/files/otherpublications/KnowingKnown/KnowingKnownFullText.pdf [accessed 10 October 2013], p. 187.
173. This point is explicitly addressed in Chapter 5, below.
174. P. Tillich, 'The Two Types of Philosophy of Religion', in *Theology of Culture*, ed. R. C. Kimball (New York: Oxford University Press, 1959), pp. 10–29, on p. 25.

175. P. Tillich, 'Existential Philosophy: Its Historical Meaning', in *Theology of Culture*, ed. Kimball, pp. 76–111, on p. 94.
176. It seems doubtful whether a claim like this would really make sense. It would be a charitable concession, too, to allow this slack use of 'ineffable'.
177. P. Tillich, 'The Meaning and Justification of Religious Symbols', in Hook (ed.), *Religious Experience and Truth*, pp. 3–11, on p. 11. Italics mine.
178. Tillich, *Systematic Theology*, vol. 1, p. 148.
179. Ibid.
180. Tillich, 'The Meaning and Justification of Religious Symbols', p. 10.
181. Tillich, 'The Two Types of Philosophy of Religion', p. 29.
182. P. Tillich, 'The Religious Symbol', in Hook (ed.), *Religious Experience and Truth*, pp. 301–21, on p. 303.
183. Ibid., p. 314.
184. Ibid., p. 315.
185. Ibid.
186. Tillich, *Dynamics of Faith*, p. 46.
187. Tillich, 'The Religious Symbol', p. 315.
188. Whether this object really exists or is imaginary makes no difference to its symbolic function. Although we cannot know for sure whether a Highest Being does exist, there is no difference relevant to the argument between this kind of symbol and one that is most certainly not just a creation of the human imagination – a golden cross or a Eucharistic wafer, for example.
189. Tillich, 'The Religious Symbol', p. 316.
190. Ibid.
191. Ibid., p. 317.
192. Ibid., p. 319.
193. Ibid., p. 320.
194. Ibid.
195. Ibid.
196. Ibid., p. 321.
197. Ibid., p. 320.
198. W. Schüßler, 'Where Does Religion Come From? Paul Tillich's Concept of *Grundoffenbarung*', in M. Despland, J. C. Petit and J. Richard (eds), *Religion et Culture. Actes du Colloque international du centinaire Paul Tillich, université Laval, Québec, 18–22 Août 1986* (Québec: Presses de l'Université Laval, 1987), pp. 159–71.
199. Tillich, *The Courage to Be*, p. 168.
200. Schüßler, 'Where Does Religion Come From?', p. 161.
201. Tillich, *The Courage to Be*, p. 169.
202. As Tillich expresses it, it is without 'special', i.e. determinate, content, the content being the ineffable 'God above God' (Tillich, cited in M. Leiner, 'Tillich on God', in R. Re Manning (ed.), *The Cambridge Companion to Paul Tillich* (Cambridge: Cambridge University Press, 2009), pp. 37–55, on p. 50.
203. Tillich, *The Courage to Be*, p. 179.
204. Tillich, 'The Religious Symbol', p. 321.
205. Ibid.
206. P. Tillich, 'The Problem of Theological Method', *Journal of Religion*, 27 (1947), pp. 16–26, on p. 17.
207. Ibid., p. 19.

208. Ibid.
209. O. Wilde, 'De Profundis', in *De Profundis, The Ballad of Reading Gaol and Other Writings* (Ware: Wordsworth Classics, 1999), pp. 1–114, on p. 83.
210. Tillich, 'The Problem of Theological Method', p. 25.
211. Another possibility is that Tillich's motive in clinging to the subject–object dichotomy is so as not to appear theologically predisposed against scientific or historical research. But existential phenomenology is not an anti-scientific alternative to Tillich's view but is, rather, anti-scientistic and in potential harmony with it. It challenges the Cartesian spectatorial premise but, far from denying that scientific enquiry has any value, it draws out the implications of this challenge by reinterpreting what scientists are doing and why. Its purpose is simply to point out the inseparability of scientific investigation from 'the stream of life'. The concerns, practices and projects that make up life are the reasons why we choose to carve up and constitute the world in certain ways – and, as the pragmatists were well aware, the various scientific ways are no exception.

4 Karl Jaspers's Philosophical Position

1. K. Jaspers, *Philosophical Faith and Revelation*, trans. E. B. Ashton (London: Collins, 1967), p. 75. This term is intended to mean something like 'ontology of the Encompassing'.
2. Ibid.
3. Jaspers, *Philosophy*, vol. 1, pp. 55–6. He claims here that his notion of *Existenz* is similar to Heidegger's and Sartre's notion of 'authentic being', arguing that *Existenz* should never be reduced to an object ('To be means to decide about being') and that such a decision is made possible by the 'freedom of possible *Existenz*'.
4. Jaspers, *Philosophy*, vol. 1, p. 88.
5. Philosophical world orientation is contrasted with its less reflective scientific counterpart.
6. Jaspers, *Philosophy*, vol. 1, p. 69 ff.
7. K. Jaspers, *Truth and Symbol: From* Von der Warheit, trans. J. T. Wilde, W. Kluback and W. Kimmel (London: Vision, 1959), p. 57; Jaspers, *Philosophy*, vol. 3, p. 7.
8. F. Buri, 'Concerning the Relation of Philosophical Faith and Christian Faith', trans. C. D. Hardwick, *Journal of the American Academy of Religion*, 40 (1972), pp. 454–7, on p. 454.
9. Ibid., pp. 455–6.
10. Ibid., p. 457.
11. E. T. Long, 'Jaspers' [*sic*] Philosophy of Existence as a Model for Theological Reflection', *International Journal for Philosophy of Religion*, 3 (1972), pp. 35–43, on p. 36.
12. D. R. Law, 'Jaspers and Theology', *Heythrop Journal*, 46 (2005), pp. 334–51, on p. 337.
13. Jaspers, *Philosophy*, vol. 3, p. 131. There is an ambiguity surrounding the precise mode in which ciphers appear to which we shall return in the next section.
14. K. Jaspers, *Philosophy is for Everyman: A Short Course in Philosophical Thinking*, trans. R. F. C. Hull and G. Wels (London: Hutchinson, 1969), p. 28; Jaspers, *Philosophy*, vol. 1, p. 75; Law, 'Jaspers and Theology', p. 341.
15. Jaspers, *Philosophical Faith and Revelation*, p. 95, n. 1.
16. D. R. Law, *Inspiration* (London: Continuum, 2001), p. 173.
17. Ibid.
18. Tillich, 'The Two Types of Philosophy of Religion', p. 25.
19. Jaspers, *Philosophy*, vol. 3, p. 15.
20. Ibid.

21. Ibid., p. 121. Here, Jaspers's own expression is 'the world and transcendence are one without being identical'. A little later, he puts it like this: 'transcendence only appears to me in the cipher script; it is not the cipher script'. (Ibid., p. 124.)
22. Ibid., p. 113.
23. Ibid., pp. 121–2.
24. Ibid., pp. 113–4.
25. Ibid., p. 126.
26. Ibid.
27. Ibid.
28. Ibid.
29. Ibid., p. 21.
30. Ibid., p. 124. I quote the word 'man' here with the intention of its being understood in the gender inclusive sense of 'humanity'.
31. Ibid., p. 125.
32. Ibid., p. 134.
33. Merleau-Ponty is the existential phenomenologist who has most famously given extensive treatment to the topic of physiognomy and the body.
34. M. Merleau-Ponty, *The World of Perception*, trans. O. Davies (London: Routledge, 2004), p. 83.
35. Ibid., pp. 83–5.
36. H.-G. Gadamer, 'Image and Gesture', in *The Relevance of the Beautiful and Other Essays*, ed. R. Bernasconi (Cambridge: Cambridge University Press, 1986), pp. 74–82, on p. 79.
37. Jaspers, *Philosophy is for Everyman*, p. 93.
38. Ibid.
39. Jaspers, *Truth and Symbol*, p. 42.
40. Jaspers, *Philosophy*, vol. 3, p. 128.
41. Ibid.
42. Ibid.
43. Ibid., p. 129.
44. Jaspers, *Truth and Symbol*, p. 42.
45. Jaspers, *Philosophy*, vol. 3, pp. 130–1.
46. If the ineffable is to be signified at all, the signification must be inexhaustible or, otherwise, empty.
47. Jaspers, *Truth and Symbol*, p. 42.
48. Jaspers, *Philosophy*, vol. 3, p. 16.
49. Jaspers, *Truth and Symbol*, p. 41. Idiosyncratically, the translators of this volume use the spelling 'cypher'. For the sake of consistency, I have silently changed it to the more usual 'cipher' in my own citations.
50. Jaspers, *Philosophy*, vol. 3, p. 18.
51. Ibid., p. 17.
52. Ibid., p. 12.
53. Ibid., p. 145.
54. Ibid., p. 146.
55. Ibid., p. 36.
56. Ibid.
57. Jaspers, *Truth and Symbol*, p. 46. Compare Jaspers's description of ciphers as 'world images' mentioned below in connection with the difference between the theological and philosophical perspectives (ibid., p. 63).

58. Jaspers, *Philosophy*, vol. 3, p. 144.
59. Tillich, *Dynamics of Faith*, p. 51.
60. Law, 'Jaspers and Theology', p. 341.
61. Jaspers, *Philosophical Faith and Revelation*, p. 92.
62. Jaspers, *Truth and Symbol*, p. 76.
63. Ibid.
64. Ibid., pp. 58–60.
65. Jaspers, *Philosophy*, vol. 1, p. 74.
66. Ibid., vol. 3, p. 133. I cannot help being reminded by this passage of Odilon Redon's 1878 lithograph, *Guardian Spirit of the Waters*.
67. Jaspers, *Philosophical Faith and Revelation*, p. 92.
68. Ibid., p. 104.
69. Ibid.
70. Jaspers, *Philosophy*, vol. 1, p. 313.
71. Jaspers, *Philosophical Faith and Revelation*, p. 92.
72. Jaspers, *Truth and Symbol*, p. 63.
73. Jaspers, *Philosophy*, vol. 3, p. 131.
74. Jaspers, *Philosophy is for Everyman*, p. 90.
75. Jaspers, *Philosophy*, vol. 3, p. 131.
76. A 'philosophical symbol' might be an objectification of the ineffable ultimate reality in a metaphysical concept that occurred at some point in the history of philosophy, for example seventeenth- and eighteenth-century notions of 'substance'. For a system of such symbols to become a cipher, the history of philosophy would have to be read existentially in the kind of way advocated by Heidegger (see Bennett-Hunter, 'Heidegger on Philosophy and Language', pp. 9–11).
77. Jaspers, *Philosophical Faith and Revelation*, p. 100.
78. Ibid.
79. Jaspers, *Truth and Symbol*, p. 77.
80. Ibid., p. 63.
81. Ibid., p. 64.
82. Ibid., p. 71.
83. Jaspers is well known to have coined this term, which translates as 'the philosophy of existence'.
84. Jaspers, *Truth and Symbol*, p. 77.
85. Cooper, *Existentialism*, p. 82. It is for this reason that Jaspers is relatively neglected in Cooper's book on existentialism. Cooper seems to be of the opinion that, unless the subject–object dichotomy is abandoned, there is no hope of overcoming the sense of 'homelessness' and alienation to which the existentialists were responding. But there is a crucial question concerning the relation of the subject–object dichotomy to Cooper's own arguments, which the present engagement with Jaspers's ideas will help to bring into focus.
86. Jaspers, *Philosophical Faith and Revelation*, p. 7.
87. Ibid.
88. Ibid.
89. Jaspers, *Philosophy*, vol. 1, p. 81.
90. Ibid., p. 82.
91. Ibid., vol. 3, p. 135.
92. K. Jaspers, *The Perennial Scope of Philosophy*, trans. R. Manheim (London: Routledge & Kegan Paul, 1950), p. 29.

93. K. Jaspers, *Way to Wisdom: An Introduction to Philosophy*, trans. R. Manheim (London: Victor Gollancz, 1951), p. 29.
94. Jaspers, *Philosophical Faith and Revelation*, p. 94. 'Without the dichotomy', he writes here, a person 'becomes unconscious and stops thinking'.
95. Ibid., p. 61.
96. Ibid.
97. Jaspers, *Way to Wisdom*, p. 30.
98. Faith, says Jaspers, is 'rooted in the vehicle phenomenality', in the Encompassing, neither subject nor object but manifest in the duality. (Jaspers, *The Perennial Scope of Philosophy*, p. 14.)
99. Ibid., p. 31.
100. Jaspers, *Truth and Symbol*, p. 23.
101. Jaspers, *Philosophy is for Everyman*, pp. 93–4.
102. Jaspers, *Truth and Symbol*, p. 24.
103. Jaspers, *Philosophy*, vol. 3, p. 7.
104. Jaspers, *Truth and Symbol*, p. 24.
105. Ibid., p. 35.
106. Jaspers, *Philosophy*, vol. 3, p. 120.
107. Ibid.
108. Ibid., vol. 1, p. 72.
109. Ibid., p. 73.
110. Ibid.
111. Ibid., p. 74.
112. Ibid., vol. 3, p. 124.
113. Ibid., p. 7. Italics mine.
114. Ibid., vol. 1, p. 78.
115. Ibid., vol. 3, p. 151.
116. Ibid., p. 36.
117. Ibid., vol. 1, p. 74.
118. Jaspers, *The Perennial Scope of Philosophy*, p. 22.
119. Jaspers, *Way to Wisdom*, p. 35.
120. Jaspers, *Truth and Symbol*, p. 38.
121. Jaspers, *Philosophical Faith and Revelation*, p. 79.
122. Jaspers, *Truth and Symbol*, p. 59.
123. Jaspers, *Philosophy*, vol. 3, pp. 16–17.
124. Jaspers, *Truth and Symbol*, p. 47.
125. Jaspers, *Philosophy*, vol. 2, p. 295.
126. See Chapter 2, above.
127. Reproduced in S. Kirkbright, *Karl Jaspers: A Biography: Navigations in Truth* (New Haven, CT: Yale University Press, 2004), illustration 6.
128. Ibid., p. viii.
129. Ibid., p. 21.
130. H. Horn, 'Karl Jaspers', *Prospects: the Quarterly Review of Comparative Education*, 23 (1993), pp. 721–39, on p. 721. This is supported by Jaspers's own retrospective comment on his, still classic, two-volume psychiatric work, *General Psychopathology*. He writes: 'As regards its contents this book is a scientific work; with respect to the deliberately chosen form in which it is written it is a work of philosophy'. (K. Jaspers, *Reason and Anti-Reason in Our Time*, trans. S. Goodman (London: SCM, 1952), p. 30.)

131. Jaspers, *Way to Wisdom*, p. 35.
132. Cooper, *Existentialism*, p. 82.
133. Ibid.
134. Jaspers, *Way to Wisdom*, p. 33.
135. Jaspers, *Philosophical Faith and Revelation*, p. 62.
136. Specifically, I have in mind here the sharp differentiation of *Existenz* and Transcendence from mundane existence.
137. Jaspers, *Philosophical Faith and Revelation*, p. 71.
138. Ibid.
139. Jaspers, *The Perennial Scope of Philosophy*, p. 20.
140. This essentiality is even reflected in the etymology of the name Jaspers gives to his philosophical system: 'periechontology'. See n. 1, above.
141. It is worth stressing that this alternative perspective is itself an important aspect of Jaspers's system alongside his affirmation of the validity of the subject–object dichotomy and is by no means alien to it.
142. Merleau-Ponty, *Phenomenology of Perception*, p. 109.
143. Ibid., p. 105.
144. Ibid.
145. He writes, 'experience of one's own body runs counter to the reflective procedure which detaches subject and object from each other, and which gives us only the thought about the body, or the body as an idea, and not the experience of the body or the body in reality'. (Merleau-Ponty, *Phenomenology of Perception*, p. 231.)
146. Ibid., p. 106.
147. Jaspers, *Philosophy*, vol. 1, p. 58.
148. Jaspers, *Philosophy is for Everyman*, p. 27.
149. Ibid.
150. Ibid., p. 29.
151. Jaspers, *Truth and Symbol*, p. 43.
152. Jaspers, *Philosophy*, vol. 1, p. 82.
153. Ibid., p. 17.
154. Ibid., vol. 3, p. 17.
155. Ibid., vol. 1, p. 119.
156. Jaspers, *Truth and Symbol*, p. 38.
157. Ibid., p. 39.
158. Ibid.
159. Ibid.
160. Jaspers, *Philosophy*, vol. 3, p. 16.
161. Ibid., p. 60.
162. These terms are experiential but experience, for the existential phenomenologists, is not reducible to the subject–object dichotomy, which is an abstraction incapable of adequately accounting for such experience. This inadequacy is made especially clear by Merleau-Ponty's remarks, quoted above, on the experiences of vision and touch.
163. The very idea of there being a way in which things 'really' are, apart from our contribution, would not make sense to an existential phenomenologist.
164. Jaspers, *Philosophy*, vol. 1, p. 122.

5 The Nature of Philosophical Evocation of the Ineffable

1. Heidegger, *Being and Time*, p. 87.
2. Ibid., p. 89.
3. D. R. Hofstadter and D. C. Dennett, *The Mind's I: Fantasies and Reflections on Self and Soul* (London: Penguin, 1982), p. 388.
4. Jaspers, *Philosophy*, vol. 3, p. 60.
5. R. Descartes, *Meditations on First Philosophy*, in *Selected Philosophical Writings*, trans. J. Cottingham, R. Stoothoff and D. Murdoch (Cambridge: Cambridge University Press, 1988), pp. 73–122, on p. 76.
6. J. Annas and J. Barnes, *The Modes of Scepticism: Ancient Texts and Modern Interpretations* (Cambridge: Cambridge University Press, 1985), p. 24.
7. Descartes, *Meditations*, p. 90.
8. Sextus Empiricus, *Outlines of Scepticism*, ed. J. Annas and J. Barnes (Cambridge: Cambridge University Press, 2002), p. 5.
9. See, for example, Pihlström, *Structuring the World*, ch. 4.6: 'Things in Themselves and the Problem of the "Measure"'.
10. E. Husserl, *Cartesian Meditations: An Introduction to Phenomenology*, trans. D. Cairns (Dordrecht: Kluwer, 1999), p. 7 ff: 'First Meditation'.
11. This, very arguably, is the only good kind of philosophical argument, even the only kind of argument that properly deserves to be called 'philosophical'. Elsewhere, I have criticized Camus's 'argument' that human life is absurd on these grounds: that it could not even possibly convince anyone who did not agree with him already. It is therefore not really an argument at all and there is nothing in it that could sustain serious philosophical discussion. See Bennett-Hunter, 'Absurd Creation', p. 51.
12. I am thinking particularly of his 1929 essay 'What is Metaphysics?' to which I also refer.
13. In a phenomenological description of his first visit to Paris, Merleau-Ponty interprets his perception of the city not as a flow of perceptions of distinct objects, nor the law which might govern such a flow, but rather as the supposedly distinct perceptions (of cafés, people and so on) only standing out against the 'city's whole being'. He concludes that 'an initial perception independent of any background is inconceivable'. (Merleau-Ponty, *Phenomenology of Perception*, pp. 327–8.)
14. J.-P. Sartre, *Being and Nothingness: An Essay on Phenomenological Ontology*, trans. H. E. Barnes (London: Routledge, 2003), p. 33. As Stephen Vizinczey puts it, in the fictional context of a more obviously emotionally charged encounter, 'I asked her to show me the apartment, but it impressed me only as a blue and green background to her figure, until we came to a huge round bed'. (S. Vizinczey, *In Praise of Older Women: The Amorous Recollections of András Vajda* (London: Penguin, 2010), p. 181.)
15. Sartre, *Being and Nothingness*, p. 34.
16. Ibid.
17. M. Heidegger, 'What is Metaphysics?', trans. R. F. C. Hull and A. Crick, in *Existence and Being*, pp. 355–92, on pp. 368–9.
18. Ibid., p. 366.
19. Sartre, *Being and Nothingness*, p. 40.
20. Heidegger, 'What is Metaphysics?', p. 361. This particular argument for the primacy of experience over logic is not very convincing.
21. Ibid., pp. 362, 363.
22. Ibid., p. 372.

23. Sartre, *Being and Nothingness*, p. 35.
24. Ibid.
25. Ibid., pp. 40, 42, 45.
26. Heidegger, 'What is Metaphysics?', pp. 368–9.
27. Ibid., p. 369.
28. Ibid.
29. Ibid.
30. Ibid., p. 371.
31. Heidegger, *Being and Time*, p. 333.
32. Cooper, *Existentialism*, p. 142; Bennett-Hunter, 'Absurd Creation', p. 54.
33. Sartre, *Being and Nothingness*, p. 34.
34. Cooper, 'Life and Meaning', p. 128.
35. Ibid.
36. Cooper, 'Mystery, World and Religion', p. 53.
37. We are familiar with Heidegger's position (see Chapter 2, above). Marcel thinks of those phenomena that it is distorting to objectify as 'mysteries', which are modes of the all-encompassing ontological mystery, to recall the title of his Gifford Lectures, the 'mystery of being'.
38. G. H. Langley, 'Reason', *Proceedings of the Aristotelian Society*, 39 (1939), pp. 85–98, on p. 85.
39. Ibid., p. 92.
40. I. McGilchrist, *The Master and his Emissary: The Divided Brain and the Making of the Western World* (London: Yale University Press, 2009), p. 31.
41. See Cooper, *Existentialism*, ch. 5: 'Dualisms Dissolved'. For a strikingly similar pragmatist perspective, see also Pihlström, *Structuring the World*, ch. 5.1.4: 'Facts and Values'.
42. Cooper, *Existentialism*, p. 89.
43. H. Putnam, cited in Pihlström, *Structuring the World*, p. 274.
44. McGilchrist, *The Master and his Emissary*. The discussion of philosophy and the phenomenological tradition may be found in ch. 4: 'The Nature of the Two Worlds'. I am not qualified to endorse, or otherwise assess, the neuroscientific component of McGilchrist's argument. Here, I simply repeat the neurological terms in which his argument is cast and try to emphasize my agreement with the more philosophical dimension.
45. Ibid., p. 133.
46. Ibid., p. 168.
47. Ibid., p. 135.
48. Ibid., p. 137.
49. Similar, and in some cases the same, paradoxes are mentioned by Jaspers in support of the same point. See K. Jaspers, *Reason and Existenz: Five Lectures*, trans. W. Earle (London: Routledge & Kegan Paul, 1956), pp. 113–7.
50. Perhaps, in this context, (ultimate) 'reality' should be written with a capital 'R'. In the argument to ineffability that I endorse, the claim is the stronger one that our ways of thinking are necessarily inadequate to the nature of Reality.
51. McGilchrist, *The Master and his Emissary*, p. 140.
52. Ibid. It is interesting to compare this with the thoroughly repeated clinical findings of Deglin and Kinsbourne reported by McGilchrist. The patient is shown a syllogism that is formally valid but unsound (the minor premise is false) and asked whether the conclusion is true. When the patient's right hemisphere is experimentally inactivated (and she is therefore reliant solely on the left), she replies that the conclusion is true even though she knows from experience that the minor premise is false. Her reply, reliant on the left

hemisphere, is logically coherent but inconsistent with experience. But when the left hemisphere is inactivated in the very same individual, and the question is repeated, she correctly replies that the conclusion is false as her right hemisphere prioritizes experience over logic. (McGilchrist, *The Master and his Emissary*, pp. 192–3.)
53. Compare the point, made above, that the Cartesian premise which subjects lived experience to scepticism (that the senses sometimes deceive us) is not itself defensible on its own terms. Compare also Merleau-Ponty's suggestion that disparities between logic and experience always be resolved in favour of experience.
54. McGilchrist, *The Master and his Emissary*, p. 70.
55. Ibid., p. 174.
56. Ibid., p. 71.
57. Ibid., p. 182. The terminology here is strikingly reminiscent of Jaspers.
58. Ibid., p. 139.
59. Ibid., p. 182.
60. Ibid., p. 135.
61. Ibid., pp. 185, 354, 139–40. In the notes, he draws an analogy with Russell's paradox (p. 486, n. 7).
62. Cooper, 'Life and Meaning', p. 126.
63. Cooper, 'Mystery, World and Religion', p. 54.
64. Ibid., pp. 56–7.
65. One 'cannot be content simply to announce that [it] is the mysterious and then stay *stumm*'. (Cooper, 'Mystery, World and Religion', p. 55.)
66. Cooper, 'Life and Meaning', p. 137.
67. Cooper, 'Mystery, World and Religion', p. 58.
68. Cooper, 'Life and Meaning', p. 137.
69. Cooper, 'Mystery, World and Religion', p. 55.
70. Cooper, *The Measure of Things*, p. 322.
71. L. Wittgenstein, *Tractatus Logico-Philosophicus*, trans. D. Pears and B. McGuiness (London: Routledge, 1988), §6.54.
72. Heidegger, 'The Origin of the Work of Art', p. 159.
73. Cooper, 'Life and Meaning', pp. 135–6.
74. Ibid., p. 137.
75. Jaspers, *Reason and Existenz*, p. 119. Here, Jaspers seems to be using 'rationality' in a broader sense than my pejorative one.
76. Jaspers, *Philosophy*, vol. 3, p. 49.
77. Ibid., p. 205.
78. Ibid., p. 206.
79. Ibid.
80. I call it 'phenomenological nihilism' because it is a nihilism of meaning as well as (since this is inseparable from) being. It is not merely the idea that the ineffable is not an object and transcends the subject–object dichotomy. It is the thought, too, that, as truly beyond the immediately meaningful human world, the ineffable has to be thought of as determinately meaningless. The concept of ineffability is determinately empty not only with regard to being but also meaning. A rational nihilism is ruled out on the grounds that it could only result from a failure to push reason far enough, i.e. to the point where the validity of the notion of ineffability beyond the human is demonstrated, and from kicking it away too soon. Sartre's supposed 'nihilism' is not explicitly rational at all and is therefore, as I have tried to show, philosophically insubstantial.

81. Compare Tillich's claim that there 'is no reality, thing or event which cannot become a bearer of the mystery of being and enter into a revelatory correlation'. (Tillich, *Systematic Theology*, vol. 1, p. 131.)
82. Jaspers, *Truth and Symbol*, p. 42.
83. Jaspers, *Philosophy*, vol. 3, p. 36.
84. Jaspers, *Philosophical Faith and Revelation*, p. 114.
85. Ibid., p. 166; Macquarrie, *In Search of Deity*, p. 172.
86. Jaspers, *Philosophical Faith and Revelation*, p. 166.
87. Ibid., p. 114.
88. Turner, *The Darkness of God*, esp. pp. 38 ff., 253; D. Turner, 'The Darkness of God and the Light of Christ: Negative Theology and Eucharistic Presence', *Modern Theology*, 15 (1999), pp. 143–58, on p. 147. Of historical interest is the fact that Turner believes that apophatic and cataphatic ways were held in tension and dialogue in this way in the Middle Ages.
89. Jaspers, *Reason and Existenz*, p. 115.
90. Jaspers, *Reason and Anti-Reason in Our Time*, p. 47. Compare R. W. Hepburn, 'Humanist Religion II: Some Possible Approaches', in R. W. Hepburn et al., *Religion and Humanism* (London: BBC, 1964), pp. 83–90, on p. 85.
91. Jaspers, *Reason and Anti-Reason in Our Time*, p. 63.
92. Ibid., p. 52.
93. It is worth noting again that, in this later stage of his thinking, Heidegger was no longer overtly interested in the historical concreteness of the Christian tradition.
94. Compare Hick's recent defence of his 'Ineffability' thesis. He describes that thesis as being more radical than the claim that the divine names are not literally true of God: 'They are not literally true, or literally false, because they do not [literally] apply to God at all'. (J. Hick, 'Response to Knepper', *Religious Studies*, 45 (2009), pp. 223–6, on p. 224.)
95. Jaspers, *Philosophical Faith and Revelation*, p. 340.
96. Ibid., p. 341.
97. Ibid., p. 342.
98. Ibid., p. 340.

6 The Aesthetic and Ritual Embodiment of the Ineffable

1. Macquarrie, *Principles of Christian Theology*, p. 364.
2. Ibid., p. 378.
3. Ibid., p. 401.
4. D. W. Brown, *God and Enchantment of Place: Reclaiming Human Experience* (Oxford: Oxford University Press, 2004), p. 2.
5. One reference is to Heidegger, 'Letter on Humanism', p. 234.
6. R. W. Hepburn, 'Restoring the Sacred: Sacred as a Concept of Aesthetics', in R. W. Hepburn, *The Reach of the Aesthetic: Collected Essays on Art and Nature* (Aldershot: Ashgate, 2001), pp. 113–29, on p. 116.
7. Ibid., p. 127.
8. Ibid.
9. L. Wittgenstein, *Remarks on Frazer's Golden Bough*, ed. R. Rhees, trans. A. C. Miles (Retford: Brynmill, 1979), p. 2e.
10. Ibid., p. 4e.
11. Ibid.

12. Ibid., p. 12e.
13. J. Bouveresse, 'Wittgenstein's Critique of Frazer', *Ratio*, 20 (2007), pp. 357–76, on pp. 359–60.
14. S. K. Langer, *Philosophy in a New Key: A Study in the Symbolism of Reason, Rite and Art*, 3rd edn (Cambridge, MA: Harvard University Press, 1957), pp. 45, 157.
15. Ibid., p. 158.
16. Ibid.
17. Ibid., p. 159.
18. Ibid.
19. Ibid., pp. 154–5.
20. Wittgenstein, *Culture and Value*, p. 8e.
21. Wittgenstein, *Remarks on Frazer's* Golden Bough, p. 7e.
22. Cottingham, *The Spiritual Dimension*, p. 5.
23. J. G. Cottingham, *On the Meaning of Life* (Oxford: Routledge, 2003), p. 98.
24. Cottingham, 'What Difference Does it Make?', p. 418; Cottingham, *The Spiritual Dimension*, p. 12.
25. Pascal, Penseés, no. 418, quoted in Cottingham, *On the Meaning of Life*, p. 94.
26. Cottingham, *The Spiritual Dimension*, p. 9. He refers to the final paragraph of Orwell's *Nineteen Eighty-Four*.
27. Cottingham, *The Spiritual Dimension*, p. 24.
28. Cottingham, *On the Meaning of Life*, p. 99.
29. B. Kapferer, 'Sorcery and the Beautiful: A Discourse on the Aesthetics of Ritual', in A. Hobart and B. Kapferer (eds), *Aesthetics in Performance: Formations of Symbolic Construction and Experience* (New York: Berhahn, 2005), pp. 129–60, on pp. 134–5.
30. Langer, *Philosophy in a New Key*, p. 49.
31. Wittgenstein, *Remarks on Frazer's* Golden Bough, p. 7e. I am grateful to Professor Howie Wettstein for drawing my attention to this passage.
32. Macquarrie, *In Search of Deity*, p. 192.
33. It should be clear that my focus is on the experience of artistic meaning and not necessarily on experiences of beauty or the beautiful. My use of the term 'aesthetic' is in spite of the almost pejorative use identified by Heidegger, 'The Origin of the Work of Art', p. 162.
34. My approach in this section is, as usual, phenomenological. Most of the thinkers with whom I engage in this section self-consciously fall into the 'phenomenological tradition', with the exception of Wittgenstein, whose later thought resists straightforward classification.
35. H.-G. Gadamer, *Truth and Method*, trans. J. Weinsheimer and D. G. Marshall, 2nd edn (London: Continuum, 2004), p. 102.
36. J. M. Connolly, 'Gadamer and the Author's Authority: A Language-Game Approach', *Journal of Aesthetics and Art Criticism*, 44 (1986), pp. 271–7, on p. 271. The Gadamerian terms 'understanding' and 'interpretation' are equivalent to the phrase 'experience of meaning'.
37. Gadamer, *Truth and Method*, p. 110.
38. Ibid., p. 115.
39. M. Dufrenne, 'The Aesthetic Object and the Technical Object', *Journal of Aesthetics and Art Criticism*, 23 (1964), pp. 113–22, on p. 116.
40. Gadamer, *Truth and Method*, p. 118.
41. Ibid., p. 129.
42. H.-G. Gadamer, 'Composition and Interpretation', in *The Relevance of the Beautiful*, pp. 66–73, on p. 69.

43. M. Budd, 'Wittgenstein on Aesthetics', in M. Budd, *Aesthetic Essays* (Oxford: Oxford University Press, 2008), pp. 252–77, on p. 271.
44. L. Wittgenstein, *Lectures and Conversations on Aesthetics, Psychology and Religious Belief*, ed. C. Barrett (Oxford: Blackwell, 1966), p. 29.
45. Ibid., p. 34.
46. Ibid.
47. L. Wittgenstein, *Philosophical Investigations*, trans. G. E. M. Anscombe, 3rd edn (Oxford: Blackwell, 2001), §523.
48. Ibid., §610.
49. See L. Tolstoy, *What is Art?*, trans. R. Pevear and L. Volokhonsky (London: Penguin, 1995), pp. 39–40.
50. Wittgenstein, *Culture and Value*, p. 58e.
51. M. Budd, 'Wittgenstein, Ludwig', in S. Davies et al. (eds), *A Companion to Aesthetics* (Oxford: Wiley-Blackwell, 2009), pp. 593–6, on p. 595. Compare Cooper, *Meaning*, p. 68 ff.
52. Wittgenstein, *Lectures and Conversations*, p. 29.
53. M. Dufrenne, 'Perception, Meaning and Convention', *Journal of Aesthetics and Art Criticism*, 42 (1983), pp. 209–11, on p. 210.
54. E. F. Kaelin, *An Existentialist Aesthetic: The Theories of Sartre and Merleau-Ponty* (Madison, WI: The University of Wisconsin Press, 1962), p. 251.
55. Merleau-Ponty, *Phenomenology of Perception*, pp. 208, 211.
56. Ibid., p. 210.
57. Ibid.
58. Ibid., p. 214.
59. Ibid., p. 172.
60. Ibid., p. 175.
61. Merleau-Ponty, *The World of Perception*, p. 101.
62. Ibid., pp. 94–5.
63. Ibid., p. 95.
64. Ibid., p. 97.
65. Ibid., p. 96.
66. Compare the reference to 'all the innumerable gestures made with the voice' (L. Wittgenstein, *Zettel*, ed. G. E. M. Anscombe and G. H. Von Wright (Berkeley, CA: University of California Press, 2007), §161. Wittgenstein's proximity to Merleau-Ponty in this area has been briefly but perceptively drawn out by Lüdeking in K. Lüdeking, 'Pictures and Gestures', *British Journal of Aesthetics*, 30 (1990), pp. 218–32.
67. Wittgenstein, *Culture and Value*, p. 48e. Compare Wittgenstein, *Lectures and Conversations*, p. 40.
68. Wittgenstein, *Culture and Value*, p. 70e.
69. Steiner, *Heidegger*, p. 44.
70. Lüdeking, 'Pictures and Gestures', p. 218.
71. Gadamer takes this distinction from Valéry (H.-G. Gadamer, 'Philosophy and Poetry', in *The Relevance of the Beautiful*, pp. 131–9, on p. 132) but Merleau-Ponty claims that he in turn took it from Mallarmé (Merleau-Ponty, *The World of Perception*, p. 100). 'Poetry' is not understood in the narrow sense of prosody but also to incorporate the kind of language in which, for example, novels are written.
72. Ibid., pp. 100–1.
73. Ibid., p. 100.

74. C. Lawn, 'Gadamer on Poetic and Everyday Language', *Philosophy and Literature*, 25 (2001), pp. 113–26, on p. 116.
75. Gadamer, 'Composition and Interpretation', p. 67.
76. Ibid.
77. Heidegger, 'The Origin of the Work of Art', p. 172.
78. Gadamer, 'Philosophy and Poetry', p. 134.
79. Gadamer, *Truth and Method*, p. 153.
80. Gadamer, 'Philosophy and Poetry', p. 134.
81. Ibid., p. 135.
82. Ibid., p. 136.
83. Gadamer, 'Composition and Interpretation', p. 72.
84. Gadamer, 'Philosophy and Poetry', p. 132. Compare McGilchrist, *The Master and his Emissary*, p. 373: 'A too great emphasis on the sound and feel of words as "things" separate from their meaning, or alternatively on the meaning as something separate from the sound and feel of the words in which it exists, destroys poetry'.
85. Gadamer, 'Philosophy and Poetry', p. 135.
86. H.-G. Gadamer, 'The Relevance of the Beautiful: Art as Play, Symbol and Festival', in *The Relevance of the Beautiful*, pp. 3–53, on p. 35.
87. Compare Cooper, *Meaning*, p. 115 ff. Cooper here points out that, ironically like the thinkers I have been considering, formalists sometimes appeal to an apparent analogy between language and art.
88. Merleau-Ponty, *The World of Perception*, pp. 96–7.
89. Wittgenstein, *Zettel*, §175.
90. Lüdeking, 'Pictures and Gestures', pp. 224–6.
91. Wittgenstein, *Lectures and Conversations*, p. 8.
92. Cooper, *Meaning*, p. 109.
93. Heidegger, 'The Origin of the Work of Art', p. 168.
94. Cooper, *Meaning*, p. 111.
95. Merleau-Ponty, *Phenomenology of Perception*, pp. 225–6.
96. Ibid., pp. 226, 216.
97. Cited in Cooper, 'The Inaugural Address: Ineffability', p. 15.
98. McGilchrist, *The Master and his Emissary*, p. 316.
99. Compare the following remark, which may help to ease the shift into more theological territory, from Merleau-Ponty's inaugural lecture: 'we must admit that all thinking which displaces, or otherwise defines, the sacred has been called atheistic, and that philosophy which does not place it here or there, like a thing, but at the joining of things and words, will always be exposed to this reproach without ever being touched by it'. (M. Merleau-Ponty, *In Praise of Philosophy*, trans. J. Wilde and J. M. Edie (Evanston, IL: Northwestern University Press, 1968), p. 46.
100. Heidegger, 'The Origin of the Work of Art', p. 174. Compare Young, *Heidegger's Philosophy of Art*, p. 45.
101. M. Merleau-Ponty, 'Eye and Mind', trans. C. Dallery, in *The Primacy of Perception*, ed. J. M. Edie (Evanston, IL: Northwestern University Press, 1964), pp. 159–90, on p. 164.
102. R. Kearney, 'Merleau-Ponty and the Sacramentality of the Flesh', in K. Semonovitch and N. De Roo (eds), *Merleau-Ponty at the Limits of Art, Religion and Perception* (London: Continuum, 2010), pp. 147–66, esp. p. 151. He describes Merleau-Ponty's use of such language as particularly bold and remarkable given the atheism that pervaded his Parisian context.

103. M. Merleau-Ponty, 'Faith and Good Faith', in *Sense and Non-Sense*, trans. H. L. Dreyfus and P. A. Dreyfus (Evanston, IL: Northwestern University Press, 1964), pp. 172–81, on p. 175.
104. Merleau-Ponty, *Phenomenology of Perception*, p. 212.
105. Merleau-Ponty, 'Eye and Mind', p. 162.
106. M. Merleau-Ponty, *Signs*, trans. R. C. McCleary (Evanston, IL: Northwestern University Press, 1964), p. 64, cited in Kearney, 'Merleau-Ponty and the Sacramentality of the Flesh', p. 153. For a pertinent example of such 'consecration', strikingly reminiscent of Merleau-Ponty's language here, see J.-K. Huysmans, 'Le Marchand de Marrons', in *Croquis Parisiens* (Paris: La Bibliothéque des Arts, 1994), pp. 97–100, on p. 99.
107. Kearney, 'Merleau-Ponty and the Sacramentality of the Flesh', p. 155.
108. P. J. FitzPatrick, *In Breaking of Bread: The Eucharist and Ritual* (Cambridge: Cambridge University Press, 1993), pp. 103–4.
109. B. Russell, *The Problems of Philosophy*, 2nd edn (Oxford: Oxford University Press, 1998), p. 6.
110. FitzPatrick, *In Breaking of Bread*, p. 98. Compare Russell, *The Problems of Philosophy*, p. 7.
111. FitzPatrick, *In Breaking of Bread*, p. 100.
112. Ibid., p. 103.
113. Ibid., p. 101.
114. Ibid., p. 103.
115. Ibid., pp. 104–5.
116. Ibid., p. 148.
117. Ibid., p. 143.
118. Ibid., p. 144.
119. Ibid., p. 47.
120. Ibid., p. 155.
121. D. E. Cooper, *A Philosophy of Gardens* (Oxford: Clarendon Press, 2006), p. 136.
122. FitzPatrick, *In Breaking of Bread*, p. 201. Here he is clearly not following the Heideggerian terminology of 'world' and 'earth'.
123. D. E. Cooper, *Sunlight on the Sea: Reflecting on Reflections* (n.p.: n.p., 2013), p. 81.
124. FitzPatrick, *In Breaking of Bread*, p. 201.
125. Ibid.
126. Ibid., p. 204.
127. Ibid., p. 206.
128. Ibid., pp. 204, 19.
129. Ibid., p. 205.
130. Ibid., p. 207.
131. Ibid., p. 206.
132. H. Brody, 'Ritual, Medicine, and the Placebo Response', in W. S. Sax, J. Quack and J. Weinhold (eds), *The Problem of Ritual Efficacy* (Oxford: Oxford University Press, 2010), pp. 151–67, on p. 163.
133. Cottingham, *On the Meaning of Life*, p. 98.
134. Cooper, *A Philosophy of Gardens*, p. 31. But see here, by contrast, his remarks on the experience of gardens, some of which, notably Zen gardens, have a ritual significance.
135. If there is any doubt about this, consider that the opening lines of many of the collects of the Church of England are dedicated to informing God of things he must know already.

136. Compare D. W. Brown, *God and Grace of Body: Sacrament in Ordinary* (Oxford: Oxford University Press, 2007), pp. 424–5; Brown, *God and Mystery in Words*, ch. 7: 'Performance, Costume, Staging'.
137. See his essay 'The Festive Character of Theater [*sic*]', in *The Relevance of the Beautiful*, pp. 57–65.
138. G. Steiner, 'Real Presences', in G. Steiner, *No Passion Spent: Essays 1978–1996* (London: Faber & Faber, 1996), pp. 20–39; G. Steiner, *Real Presences* (London: Faber & Faber, 1989); S. Mulhall, *On Being in the World: Wittgenstein and Heidegger on Seeing Aspects* (London: Routledge, 1990), esp. ch. 6: 'Icons, Gestures and Aesthetics'. For some of the controversy, see R. W. Hepburn, 'Aesthetic and Religious: Boundaries, Overlaps and Intrusions', in Hepburn, *The Reach of the Aesthetic*, pp. 96–112.
139. Gadamer, 'The Relevance of the Beautiful', p. 35: 'I am simply making use of this problem of dogma to claim that, if we really want to think about the experience of art, we can, indeed must, think along these lines: the work of art does not simply refer to something, because what it refers to is actually there. We could say that the work of art signifies an increase in being.'
140. Brown, *God and Enchantment of Place*, p. 3.
141. Ibid., p. 33. See Cooper, *A Philosophy of Gardens* on the experience of gardens as a philosophical challenge to such a division.
142. Brown, *God and Enchantment of Place*, p. 23.
143. Brody, 'Ritual, Medicine and the Placebo Response', pp. 153, 160–4. On p. 163, Brody explicitly notes the religious parallel. Relatedly, Quack's reading of the Wittgensteinian perspective on ritual implies that ritual be understood 'not as a distinct class of actions of behavior, but as a central aspect of some human actions'. J. Quack, 'Bell, Bourdieu, and Wittgenstein on Ritual Sense', in Sax, Quack and Weinhold (eds), *The Problem of Ritual Efficacy*, pp. 169–88, on p. 183.
144. Wittgenstein's late work on hinge commitments, and Pritchard's recent application of this work in philosophy of religion also make this point in a way that I find congenial. If rationally unjustifiable hinge commitments lie at the foundations of our epistemic practices then those practices are, in an important sense, groundless – if the sought-after foundations comprise knowledge or certainty conceived as a special and particularly secure kind of knowledge. L. Wittgenstein, *On Certainty*, ed. G E. M. Anscombe and G. H. von Wright, trans. D. Paul and G. E. M. Anscombe (Oxford: Blackwell, 1969), § 166. See also D. Pritchard, 'Is "God Exists" a "Hinge Proposition" of Religious Belief?', *International Journal for Philosophy of Religion*, 47 (2000), pp. 129–40; D. Pritchard, 'Wittgensteinian Quasi-Fideism', in J. L. Kvanvig (ed.), *Oxford Studies in Philosophy of Religion: Volume IV* (Oxford: Clarendon Press, 2011), pp. 146–60; D. Pritchard, 'Wittgenstein on Scepticism', in O. Kuusela and M. McGinn (eds), *The Oxford Handbook of Wittgenstein* (Oxford: Oxford University Press, 2011), pp. 523–49; 'Wittgenstein and the Groundlessness of our Believing', *Synthese*, 189 (2012), pp. 255–72. G. A. Bennett-Hunter, 'A Pragmatist Conception of Certainty: Wittgenstein and Santayana', in C. Chauviré and S. Plaud (eds), 'Wittgenstein and Pragmatism: a Reassessment', special issue, *European Journal of Pragmatism and American Philosophy*, 4 (2012), pp. 146–57.

WORKS CITED

Heidegger's works are ordered by date of composition, which is given in square brackets.

Abbott, E. A., *Flatland: A Romance of Many Dimensions* (Oxford: Oxford University Press, 2006).

Abrams, M. H., *The Mirror and the Lamp: Romantic Theory and the Critical Tradition* (New York: Oxford University Press, 1953).

Alston, W. P., 'Ineffability', *Philosophical Review*, 65 (1956), pp. 506–22.

—, *Perceiving God: The Epistemology of Religious Experience* (Ithaca, NY: Cornell University Press, 1991).

—, 'Lecture I: The Divine Mystery Thesis', *Divine Mystery and Our Knowledge of God*, Nathaniel William Taylor Lectures, Yale Divinity School, 11 October 2005, at http://www.goodnewsline.com/pastoral_resource/lecture_in.htm [accessed October 2008].

—, 'Lecture II: Why We Should Take Divine Mystery Seriously', *Divine Mystery and Our Knowledge of God*, Nathaniel William Taylor Lectures, Yale Divinity School, 12 October 2005, at mms://128.36.128.39/convo2005/alston/alston_2_audio.wma [accessed October 2008].

—, 'Lecture III: 'The Need for True Statements about God and How to Reconcile This with Divine Mystery', *Divine Mystery and Our Knowledge of God*, Nathaniel William Taylor Lectures, Yale Divinity School, 13 October 2005, at http://www.yale.edu/divinity/video/convo2005/alston_lecture_03.shtml [accessed October 2008].

Annas, J. and J. Barnes, *The Modes of Scepticism: Ancient Texts and Modern Interpretations* (Cambridge: Cambridge University Press, 1985).

Bartky, S. L., 'Originative Thinking in the Later Philosophy of Heidegger', *Philosophy and Phenomenological Research*, 30 (1970), pp. 368–81.

Beckett, S., *Acte Sans Parole II*, translated in *The Complete Dramatic Works* (London: Faber & Faber, 1986), pp. 207–11.

Bennett-Hunter, G. A., 'Heidegger on Philosophy and Language', *Philosophical Writings*, 35 (2007), pp. 5–16.

—, 'Absurd Creation: An Existentialist View of Art?', *Philosophical Frontiers*, 4 (2009), pp. 49–58.

—, 'A Pragmatist Conception of Certainty: Wittgenstein and Santayana', in C. Chauviré and S. Plaud (eds), 'Wittgenstein and Pragmatism: a Reassessment', special issue, *European Journal of Pragmatism and American Philosophy*, 4 (2012), pp. 146–57.

—, 'Natural Theology and Literature', in R. Re Manning (ed.), *The Oxford Handbook of Natural Theology* (Oxford: Oxford University Press, 2013), pp. 551–65.

Bouveresse, J., 'Wittgenstein's Critique of Frazer', *Ratio*, 20 (2007), pp. 357–76.

Bouyer, L., 'Mysterion', in A. Plé (ed.), *Mystery and Mysticism: A Symposium* (London: Blackfriars Publications, 1956), pp. 18–32.

—, 'Mysticism: An Essay on the History of a Word', in Plé (ed.), *Mystery and Mysticism*, pp. 119–37.

Boyer, S. D., 'The Logic of Mystery', *Religious Studies*, 43 (2007), pp. 89–102.

Brody, H., 'Ritual, Medicine, and the Placebo Response', in W. S. Sax, J. Quack and J. Weinhold (eds), *The Problem of Ritual Efficacy* (Oxford: Oxford University Press, 2010), pp. 151–67.

Brown, D. W., *God and Enchantment of Place: Reclaiming Human Experience* (Oxford: Oxford University Press, 2004).

—, *God and Grace of Body: Sacrament in Ordinary* (Oxford: Oxford University Press, 2007).

—, *God and Mystery in Words: Experience through Metaphor and Drama* (Oxford: Oxford University Press, 2008).

Budd, M., 'Wittgenstein on Aesthetics', in M. Budd, *Aesthetic Essays* (Oxford: Oxford University Press, 2008), pp. 252–77.

—, 'Wittgenstein, Ludwig', in S. Davies et al. (eds), *A Companion to Aesthetics* (Oxford: Wiley-Blackwell, 2009), pp. 593–6.

Buri, F., 'Concerning the Relation of Philosophical Faith and Christian Faith', trans. C. D. Hardwick, *Journal of The American Academy of Religion*, 40 (1972), pp. 454–7.

Calder, J., *The Philosophy of Samuel Beckett* (London: Calder Publications, 2001).

Carlson, T. A., 'Postmetaphysical Theology', in K. J. Vanhoozer (ed.), *The Cambridge Companion to Postmodern Theology* (Cambridge: Cambridge University Press, 2003), pp. 58–78.

Casel, O., *The Mystery of Christian Worship and Other Writings*, ed. B. Neunheuser (London: Darton, Longman and Todd, 1962).

Clark, T., *Martin Heidegger* (London: Routledge, 2002).

Connolly, J. M., 'Gadamer and the Author's Authority: A Language-Game Approach', *Journal of Aesthetics and Art Criticism*, 44 (1986), pp. 271–7.

Cooper, D. E., 'Ineffability and Religious Experience', in A. de Nicholás and E. Moutsopoulos (eds), *God: Experience or Origin?* (New York: Paragon House, 1985), pp. 189–99.

—, 'The Inaugural Address: Ineffability', *Proceedings of the Aristotelian Society, Supplementary Volume*, 65 (1991), pp. 1–15.

—, *Heidegger* (London: Claridge, 1996).

—, *Existentialism: A Reconstruction*, 2nd edn (Oxford: Blackwell, 1999).

—, *The Measure of Things: Humanism, Humility, and Mystery* (Oxford: Clarendon Press, 2002).

—, *Meaning* (Chesham: Acumen, 2003).

—, 'Life and Meaning', *Ratio*, 18 (2005), pp. 125–37.

—, *A Philosophy of Gardens* (Oxford: Clarendon Press, 2006).

—, 'Mystery, World and Religion', in J. Cornwell and M. McGhee (eds), *Philosophers and God: At the Frontiers of Faith and Reason* (London: Continuum, 2009), pp. 51–62.

—, *Sunlight on the Sea: Reflecting on Reflections* (n.p: n.p., 2013).

Cottingham, J. G., *On the Meaning of Life* (Oxford: Routledge, 2003).

—, *The Spiritual Dimension: Religion, Philosophy and Human Value* (Cambridge: Cambridge University Press, 2005).

—, 'What Difference Does it Make?: The Nature and Significance of Theistic Belief', *Ratio*, 19 (2006), pp. 401–20.

—, 'What is Humane Philosophy and Why is it at Risk?', in A. O'Hear (ed.), *Conceptions of Philosophy*, Royal Institute of Philosophy Supplement, 65 (2009), pp. 233–55.

Descartes, R., *Meditations on First Philosophy*, in *Selected Philosophical Writings*, trans. J. Cottingham, R. Stoothoff and D. Murdoch (Cambridge: Cambridge University Press, 1988), pp. 73–122.

Dewey, J. and A. F. Bentley, *Knowing and the Known*, at https://www.aier.org/sites/default/files/otherpublications/KnowingKnown/KnowingKnownFullText.pdf [accessed 10 October 2013].

Dufrenne, M., 'The Aesthetic Object and the Technical Object', *Journal of Aesthetics and Art Criticism*, 23 (1964), pp. 113–22.

—, 'Perception, Meaning and Convention', *Journal of Aesthetics and Art Criticism*, 42 (1983), pp. 209–11.

FitzPatrick, P. J., *In Breaking of Bread: The Eucharist and Ritual* (Cambridge: Cambridge University Press, 1993).

Freud, S., *The Future of an Illusion*, trans. J. A. Underwood (London: Penguin, 2004).

Gadamer, H.-G., 'The Relevance of the Beautiful: Art as Play, Symbol and Festival', in *The Relevance of the Beautiful and Other Essays*, ed. R. Bernasconi (Cambridge: Cambridge University Press, 1986), pp. 3–53.

—, 'The Festive Character of Theater [sic]', in *The Relevance of the Beautiful*, pp. 57–65.

—, 'Composition and Interpretation', in *The Relevance of the Beautiful*, pp. 66–73.

—, 'Image and Gesture', in *The Relevance of the Beautiful*, pp. 74–82.

—, 'Philosophy and Poetry', in *The Relevance of the Beautiful*, pp. 131–9.

—, *Truth and Method*, trans. J. Weinsheimer and D. G. Marshall, 2nd edn (London: Continuum, 2004).

Godzieba, A. J., 'Ontotheology to Excess: Imagining God without Being', *Theological Studies*, 56 (1995), pp. 3–20.

Gordon-Taylor, B. N., 'Mystery: A Neglected Aspect of First-Millennium Western Liturgy' (PhD dissertation, Durham University, 2007).

Guiver, G., *Pursuing the Mystery: Worship and Daily Life as Presences of God* (London: SPCK, 1996).

Hall, C. A. and S. D. Boyer, *The Mystery of God: Theology for Knowing the Unknowable* (Grand Rapids, MI: Baker Academic, 2012).

Heidegger, M., *Being and Time*, trans. J. Macquarrie and E. Robinson (New York: Harper & Row, 1962) [1927].

—, 'What is Metaphysics?', trans. R. F. C. Hull and A. Crick, in *Existence and Being* (London: Vision, 1949), pp. 355–92 [1929].

—, 'On the Essence of Truth', in *Basic Writings*, ed. D. F. Krell, 2nd edn (London: Routledge, 1993), pp. 115–38 [1930].

—, 'The Origin of the Work of Art', in *Basic Writings*, ed. Krell, 2nd edn, pp. 139–212 [1935].

—, 'Hölderlin and the Essence of Poetry', trans. D. Scott, in *Existence and Being*, pp. 293–315 [1936].

—, *Contributions to Philosophy (From Enowning)*, trans. P. Emad and K. Maly (Bloomington, IN: Indiana University Press, 1999) [1936–8].

—, 'The Way to Language', in *Basic Writings*, ed. Krell, 2nd edn, pp. 393–426 [1937].

—, 'Letter on Humanism', in *Basic Writings*, ed. Krell, 2nd edn, pp. 213–65 [1947].

—, *Existence and Being*, intro. W. Brock (London: Vision Press, 1949).

—, 'The Thing', in *Poetry, Language, Thought*, trans. A. Hofstadter (New York: Harper & Row, 2001), pp. 161–84 [1950].

—, 'Building, Dwelling, Thinking', in *Poetry, Language, Thought*, trans. Hofstadter, pp. 141–59 [1951].

—, '" ... Poetically Man Dwells..."', in *Poetry, Language, Thought*, trans. Hofstadter, pp. 209–27 [1951].

—, *What is Called Thinking?*, trans. J. G. Gray (New York: Harper & Row, 1968) [1951–2].

—, *Discourse on Thinking*, trans. J. M. Anderson and E. H. Freund (New York: Harper & Row, 1966) [1955/1944–5].

—, 'On the Question of Being', in *Pathmarks*, ed. W. McNeill (Cambridge: Cambridge University Press, 1998), pp. 291–322 [1955].

—, *What is Philosophy?*, trans. W. Kluback and J. T. Wild (London: Vision, 1958) [1955].

—, *Identity and Difference*, trans. J. Stambaugh (New York: Harper & Row, 1969) [1957].

—, 'The Nature of Language', in *On the Way to Language*, trans. P. D. Hertz (San Francisco, CA: Harper & Row, 1971), pp. 55–108 [1957–8].

—, *Basic Writings*, ed. D. F. Krell, 2nd edn (London: Routledge, 1993).

—, *Poetry, Language, Thought*, trans. A. Hofstadter (New York: Harper & Row, 2001).

Hemming, L. P., *Heidegger's Atheism: The Refusal of a Theological Voice* (Notre Dame, IN: University of Notre Dame Press, 2002).

Hepburn, R. W., 'Humanist Religion II: Some Possible Approaches', in R. W. Hepburn et al., *Religion and Humanism* (London: BBC, 1964), pp. 83–90.

—, 'Aesthetic and Religious: Boundaries, Overlaps and Intrusions', in R. W. Hepburn, *The Reach of the Aesthetic: Collected Essays on Art and Nature* (Aldershot: Ashgate, 2001), pp. 96–112.

—, 'Restoring the Sacred: Sacred as a Concept of Aesthetics', in Hepburn, *The Reach of the Aesthetic*, pp. 113–29.

Hick, J., 'Ineffability', *Religious Studies*, 36 (2002), pp. 35–46.

—, 'Response to Knepper', *Religious Studies*, 45 (2009), pp. 223–6.

Hofstadter, D. R. and D. C. Dennett, *The Mind's I: Fantasies and Reflections on Self and Soul* (London: Penguin, 1982).

Hook, S., 'The Atheism of Paul Tillich', in S. Hook (ed.), *Religious Experience and Truth: A Symposium* (London: Oliver & Boyd, 1962), pp. 59–64.

— (ed.), *Religious Experience and Truth: A Symposium* (London: Oliver & Boyd, 1962).

Horn, H., 'Karl Jaspers', *Prospects: the Quarterly Review of Comparative Education*, 23 (1993), pp. 721–39.

Hume, D., *Dialogues Concerning Natural Religion* (Edinburgh: William Blackwood and Sons, 1907).

Husserl, E., *Cartesian Meditations: An Introduction to Phenomenology*, trans. D. Cairns (Dordrecht: Kluwer, 1999).

Huysmans, J.-K., 'Le Marchand de Marrons', in *Croquis Parisiens* (Paris: La Bibliothéque des Arts, 1994), pp. 97–100.

James, W., *The Varieties of Religious Experience* (New York: Mentor Books, 1958).

Jaspers, K., *The Perennial Scope of Philosophy*, trans. R. Manheim (London: Routledge & Kegan Paul, 1950).

—, *Way to Wisdom: An Introduction to Philosophy*, trans. R. Manheim (London: Victor Gollancz, 1951).

—, *Reason and Anti-Reason in Our Time*, trans. S. Goodman (London: SCM, 1952).

—, *Reason and Existenz: Five Lectures*, trans. W. Earle (London: Routledge & Kegan Paul, 1956).

—, *Truth and Symbol: From* Von der Warheit, trans. J. T. Wilde, W. Kluback and W. Kimmel (London: Vision, 1959).

—, *Philosophical Faith and Revelation*, trans. E. B. Ashton (London: Collins, 1967).

—, *Philosophy*, trans. E. B. Ashton, 3 vols (Chicago, IL: University of Chicago Press, 1969).

—, *Philosophy is for Everyman: A Short Course in Philosophical Thinking*, trans. R. F. C. Hull and G. Wels (London: Hutchinson, 1969).

Kant, I., *Critique of Pure Reason*, trans. F. Heywood (London: William Pickering, 1848).

Kaelin, E. F., *An Existentialist Aesthetic: The Theories of Sartre and Merleau-Ponty* (Madison, WI: The University of Wisconsin Press, 1962).

Kapferer, B., 'Sorcery and the Beautiful: A Discourse on the Aesthetics of Ritual', in A. Hobart and B. Kapferer (eds), *Aesthetics in Performance: Formations of Symbolic Construction and Experience* (New York: Berhahn, 2005), pp. 129–60.

Kearney, R., 'Merleau-Ponty and the Sacramentality of the Flesh', in K. Semonovitch and N. De Roo (eds), *Merleau-Ponty at the Limits of Art, Religion, and Perception* (London: Continuum, 2010), pp. 147–66.

Kellenburger, J., 'The Ineffabilities of Mysticism', *American Philosophical Quarterly*, 16 (1979), pp. 307–15.

Kenny, A., 'Worshipping an Unknown God', *Ratio*, 19 (2006), pp. 441–53.

Kidd, I. J., 'Humane Philosophy and the Question of Progress', *Ratio*, 25 (2012), pp. 277–90.

Kirkbright, S., *Karl Jaspers: A Biography: Navigations in Truth* (New Haven, CT: Yale University Press, 2004).

Kołakowski, L., *Husserl and the Search for Certitude* (London: Yale University Press, 1975).

—, *Metaphysical Horror* (Oxford: Blackwell, 1988).

Kukla, A., *Ineffability and Philosophy* (London: Routledge, 2005).

Langer, S. K., *Philosophy in a New Key: A Study in the Symbolism of Reason, Rite, and Art*, 3rd edn (Cambridge, MA: Harvard University Press, 1957).

Langley, G. H., 'Reason', *Proceedings of the Aristotelian Society*, 39 (1939), pp. 85–98.

Law, D. R., *Inspiration* (London: Continuum, 2001).

—, 'Jaspers and Theology', *Heythrop Journal*, 46 (2005), pp. 334–51.

Lawn, C., 'Gadamer on Poetic and Everyday Language', *Philosophy and Literature*, 25 (2001), pp. 113–26.

Le Poidevin, R., *Arguing for Atheism: An Introduction to the Philosophy of Religion* (London: Routledge, 1996).

Leiner, M., 'Tillich on God', in Re Manning, R. (ed.), *The Cambridge Companion to Paul Tillich* (Cambridge: Cambridge University Press, 2009), pp. 37–55.

Long, E. T., 'Jaspers' [sic] Philosophy of Existence as a Model for Theological Reflection', *International Journal for Philosophy of Religion*, 3 (1972), pp. 35–43.

Lowe, E. J., 'The Ontological Argument', in C. Meister and P. Copan (eds), *The Routledge Companion to Philosophy of Religion* (Oxford: Routledge, 2007), pp. 331–40.

Lüdeking, K., 'Pictures and Gestures', *British Journal of Aesthetics*, 30 (1990), pp. 218–32.

McGilchrist, I., *The Master and his Emissary: The Divided Brain and the Making of the Western World* (London: Yale University Press, 2009).

MacKinnon, D. M., 'Some Epistemological Reflections on Mystical Experience', in S. T. Katz (ed.), *Mysticism and Philosophical Analysis* (London: Sheldon Press, 1978), pp. 132–40.

Macquarrie, J., *Principles of Christian Theology* (London: SCM, 1966).

—, *Mystery and Truth: The 1970 Pere Marquette Theology Lecture* (Milwaukee, WI: Marquette University Theology Department, 1973), pp. 55–98.

—, *In Search of Deity: An Essay in Dialectical Theism (The Gifford Lectures Delivered at the University of St Andrews in Session 1983-4)* (London: SCM, 1984).

—, *Two Worlds are Ours: An Introduction to Christian Mysticism* (London: SCM, 2004).

Marcel, G., 'On the Ontological Mystery', in *The Philosophy of Existence*, trans. M. Harari (London: Harvill Press, 1948), pp. 1–31.

Marion, J.-L., *God Without Being* (Chicago, IL: University of Chicago Press, 1991).

Mason, R., *Understanding Understanding* (Albany: State University of New York Press, 2003).

Merleau-Ponty, M., 'Eye and Mind', trans. C. Dallery, in *The Primacy of Perception*, ed. J. M. Edie (Evanston, IL: Northwestern University Press, 1964), pp. 159–90.

—, 'Faith and Good Faith', in *Sense and Non-Sense*, trans. H. L. Dreyfus and P. A. Dreyfus (Evanston, IL: Northwestern University Press, 1964), pp. 172–81.

—, *Signs*, trans. R. C. McCleary (Evanston, IL: Northwestern University Press, 1964).

—, *In Praise of Philosophy*, trans. J. Wilde and J. M. Edie (Evanston, IL: Northwestern University Press, 1968).

—, *Phenomenology of Perception*, trans. C. Smith (London: Routledge, 2002).

—, *The World of Perception*, trans. O. Davies (London: Routledge, 2004).

Moore, A. W., 'Ineffability and Religion', *European Journal of Philosophy*, 11 (2003), pp. 161–76.

Mulhall, S., *On Being in the World: Wittgenstein and Heidegger on Seeing Aspects* (London: Routledge, 1990).

—, '"The Presentation of the Infinite in the Finite": The Place of God in Post-Kantian Philosophy', in B. Leiter and M. Rosen (eds), *The Oxford Companion to Continental Philosophy* (Oxford: Oxford University Press, 2007), pp. 494–522.

—, 'The Ontological Argument: Wittgensteinian Variations', paper read to the D Society, University of Cambridge, 17 October 2008.

Olson, D., 'Paul Tillich and the Ontological Argument', *Quodlibet Journal*, 6 (2004), at http://www.quodlibet.net/olson-tillich.shtml [accessed 21 January 2009].

Pailin, D. A., *Groundwork of Philosophy of Religion* (Peterborough: Epworth, 1986).

Philipse, H., *Heidegger's Philosophy of Being* (Princeton, NJ: Princeton University Press, 1998).

Pihlström, S., *Structuring the World: The Issue of Realism and the Nature of Ontological Problems in Classical and Contemporary Pragmatism*, Acta Philosophical Fennica, vol. 59 (Helsinki: The Philosophical Society of Finland, 1996).

Plé, A. (ed.), *Mystery and Mysticism: A Symposium* (London: Blackfriars Publications, 1956).

—, 'Mysticism and Mystery', in Plé (ed.), *Mystery and Mysticism*, pp. 1–17.

Pritchard, D., 'Is "God Exists" a "Hinge Proposition" of Religious Belief?', *International Journal for Philosophy of Religion*, 47 (2000), pp. 129–40.

—, 'Wittgenstein on Scepticism', in O. Kuusela and M. McGinn (eds), *The Oxford Handbook of Wittgenstein* (Oxford: Oxford University Press, 2011), pp. 523–49.

—, 'Wittgensteinian Quasi-Fideism', in J. L. Kvanvig (ed.), *Oxford Studies in Philosophy of Religion: Volume IV* (Oxford: Clarendon Press, 2011), pp. 146–60.

—, 'Wittgenstein and the Groundlessness of our Believing', *Synthese*, 189 (2012), pp. 255–72.

Pseudo-Dionysius the Areopagite, *The Complete Works*, trans. C. Luibheid (New York: Paulist Press, 1987).

Quack, J., 'Bell, Bourdieu, and Wittgenstein on Ritual Sense', in Sax, Quack and Weinhold (eds), *The Problem of Ritual Efficacy*, pp. 169–88.

Rahner, K., 'The Hiddenness of God', in *Theological Investigations*, trans. D. Morland, 23 vols (London: Darton, Longman & Todd, 1979), vol. 16, pp. 227–43.

Re Manning, R., *Theology at the End of Culture: Paul Tillich's Theology of Culture and Art* (Leuven: Peeters, 2005).

Richardson, W. J., *Heidegger: Through Phenomenology to Thought* (The Hague: Nijhoff, 1963).

Robins, J. W., 'The Problem of Ontotheology: Complicating the Divide between Philosophy and Theology', *Heythrop Journal*, 43 (2002), pp. 139–51.

Russell, B., *The Problems of Philosophy*, 2nd edn (Oxford: Oxford University Press, 1998).

Russell, J. M., 'Tillich's Implicit Ontological Argument', *Sophia*, 32 (1993), pp. 1–16.

Santayana, G., *The Unknowable: The Herbert Spencer Lecture Delivered at Oxford, 24 October, 1923* (Oxford: Clarendon Press, 1923).

Sartre, J.-P., *Nausea*, trans. R. Baldick (Harmondsworth: Penguin, 1965).

—, *Being and Nothingness: An Essay on Phenomenological Ontology*, trans. H. E. Barnes (London: Routledge, 2003).

Schrag, C. O., 'The Three Heideggers', in C. O. Scrag, *Philosophical Papers: Betwixt and Between* (Albany, NY: State University of New York Press, 1994), pp. 159–73.

—, *God as Otherwise Than Being: Toward a Semantics of the Gift* (Evanston, IL: Northwestern University Press, 2002).

Schüßler, W., 'Where Does Religion Come From? Paul Tillich's Concept of *Grundoffenbarung*', in M. Despland, J. C. Petit and J. Richard (eds), *Religion et Culture. Actes du Colloque international du centenaire Paul Tillich, université Laval, Québec, 18–22 Août 1986* (Québec: Presses de l'Université Laval, 1987), pp. 159–71.

Sextus Empiricus, *Outlines of Scepticism*, ed. J. Annas and J. Barnes (Cambridge: Cambridge University Press, 2002).

Steiner, G., *Real Presences* (London: Faber & Faber, 1989).

—, *Heidegger*, 2nd edn (London: Fontana, 1992).

—, 'Real Presences', in G. Steiner, *No Passion Spent: Essays 1978–1996* (London: Faber & Faber, 1996), pp. 20–39.

—, 'A Reading against Shakespeare', in *No Passion Spent: Essays 1978–1996*, pp. 108–28.

Tertullian, *De Praescriptione Haereticorum*, ed. T. H. Bindley (Oxford: Clarendon Press, 1893).

Thatcher, A., *The Ontology of Paul Tillich* (Oxford: Oxford University Press, 1978).

Thomson, I. D., *Heidegger on Ontotheology: Technology and the Politics of Education* (Cambridge: Cambridge University Press, 2005).

Tillich, P., 'The Problem of Theological Method', *Journal of Religion*, 27 (1947), pp. 16–26.

—, *The Courage to Be* (London: Nisbet, 1952).

—, *Dynamics of Faith* (London: George Allen & Unwin, 1957).

—, 'The Two Types of Philosophy of Religion', in *Theology of Culture*, ed. R. C. Kimball (New York: Oxford University Press, 1959), pp. 10–29.

—, 'Existential Philosophy: Its Historical Meaning', in *Theology of Culture*, pp. 76–111.

—, 'The Meaning and Justification of Religious Symbols', in Hook (ed.), *Religious Experience and Truth*, pp. 3–11.

—, 'The Religious Symbol', in Hook (ed.), *Religious Experience and Truth*, pp. 301–21.

—, *Systematic Theology*, 3 vols (Welwyn: James Nisbet & Co., 1968).

Toland, J., *Christianity Not Mysterious: Or, a Treatise Shewing, That There is Nothing in the Gospel Contrary to Reason Nor Above it: And That no Christian Doctrine can be Properly Call'd a Mystery* (New York: Garland Publishing, 1978).

Tolstoy, L., *What is Art?*, trans. R. Pevear and L. Volokhonsky (London: Penguin, 1995).

Turner, D., *The Darkness of God: Negativity in Christian Mysticism* (Cambridge: Cambridge University Press, 1995).

—, 'The Darkness of God and the Light of Christ: Negative Theology and Eucharistic Presence', *Modern Theology*, 15 (1999), pp. 143–58.

—, *Faith, Reason and the Existence of God* (Cambridge: Cambridge University Press, 2004).

Vizinczey, S., *In Praise of Older Women: The Amorous Recollections of András Vajda* (London: Penguin, 2010).

Westphal, M., 'Overcoming Onto-theology [sic]', in M. Westphal, *Overcoming Onto-theology [sic]: Toward a Postmodern Christian Faith* (New York: Fordham University Press, 2001), pp. 1–28.

Wilde, O., 'De Profundis', in *De Profundis, The Ballad of Reading Gaol and Other Writings* (Ware: Wordsworth Classics, 1999), pp. 1–114.

Williams, R., 'Simone Weil and the Necessary Non-Existence of God', in *Wrestling with Angels: Conversations in Modern Theology* (London: SCM, 2007), pp. 203–27.

Wittgenstein, L., *Lectures and Conversations on Aesthetics, Psychology and Religious Belief*, ed. C. Barrett (Oxford: Blackwell, 1966).

—, *On Certainty*, ed. G. E. M. Anscombe and G. H. von Wright, trans. D. Paul and G. E. M. Anscombe (Oxford: Blackwell, 1969).

—, *Remarks on Frazer's* Golden Bough, ed. R. Rhees, trans. A. C. Miles (Retford: Brynmill, 1979).

—, *Culture and Value*, trans. P. Winch (Oxford: Blackwell, 1980).

—, *Tractatus Logico-Philosophicus*, trans. D. Pears and B. McGuiness (London: Routledge, 1988).

—, *Philosophical Investigations*, trans. G. E. M. Anscombe, 3rd edn (Oxford: Blackwell, 2001).

—, *Zettel*, ed. G. E. M. Anscombe and G. H. von Wright (Berkeley, CA: University of California Press, 2007).

Yandell, K. E., *The Epistemology of Religious Experience* (Cambridge: Cambridge University Press, 1993).

Yannaras, C., *On the Absence and Unknowability of God: Heidegger and the Areopagite*, ed. A. Louth, trans. H. Ventis (London: T&T Clark International, 2005).

Young, J., *Heidegger's Philosophy of Art* (Cambridge: Cambridge University Press, 2001).

—, *Heidegger's Later Philosophy* (Cambridge: Cambridge University Press, 2002).

—, 'The Fourfold', in C. B. Guignon (ed.), *The Cambridge Companion to Heidegger*, 2nd edn (Cambridge: Cambridge University Press, 2006), pp. 373–92.

INDEX

Abbott, Edwin, 10, 12
   Flatland, 10, 12
Abraham, 74
absolute, the, 13, 16, 27, 55, 57, 64–5, 68–9, 73–4, 77, 85, 89, 96, 102, 108–10, 117, 122, 124–5, 128–9, 151
absolute faith, 73–4, 84
absolutism, 21, 23, 26–7, 62, 100, 119
absurdity, 25–6, 107, 110–11, 123–31, 134, 152
Achilles, 116
Adam, 37
aesthetics, 6, 127, 139–48
Alston, William, 15, 17–19, 21, 39–40, 59–60
Anaximander, 125
Angst, 24, 108–9, 111, 123–6
Anselm of Canterbury, St, 51–4, 65–6
answerability, 5, 13–15, 18, 20, 24, 26–7, 31–2, 34, 38, 40, 59–60, 75, 110–11, 118–19, 129, 133–4, 139, 150
apeiron, 125
apophatic premise, 7, 13–15, 27
apophatic theology, 5, 9, 13–14, 28, 52–4, 126
   see also mysticism
Aquinas, St Thomas, 52
Aristotle, 43
art, viii, 21–2, 24–6, 121, 127, 131, 134–6, 139, 150–3
   see also phenomenology of art
Ashton, E. B., 97
atheism, 2, 44
attention, 108, 113, 115–17, 130, 145
awe, 41, 136
   see also wonder

Bachelard, Gaston, 135
Bartky, Sandra, 32, 35
Beckett, Samuel, 24–6
   Act Without Words II, 25
Being, *passim*
   translation of *Sein* in Heidegger, 29–30
   compared with being (lowercase), 29, 42, 47, 55, 56, 169
body, human, 12, 81–2, 97–9, 106, 142, 144, 148, 154
Bouyer, Louis, 8–9
Boyer, Steven, 10–13, 39
Brown, David, vii, 14, 134, 153–4
Buber, Martin, 64, 73
Budd, Malcolm, 141–2, 144
Buri, Fritz, 77–8

Calder, John, 25–6
Casel, Odo, 8–10, 14
certainty, 65, 84, 116, 154
   see also doubt
ciphers, 77–104, 124–5, 127–8, 130, 133, 151–2
   definition, 78–9
   religious, 128–31, 133–4, 139, 147, 151, 153
Clark, Timothy, 34
classical theism, 2, 45, 54
Comprehensive *see* Encompassing
Cooper, David, *passim*
Cottingham, John, 2, 5, 129, 137, 138, 151, 152

Dasein, 24, 31, 35, 56, 68–9, 108
Descartes, René (also Cartesian), 11, 105–6, 138
Dewey, John, 68, 95, 115

– 197 –

dialectic, 6, 57, 61–2, 64, 93, 125–8, 151–2, 154
  phenomenological, 123–31, 134, 151
dialectical theism, 45, 57, 59, 60, 63–4, 75, 125
Diamond, Cora, 53–4
doubt, 65, 73, 84–5, 107, 149, 154
  see also certainty
Dufrenne, Mikel, 140, 142

Eckhart, Meister, 59
Encompassing, 77, 78, 89–100, 102, 112, 125
Enlightenment, 1
Epimenides, 116
Epiphanius of Salamis, 139
epistemology, 3–4, 7, 10–12, 16–21, 58, 60, 64–6, 81, 90, 103, 105–6, 116, 138, 149, 154
equipollence, 106–7
Ereignis, 30, 35, 46, 47, 48, 59
  see also Seyn
Eucharist, 6, 8–9, 131, 133, 148–52
existentialism, 1, 40, 45, 77
experience, 3, 5–6, 12–14, 16–18, 20–2, 29–39, 58, 62–3, 68–70, 72–3, 75, 91, 98–101, 106–11, 113–17, 119, 123–7, 129, 133–4, 139, 143, 148, 153–4
  aesthetic *see* phenomenology of art
  see also perception
  priority over logic, 98–9, 109, 116–17
  see also revelation

Feuerbach, Ludwig, 94
FitzPatrick, Patrick, 148–52
formalism (aesthetics), 145–6
fourfold, 35, 49
Freud, Sigmund, 3–4

Gadamer, Hans-Georg, 82, 139–41, 144–6, 153
geometry, 11–12
Gestalt, 116
gesture, 81–2, 129, 134, 141–4, 147–8, 150–1, 153
Gifford, Adam *see* Gifford, Lord
Gifford, Lord, 4
Gifford Lectures, 3–4, 15

God, *passim*
  existence, 1–3, 20, 43–4, 54, 56, 58–9, 63, 66, 79
  necessary existence, 49–54
  necessary non-existence, 54–5
'God' (word), 6, 13, 19, 28, 39–46, 54, 56, 63, 67, 70–3, 77, 129
Gordon-Taylor, Ben, 9
Grundoffenbarung, 73
  see also absolute faith
Guiver, George, 9

Heidegger, Martin, 4, 6, 23–4, 26–44, 46–9, 51, 55–9, 68–70, 73–5, 89, 95–6, 105, 107–12, 114–15, 118, 120–2, 124, 127–30, 133, 135, 144, 146–8, 150
  Being and Time, 29, 69, 121
  Contributions to Philosophy, 48
  Identity and Difference, 41
  Kehre see Heidegger, Martin, turning
  turning, 29–30, 46–9
Hepburn, Ronald, 135–6
Heraclitus, 113
Hick, John, 14
Hitchens, Christopher, 85
Hölderlin, Friedrich, 31, 37
humane philosophy, viii, 5
humanism, existential, 23–7, 62, 69, 107, 110–12, 114, 118, 124
Hume, David, 1–2, 4, 85
  Enquiry Concerning Human Understanding, 2
Husserl, Edmund, 107, 115

imagination, 14, 54, 109, 125–6, 130, 136, 148, 154
ineffabilism, 154
ineffability, *passim*
  definition, 7
  see also mystery
ineffable, the *see* ineffability
inexhaustibility, 14, 62, 83, 111, 126, 139–41, 143, 145, 146–9, 153
isostheneia see equipollence

James, William, 5, 15, 16, 21, 27, 40, 115
  The Varieties of Religious Experience, 15

Jaspers, Karl, 6, 56–7, 75, 77–106, 112, 120, 123–30, 133–4, 151–2, 154
'oath to the spirit of science' (photograph), 96

Kant, Immanuel, 1, 4, 26, 54, 89
Kearney, Richard, 148
Kellenburger, James, 16
Kenny, Anthony, 13
Kierkegaard, Søren, 75, 120
Kripke, Saul, 17
Kukla, André, 15, 16, 20, 21

Langer, Suzanne, 136–8
Langley, G. H., 113–14
language, 5–6, 19–20, 22, 24, 33, 36–8, 40, 43, 46–7, 50, 52–3, 79–84, 86–7, 90, 92–4, 112, 116, 122, 129, 133–4, 142–4, 146–7
   poetic, 36–8, 47, 120–3, 125–9, 134, 139, 141, 143–5, 153
   religious, 5, 6, 19, 20, 22, 40, 51–4, 56, 59–60, 86, 129, 131, 134–5, 148, 153–4
   see also meaning, linguistic
language-games, 53, 146
Law, David, vii, 78, 79, 85
le Poidevin, Robin, 49–51
logic, 2, 5, 10–12, 15–17, 25, 28, 44, 52, 70, 77, 85, 94, 98, 102, 106, 109, 112, 116–19, 122–3, 135–6, 139, 141, 147, 154
   priority of experience over *see* experience, priority over logic
   limits of *see* reason, limits of
   modal, 49–51
love, vii–viii, 55–7
Lüdeking, Karlheinz, 144, 146

McGilchrist, Iain, 113, 115–17, 126, 130, 147, 152
MacKinnon, Donald, 22
Macquarrie, John, 1–4, 6, 40, 45–7, 49, 54, 57–60, 63–4, 67, 75, 103–4, 125, 133, 138–9, 148, 153
   Principles of Christian Theology, 2
magic, 85, 136–7
Malcolm, Norman, 51–2

Mallarmé, Étienne *see* Mallarmé, Stéphane
Mallarmé, Stéphane, 144–5
Marcel, Gabriel, 15, 43, 58, 112
Marion, Jean-Luc, 47–8, 55–7
Mason, Richard, 18
meaning, 6, 20–3, 25–6, 29–30, 46, 63–4, 66–73, 75, 79–83, 90, 92, 95, 102, 108–11, 114, 123–31, 134–5, 139, 143, 150, 152
   aesthetic *see* phenomenology of art
   linguistic, 81, 142, 145
   of life, 14, 23–6, 40, 44, 118, 124, 128, 129, 137, 152, 154
medicine, 96, 154
   psychiatric, 96
Merleau-Ponty, Maurice, 26, 67, 81–2, 90, 98–9, 107–9, 111, 115, 118, 142–5, 147–8, 153
metaphor, 16, 56, 80–4, 87–8, 90, 94, 109, 116, 129, 134, 137
metaphysics, 41–3, 48–9, 62, 64, 77, 80, 86, 93, 110, 135–8
miracles, 2, 61, 67, 68, 86
Moore, Adrian, 19–21
Moses, 74
Mulhall, Stephen, 51–4
mystery, 5, 7–12, 14, 17, 23, 27–37, 43, 45–6, 53, 57–8, 60–3, 112, 117, 120, 122, 138, 145, 147, 150–1
   theological conception of, 7–13, 15
   see also ineffability
mysticism, 5, 7–8, 15–16, 21–2, 28, 61, 74, 78, 86
   see also apophatic theology
mythology, 79, 85, 88, 154

naturalism, 75
natural theology, 1–5, 16–17, 45–6, 58, 153
   see also philosophy of religion
negative theology *see* apophatic theology
nihilism, 110, 124
nothingness, 15, 45, 49, 57, 60, 86, 93, 107–11, 124–5
Nothing, the *see* nothingness
Nozick, Robert, 111, 124

Olson, Duane, 65–7
ontological argument, 2, 43–4, 49–55, 64

modal version, 49–51
  implicit in Tillich, 65–7, 90, 96, 112
ontological difference, 29, 31, 39, 41, 46,
  48–9, 59
ontotheology, 40, 57–8, 75, 129, 135
  critique of, 41–55, 60, 66, 72, 77, 136
  definition, 41
Orwell, George, 138

pantheism, 80
paradox, 60, 63–4, 66, 79, 97–9, 102,
  116–17, 126–7, 130
Parmenides, 125
Pascal, Blaise, 138
perception, 17, 72, 81–3, 95, 98–9, 106,
  108, 111, 140, 142–3, 147
  see also experience
performance, 22, 136, 140, 143, 144, 146–7,
  151–3
phenomenality, 88–91
phenomenology
  existential, 3–6, 12, 20, 22, 24, 26–7,
    56–7, 63, 67–70, 75, 95, 98, 102–3,
    105, 109–15, 117–18, 120–31, 134,
    150, 153
  transcendental, 115
  of art, 139–48, 150, 152
  see also art
phenomenological dialectic *see* dialectic,
  phenomenological
philosophy, *passim*
philosophy of religion, viii, 1–2, 4–5, 53, 59,
  66, 78, 137, 153
physiognomy, 80–1, 90, 128–9, 134, 142
Plé, Albert, 7–9
Plotinus, 45
poetry *see* language, poetic
pragmatism, 5–6, 40, 68, 98, 103, 107, 112,
  114–16, 118, 126, 152
pre-Socratic philosophy, 116–17, 126
Pseudo-Denys *see* Pseudo-Dionysius the
  Areopagite
Pseudo-Dionysius the Areopagite, 13–14
Putnam, Hilary, 40, 114
Pythagoras, 32

reason, 4, 11, 16–17, 60–3, 65–6, 98, 103,
  105, 107, 109, 110–13, 123–7, 129,
  134, 138
  limits of, 4, 60, 66, 94, 103, 107, 110,
    112–23, 126, 128
  relation to rationality, 112–15, 122–3,
    128
  versus passion, vii, 113, 114, 121, 122
rationality, 63, 109–10, 112–15, 118,
  120–4, 126, 128, 138
  definition, 112–13, 120
religious experience, *passim*
  see also experience
  see also revelation
religious symbols *see* symbol
revealed theology *see* revelation
revelation, 3, 5, 8, 11, 14, 57–65, 67–8, 70,
  75, 78, 84–5, 87–8, 127–31, 153
  see also religious experience
Richardson, William, 46
ritual, 6–8, 25, 127, 130, 133–9, 145,
  148–54
Roquentin, 24
Russell, Bertrand, 149
Russell, John, 66

Sartre, Jean-Paul, 24–6, 107–11, 114, 123,
  124, 125
scepticism, 106–7, 149–50
Schopenhauer, Arthur, 26
Schrag, Calvin, 42, 46–8
Schumann, Robert, 144
Schüßler, Werner, 73
science, 4, 86, 96, 103, 112, 136
  see also medicine
Sein, 29–30
  see also Being, translation of *Sein* in
    Heidegger
Seinsfrage, 29, 32
Seinsvergessenheit, 30, 33, 35
Seyn, 35
Sextus Empiricus, 106
Shakespeare, William, 37
  King Lear, 140
significance *see* meaning
sociology, 138
Socrates, 74
Stace, Walter, 15, 16, 21

Steiner, George, 32, 36–7, 42, 153
subject–object dichotomy, 6, 21–2, 28, 33, 36, 39, 43–4, 46, 60–2, 65–80, 82–3, 88–106, 111–15, 118, 120, 127–8, 133
   compared with subject–object distinction, 68, 97–8, 103–7, 112, 118, 121–3, 128
   definition, 68
subject–object distinction, 104–5, 107, 112–13, 118–28, 151
Suzuki, Daisetsu, 150
symbol, 16, 59–61, 63–4, 67–75, 78, 80, 84, 86, 88, 103, 128
   compared with cipher, 79, 82–4, 87, 89, 92–3, 102–3, 128–9

Tertullian, 1, 4
theology, 1, 7, 39–75, 77–8, 85–6, 104–5, 126, 129–30, 149, 153
   critique of, 85, 154
Theseus, ship of, 116
Thomson, Iain, 41
Tillich, Paul, 6, 40, 42–7, 49, 54–5, 57–8, 60–75, 78–9, 83–5, 87, 89–90, 93, 96, 101–4, 112, 127–8, 154
   Systematic Theology, 42
   The Courage to Be, 44
   Dynamics of Faith, 85
Toland, John, 9–11, 14
   Christianity Not Mysterious, 9
Tolstoy, Leo, 141–2
transcendence, 13, 19–20, 26, 28, 31, 35, 43, 48, 56–7, 59–60, 64, 70–3, 77–97, 100–2, 104, 108, 115–16, 124–5, 127, 130, 133, 134, 149, 151
transparency, 22, 31, 61–2, 70, 73, 81, 84, 94, 101, 116, 125–7, 147–8, 150–1
transubstantiation, 148–50
Trinity, the, 88
Turner, Denys, 13, 41–2, 52–3, 126

ultimate reality *see* absolute, the
uncertainty *see* doubt
unconditioned, the *see* absolute, the

Valéry, Paul, 109, 144
van Gogh, Vincent, 121
von Hochheim, Eckhart *see* Eckhart, Meister

Weil, Simone, 54–5
Wilde, Oscar, 75
Williams, Rowan, 54–5
Wittgenstein, Ludwig, 21, 28, 37, 51–4, 119, 121, 136–8, 141–7, 151
   Lectures and Conversations on Aesthetics, Psychology and Religious Belief, 141
   Philosophical Investigations, 142
   Remarks on Frazer's Golden Bough, 136–7
wonder, 135–6
   see also awe
Wynn, Mark, 5

Yannaras, Christos, 13
Young, Julian, 29–30, 42, 48–9, 57

Zeno of Elea, 116

Milton Keynes UK
Ingram Content Group UK Ltd.
UKHW022042060324
438929UK00005B/238